SECRET UNDERGROUND CITIES

SECRET UNDERGROUND CITIES

An account of some of Britain's
subterranean defence, factory and
storage sites in the Second World War

by

N.J. McCamley

LEO COOPER

First published in Great Britain in 1998, Reprinted 1999
LEO COOPER
an imprint of
Pen & Sword Books Ltd
47 Church Street
Barnsley,
South Yorkshire
S70 2AS

Copyright © N.J. McCamley 1998,1999

ISBN 0 85052 585 3

Typeset in 10½/12½pt Plantin by Phoenix Typesetting,
Ilkley, West Yorkshire

Printed by
Redwood Books Limited,
Trowbridge, Wiltshire

CONTENTS

MAPS AND DIAGRAMS

ACKNOWLEDGEMENTS

Research for this book has spanned a period of thirty years since the day in July 1967 when I first stumbled upon the recently abandoned bulk of Monkton Farleigh quarry. In those far-off days when cold-war paranoia was at its peak, the prospect of gaining access to official archives concerning Corsham simply did not exist, but from the mid-1980s restrictions were gradually relaxed and since 1994 I have been privileged with access to many new and exciting resources.

Over this span of more than a generation numerous organizations and individuals have provided information, assistance and support. Inevitably, with the passage of time, the names of some of these contributors have become lost, but to all of those, and to the following, I offer my heartfelt thanks and gratitude:

Above all I must thank my wife, Vicky, who married me in 1973 despite her awareness of my subterrannean obsession, and has soldiered on with sterling fortitude ever since. Without her unwavering support and encouragement, particularly during the last six years of intensive research, this book would not have been written.

A special debt of gratitude is owed to Mr F.W. Allan who came to Corsham in 1936 from County Durham, where he had been manager at Beamish Colliery, to take charge of the construction of the Central Ammunition Depot. Mr Allan has allowed me unrestricted access to his unique collection of contemporary documents and photographs which have provided the core of this narrative, backed up by his faultless and lucid memory of events and people. Fred Allan's pride in the achievements of his fellow countrymen from the distressed areas of northern

England is tangible, and it is in recognition of their achievement that this book is written.

I would also like to thank the staff of the Public Records Office at Kew; the RAF Museum archive at Hendon; Mr Joseph T. Warden of the Royal Logistic Corps Museum; Phillip Dutton of the Imperial War Museum photographic section; Christopher Date, archivist of the British Museum; David Carter, archivist of the National Gallery; Christopher Marsden, assistant archivist at the Victoria and Albert Museum; David Edwards of the British Motor Industry Heritage Museum at Gaydon (which holds the records of the Rover Car Company); Ed Bartholomew, curator of photographs at the National Railway Museum; Emily Hamilton-Seward, of Alfred McAlpine Plc; Ray Marshall, archivist of De La Rue Plc; staff at the Welsh Office Library of Aerial Photographs, The Royal Commission on the Historical Monuments of England, Wiltshire County Archive, and the planning departments of North Wiltshire and West Wiltshire District Councils. I must also thank Trevor Allen of EMF Farming Associates, one-time owner of Monkton Farleigh and Eastlays quarries, for passing on a number of relevant plans and photographs, and for explaining the convoluted story of his firm's purchase of the quarries. John Turner has answered with great patience and goodwill my numerous enquiries about Eastlays quarry, where he is now quarry manager.

Private individuals to whom I am indebted include Peter Yarborough, who has provided transport and good company for the often long and arduous journeys to every underground site mentioned in this book; Bob Scammell, who has made easy my numerous visits to the Public Record Office; Bruce Maskery, with whom I have spent many hours deciphering clues to the development of Monkton Farleigh Quarry; the late Simon Finch, who by his sheer persistence was able to charm information from sources closed to me; and David Pollard, whose knowledge of the Bath stone industry is unsurpassed. John Heaven of the Rolls-Royce Heritage Trust gave freely of his knowledge of Bristol piston aero-engines, and on the same subject I must thank Terry Wilson, who also put me straight about the underground factories at Henley on Thames. Steve Fox has been my mentor on all Civil Defence matters, and I must admit to drawing freely upon his research. Anne Bradford, and Eddie Baker provided stunning photographs of the Royal Enfield underground factory at Westwood, and Paul Stokes, author of *Drakelow Unearthed*, pointed me towards a whole new range of source material concerning the Drakelow factory, and also arranged for me to visit and photograph the site.

After years of documentary research it was necessary to actually inspect on the ground what until then I had only read about, in order to fully understand the subject. This difficult task was made relatively easy by many past and serving Army and RAF Officers at Corsham, and employees of the Property Services Agency and its privatised successor, who arranged for me to roam underground at Corsham on a number of occasions. Among those who showed their trust in my motives were Brigadier Neave, Brigadier S.M.A. Lee, OBE, and Major R.B. Davies of the Royal Signals Corp, and Air Commodore Ferguson, Squadron Leader Wallis and Flight Sergeant Quinn of the RAF. A special thanks, also, to Colonel Bob Stark, for it is due to his enthusiasm and energy that many of my visits were made possible. Commander Tim MacDonald, beyond the call of duty, very kindly allowed me to explore and photograph Spring Quarry, both above and below ground. Of the civilian custodians of Corsham I must mention George Morley, Dick Brown, John White, Steve Tucker and Derek Hawkins, through whose efforts I was able to accompany Mr F.W. Allan on a trip around Tunnel Quarry some sixty years after he first set foot there in 1936.

GLOSSARY

AS	Air Shaft
ASD	Ammunition Supply Depot
BAC	Bristol Aircraft Company
BLC	Breech Loading Cartridge
BSA	Birmingham Small Arms Company
CAD	Central Ammunition Depot
CDI	Corsham Depot Inlet
Cfm	Cubic Feet Per Minute
COO	Commanding Ordnance Officer
DCRE	Deputy Commander, Royal Engineers
DGAFP	Director General of Airframe Production
DORA	Defence of the Realm Act
ENSA	Entertainments National Service Association
GHQ	General Headquarters
GOC	General Officer Commanding
GPO	General Post Office
GWR	Great Western Railway
HE	High Explosive
ICI	Imperial Chemical Industries
MAP	Ministry of Aircraft Production
MOS	Ministry of Supply
MOWB	Ministry of Works & Buildings
MOWT	Ministry of War Transport
MSLP	Main Surface Loading Platform
MSU	Maintenance Sub-Unit
MU	Maintenance Unit

NATO	North Atlantic Treaty Organization
PSA	Property Services Agency
QOC	Quarry Operation Centre
RAF	Royal Air Force
RAOC	Royal Army Ordnance Corps
RDF	Radio Direction Finding (Radar)
RE	Royal Engineers
RGHQ	Regional Government Headquarters
RNAD	Royal Navy Armaments Depot
RNSD	Royal Navy Storage Depot
RSG	Regional Seat of Government
RSJ	Rolled Steel Joist
SF	Special Fire or 'Starfish' decoy
SRHQ	Sub-Regional Headquarters
TISC	Treasury Inter-Service Committee
TNT	Tri-Nitro-Toluene (High Explosive)
UKWMO	United Kingdom Warning & Monitoring Organization
WAAF	Women's Auxiliary Air Force
WD	War Department

LOCATION PLAN

Showing

Principal underground factory & storage depots

and ancillary sites

1939-1945

GLASGOW

EDINBURGH

CAIRNRYAN
Departure port for
deep-sea dumping

VALLEY WORKS, RHYDYMWYN
Chemical Weapons depot

MANCHESTER

HARPUR HILL
RAF ammunition depot

LLANBERIS
RAF ammunition depot

LINLEY
RAF ammunition depot

FAULD
RAF ammunition depot

MANOD
National Gallery repository

DUDLEY
MAP factory

BIRMINGHAM

DRAKELOW
MAP factory

CORSHAM
Tunnel
Eastlays } CAD Corsham
Ridge
Elm Park - RAF storage
Spring Quarry - MAP Factory
Copenacre
Brockleaze } Admiralty
Pickwick Storage
Monks Park

LONDON

TREOWN
Admiralty ammunition depot

SHARPNESS
Departure port for
deep-sea dumping

BRISTOL

HENLEY-ON-THAMES
Warren Row
Park Place } MAP factories

BRADFORD-ON-AVON
Westwood - Museum repository
Westwood - MAP factory
Monkton Farleigh - CAD sub-depot
Hayes Wood - MAP explosive store
Bethel Quarry - Admiralty storage

CHILMARK
RAF ammunition depot

DEAN HILL
Admiralty ammunition depot

INTRODUCTION

Since the dawn of life on earth man and beast have sought refuge from their tormentors underground. As the technology of destruction has advanced man has burrowed ever deeper, from cave to catacomb to bunker reinforced with iron and concrete, seeking protection for himself and to defend his weapons of war. Out of sight, these boltholes created in themselves a new weapon – *secrecy* – with which to further confound the enemy.

This secrecy aspect gained particular significance after the First World War when it appeared that the bombing aeroplane would henceforth be the predominant weapon of aggression. Not only would underground bunkers, if deep enough, protect against the heaviest of bombs, but the enemy had first to locate the hidden target – maybe just a tiny shaft hidden in woodland or an inconspicuous adit on a hillside, leading to who knows how large a labyrinth below the ground? Then the next problem: how extensive are the tunnels, in which direction do they go, how deep are they and will the bombs penetrate to that depth, or are they just a wasteful dissipation of resources? This search for security below the ground reached its apotheosis during the early years of the Second World War and has lingered on anachronistically through the post-war years and in to the nuclear era.

This book does not pretend to be a gazetteer of *all* the Second World War underground sites in Britain, although most get at least a mention, except for the uniform series of ready-use magazines, built like short interconnected tube tunnels at the Royal Ordnance Filling Factories; the small but sinister caverns specially excavated by the Halklyn United Mining Company at Rhydymwn near Mold to store the nation's supply

1

of mustard gas, and the government bunkers and civilian air-raid shelters in London, all of which are comprehensively documented elsewhere. Little mention is made of the many Admiralty oil and ammunition depots other than those at Corsham, not because they are uninteresting but because most remain in Ministry of Defence hands and technical details are still secret. Of the sixteen Admiralty underground sites recorded in 1942, five were fuel-oil depots and eleven were ammunition magazines, ranging in size from disused railway tunnels at Colwall in Herefordshire and Hawthorn in the Forest of Dean (not to be confused with the infinitely more important underground complex at Corsham bearing the same name) to the multi-million pound extravagances at Dean Hill and Trecwn.

Two distinct phases of construction can be seen in the underground works associated with the Second World War. The first phase started before the Great War ended and was driven by a realization by the Army Council that the next war would be won predominantly by air-power, and that protection against this threat should be the government's prime concern. It is characterized by a preliminary period of meticulous analysis and planning which resulted in a series of engineering masterpieces designed to last for generations. Largest and most important among these masterpieces was the Corsham Central Ammunition Depot, the ideal to which all subsequent underground works aspired. Lesser but still substantial developments from the same phase were the five RAF underground reserve depots which followed the Army lead from 1936, and the Trecwn and Dean Hill Admiralty depots, conceived at much the same time but subject to a prolonged gestation.

The second phase is marked by blind panic and incompetent bureaucratic interference and dates from the autumn of 1940, when the threat defined by the service departments soon after the First World War was at last (and almost too late) recognized by the country at large and by the Supply Departments in particular. Its chief manifestation is in the series of vast underground aircraft engine factories situated country-wide, but, due to a quirk of geology, with its centre of gravity in the Corsham area.

CAD Corsham and its pre-war army and navy equivalents symbolize the success of engineering ambition tempered only by the exigencies of war. They were built because they were needed whether or not war came and they were built to an agreed standard to satisfy a scrupulously calculated military requirement. If they were not as perfect as they should have been it is only because the war started two years before it should have, and the carefully nurtured plans were compromised in consequence. The underground factories on the other hand represent the victory of bureaucracy over common sense. Prolonged blitz and sudden invasion, the perceived threats which were their spark of life, faded and were dead even before construction of the factories got properly under way; but once the bureaucratic engine was rolling it could not be stopped until virtually every underground space in the Kingdom larger than a cellar was converted, irrespective of cost, into some form of inconvenient store or workshop for one firm or another, coerced into unwilling tenancy by the Ministry of Works, Supply, or Aircraft Production. The building of the factories, rather than the making of guns and engines *within* the factories, became an end in itself.

The underground bunkers and depots were not built at the drop of a hat, their construction absorbed a substantial proportion of the military budget, mopped up, at a stroke, the great pool of chronically unemployed labour from the industrial black spots of the north-east, stimulated industrial output and initiated technical research in many previously neglected fields of technology. When built, these depots did not operate in isolation but impacted significantly on their surroundings. Employment and housing, roads, railways, water supply and other services in their localities were improved dramatically and the rate of rural electrification was accelerated by at least a generation. The underground sites needed to be defended, either by integration into existing home defence schemes or by new and dedicated arrangements and, although the troops are long gone, the surviving military infrastructure, particularly in the Corsham area, is a vivid reminder of the invasion panic of 1940/41.

In the pages that follow I hope not only to explain in detail the construction of the most significant of the Second World War underground works, but also to set these works in the context of their time and of the political and economic circumstances which shaped their development. I have endeavoured to describe the evolution and demise of the two main threads of this story, both in their own ways magnificent achievements of the civil engineer, and both achieved with the same raw material, resources and technology. One, however, (the ammunition depots) must be adjudged a success (if only a qualified success) and the other (the factories) a failure (but not an unqualified failure). Paradoxically, the disastrous underground factories were to outlive the technically superior ammunition depots. Abandoned as soon as decency allowed after the war on account of their patent failings, the factories were instantly seized upon by a paranoid government desperately seeking refuge from nuclear Armageddon; or so recent commentators would have us believe. In the final section of this book, however, I hope to prove that the transition from the emergency ammunition depots countering the threat of Zeppelin bombardment to the hardened nuclear-bomb shelters for central and regional government has been a logical step-by-step progression, each stage following inevitably and inexorably from the last.

1

THE CENTRAL AMMUNITION DEPOT
CORSHAM

"They built a City out of Sight . . . an underground City which has taken thousands of men seven years to construct, houses Britain's largest ammunition dump. Details are secret, but it can be said that the stocks are of incredible size."

This headline appeared in the *Daily Mail* on 23 November, 1943, and the stocks referred to were indeed incredible. Throughout the war years the vast underground depot at Corsham held over 300,000 tons of explosives in a fantastic bomb-proof ramification of air-conditioned chambers and tunnels one hundred feet below the peaceful Wiltshire countryside.

A further description, by Douglas Worth in the *Daily Express*, appeared on the same day under the headline "They Form Our Biggest Arsenal":

"Somewhere in England, Monday – A lonely looking policeman is at this very moment stamping his cold feet on a bleak railway siding. There is nothing about him to suggest that he marks the spot where two worlds meet. Yet such is the case. Before him are the familiar scenes of normal life. But behind him slopes a tunnel to the preposterous underworld built as a series of permanent ammunition depots, biggest of their kind, each a lavish Temple of Mars.

"Many thousands of lights burn continuously in this land of hidden cities; warm conditioned air flows through arterial channels of concrete and limestone. Shells painted a gay yellow rock endlessly on a conveyor belt, to be stacked in a twenty-foot honeycomb, or to be shipped to a theatre of war.

"Here, carved from the living rock, is a great bomb-proof cloister hundreds of feet long, supported by square thirty-foot columns

5

hewn out of stone. Already scurrying blobs of khaki have piled it high with war stores.

"And here on rock covered with smooth concrete, engineers have built a great powerhouse, with whirring giant dynamos, winking signal lights and shiny black controls. Fluorescent bars throw a daylight effect over the spotless asphalt floors."

A modest scheme initiated by the War Office in 1928 to provide a secure, six-acre magazine to house 12,000 tons of shell and bombs at a capital cost of £100,000 had, by 1943, evolved into a highly sophisticated underground citadel encompassing 125 acres of subterranean chambers, containing 300,000 tons of explosives, and costing well in excess of £4,500,000.

2

ATTACK BY AIR – A NEW THREAT

Prior to the development of military aviation little regard was paid to the overhead protection of home ammunition storage depots. Indeed the general practice was to design magazines with their roofs as the weakest part of the structure in order to deflect the blast from an accidental explosion upwards rather than sideways, thereby reducing the risk of damage to adjacent buildings.

Within two years of Bleriot's flight across the English Channel in 1909 European military leaders were investigating the strategic value of this aerial revolution; the War Office was eventually persuaded, in April, 1911, to purchase four Bristol Boxkites, while France, Germany, and Italy were also taking to the air, albeit with no great enthusiasm. The Italian army used its primitive aircraft to drop small bombs on the Turkish lines during the Tripolitanian campaign of 1912, inflicting great psychological but minimal material damage. During the two years leading up to the First World War Germany experimented with airships to carry much larger bomb loads over enemy territory, and on 4 August, 1914, Zeppelin ZV1 loaded with eight large, percussion-fused artillery shells approached the Belgian fort of Liège with evil intent, but, succumbing to defensive small-arms fire, was fatally damaged and crashed as it withdrew.

Paradoxically, the War Office, having shown no confidence in the efficacy of aerial bombardment and little enthusiasm for a British Air Force, was much shaken by the fear of such a force controlled by its European enemies. During the latter half of 1913 the War Office initiated an inquiry to determine the most effective way to protect existing ammunition storage sheds against attack from the air. The investigating officers concluded that the most effective protection for sheds containing shell of all descriptions was achieved by suspending light steel mesh on stout poles ten feet above the roofs, rather like a fly-sheet over a tent. The mesh would catch and explode falling bombs well outside the safety distance and the damaged mesh could then be cheaply replaced. In the case of sheds containing cordite this arrangement was augmented by thick steel sheets placed on the roofs to prevent the penetration of hot splinters.

Whilst accepting that the measures outlined would be adequate in the short term for the protection of existing surface storehouses the enquiry concluded that:

"For new magazines the only satisfactory construction appears to be by earth protection. To provide such protection on a large scale the best arrangement would seem to be a series of short tunnels entering at right angles from a steep hillside or cliff face. This arrangement would to a great extent allow freedom for the escape of gases in the event of an explosion occurring in any one of the tunnels. Such magazines would not be difficult or expensive to construct in chalk and convenient sites might be found in disused quarries or in some of the steep-sided valleys that exist in chalk formations.

"Where on account of the site it is not practicable to construct underground magazines protection can best be afforded by ordinary bomb-proof construction, i.e. arched roofs with earth cover. Such buildings are however very expensive."

Limited use *was* made of underground storage during the Great War, mainly by the Ministry of Munitions to secure supplies of TNT and other bulk explosives, which were being supplied quicker than the shell-filling factories could consume them.

A salt mine near Northwich was adapted to house 1,500 tons of explosives destined for filling factories in the north of the country, and Chislehurst Cave was acquired on 27 October, 1914, for the storage of shell fillings for Woolwich Arsenal, which was finding difficulty accommodating the great quantities of explosives and raw material accumulating there. Conditions underground were far from ideal and boxes of explosives had to be stacked on railway sleepers to raise them from the damp floor. Only the front part of the twenty-two miles of passages at Chislehurst was used for storage, separated from the rest of the cave by thick brick walls.

Deliveries of explosives began on 10 December, 1914, the material having travelled nine miles by train from Woolwich and from the station to the caves by a fleet of nine motor lorries. In response to concern expressed by local residents about the dangers of explosives being stored in such large quantities so close to domestic habitation, the War Office stated that the material to be stored "was not explosive as such, but the raw material to make explosives, rather like the chemicals used to make dyes". This disingenuous declaration indicates some economy of truth because, while some raw acid was kept at Chislehurst, the principal inventory consisted of at least 1000 tons of TNT. Within the War Office there was apprehension that perhaps such quantities *were* dangerous, and perhaps only 500 tons should be kept at Chislehurst, but this argument was dismissed as academic as the effect of 500 tons exploding *en masse* would be much the same as 1,000 tons!

There was only one entrance to the area used for ammunition storage, but beyond the cut-off wall were three air-shafts which were made secure by reducing their diameters with concrete placements and by fitting strong iron grilles at top and bottom. All three shafts surfaced in the gardens of nearby houses, one of which was tenanted by a German national who was a naturalized British subject. A guard of fifteen soldiers patrolled the site and, as these men were billeted locally, discreet arrangements were made to ensure that at least one of the guards was billeted in the house of the German national. It is recorded, however, that by 1918 the house was untenanted, the German having been 'taken away'. After the Armistice it was decided temporarily to retain Chislehurst to store 100,000 lbs of explosive for which there was still no capacity at Woolwich, but by 17 July, 1920, the caves were classified surplus to requirement and offered back to the original owner who reoccupied the site at the end of the month.

Most notable of all the Great War ventures underground was the magazine completed at the Chilwell Ordnance Factory near Nottingham just before the Armistice, at a cost of £43,579. The installation consisted of a 'T'-shaped chamber approached via a long tunnel bored into the hillside, along the lines of the concept proposed in 1913. The Chilwell filling factory has a fascinating history, its completion marking a turning point in the hitherto disastrous record of ammunition supply during the

First World War. One of the first acts of David Lloyd George after taking control of the Ministry of Munitions in 1915 was to introduce new blood from private industry into the Ministry with the aim of generating new work practices and countering the conservative reactionism of the old men who at that time reigned at Woolwich and on the Army Council. From among these new industrialists Lord Chetwynd was recommended as the man to build and run a new government factory designed to turn 1000 tons of high explosive into artillery shells each week. Chetwynd was accordingly approached by Lloyd George, and accepted the position offered on the condition that he would have a free hand to run the business in his own way without War Office interference.

A disused silk mill at Chilwell was purchased and filled with an assortment of machinery, designed originally for a range of industrial applications but adapted at Chetwynd's dictation to the manufacture of high explosives on a massive scale. Raw TNT was, for example, ground to powder in a flour mill and combined with ammonium nitrate to produce Amatol in a baker's dough mixer. This unconventional approach caused a certain amount of fear among many employees who were appalled to see high explosives treated with such apparent disrespect. Chetwynd's response was to take up residence in the former mill owner's house situated at the north corner of the site, with the comment: 'If anyone is to be blown up, I'll be the first!"

One January night in 1916 a lone Zeppelin tracked along the Trent in a fruitless search for the Chilwell factory. The following day a rumour circulated that while Lord Chetwynd was touring the factory the previous night he had caught three German agents signalling to the Zeppelin with lights and had peremptorily drawn his revolver and shot them dead. Hearing of this rumour Chetwynd decided to turn the story to his advantage and had an armed policeman stand guard over a remote and empty room in the factory. Later that night he arranged for a labourer to dig three graves on the nearby hillside, filling each with stones, then covering them over and marking the heads with black posts. From that day Lord Chetwynd's reputation was assured, and the prying eye of the would-be spy, the ill-intentioned visitor and the merely inquisitive was firmly discouraged.

Unfortunately the whole site fell into disuse shortly after the Armistice and the government was keen to rid itself of the upkeep expenses. A nominal valuation of £200,000 was put on the factory in the early

1920s, but the War Office was unwilling to part with it at that figure, arguing that its development had cost over £2,500,000 and that such a loss could not be justified. The dispute between the War Office and the Treasury over its disposal was to continue for more than two decades. In June, 1928, at a time when the Army Council was again actively debating underground ammunition storage, the War Office commented that the underground magazine at Chilwell was the only one existing in the country and was of great value on that account. With a capacity of only 200 tons Chilwell was too small to figure in the great CAD scheme.

Significantly, a small Bath-stone mine at The Ridge near Corsham in Wiltshire was taken over in 1915 for TNT and cordite storage, and an agreement reached between its owners, the Bath Stone Company, and the Director General of Explosives under which the company was appointed contractor for the necessary conversion work. The following year the workings were inspected by General Savile and Colonel Dempster, accompanied by the General Manager of the Bath and Portland Stone Company, Mr Sturge Cotterell. The War Office representatives were so impressed by Cotterell's management of the project that they requested that his services be made available to advise on the construction of underground magazines elsewhere in the country. Thus it was that Sturge Cotterell joined the Ministry of Munitions as Superintendent of Munitions Stores. Although abandoned shortly after the war Ridge Quarry was subsequently to figure as a key progenitor of the vast schemes undertaken at Corsham in preparation for the Second World War.

Experiences during the Great War raised concern about the safety and security of the Army War Reserve of ammunition. The 1st Committee of the Army Council to Consider the Revisions of the Regulations for Magazines and Care of War Materials, under the chairmanship of Lieutenant-Colonel P.K. Lewes, sat on 11 June, 1919. Fearful of the danger of large scale aerial attack, it concluded that:

"The committee are of the opinion that the only real protection for any Magazines or Depots above ground is an adequate and efficient Anti-Aircraft defence, and that it is not practicable on account of expense to make Magazines bomb-proof without employing underground storage. They consider, however, that small magazines and

11

dispersed buildings tend greatly to minimise the danger from aerial attack. They are further of the opinion that immunity from damage by aerial attack can only be assured by provision of underground magazines and ammunition depots.

"The committee has been given various estimates of subterranean Magazines differing so widely in cost that they are unable to agree on any one as a representative average. Local circumstances appear to govern the question. They understand, however, that there are various disused caves, quarries and similar workings in the United Kingdom which might be suitable for adaption."

Among the dissenting voices was the Master General of Ordnance, whose opinion was that:

"We must accept the War Risks of depots vulnerable to air attack as unavoidable:- the expense of making bomb-proof or underground storage, yet which would be a workable proposition for issues and receipts under the pressure of war would be so great as to be prohibitive, and I do not think we would be justified in embarking upon such a scheme".

The following year the matter was discussed again by the Committee on Armament Supply Depots, which concluded that absolute security could only be provided by underground storage, particularly for propellants, bulk explosives, and Lyddite, Trotyl and Amatol-filled shell. It was emphasized that protection of bulk explosive was of fundamental importance, as their destruction would inevitably affect the supply of shell and propellant.

Colonel Bainbridge presented a report analysing the future requirements for ammunition depots during the next war. He predicted the use of much heavier high explosive bombs, weighing perhaps several tons, in conjunction with large numbers of small incendiary bombs, which he suggested would greatly reduce the effectiveness of the policy of dispersal currently favoured by the War Office. Bainbridge concluded that:-

"Concealment from hostile aircraft cannot be said to have received much consideration in determining the sites of ammunition depots in this war. The necessity for it will no doubt be clear in the next."

12

The general recommendation of the committee was that the existing surface depots should be used only for immediate issues and sites with good rail access should be found for underground magazines to hold the reserve stock. The report concluded that:

"Investigations and estimates with regard to underground storage should be commenced as soon as possible, so that if the principle is approved work may start as money is available."

Particular attention was focused on the sprawling surface depot at Bramley, a rather inconvenient site near Basingstoke that had developed in a piecemeal fashion during the Great War. By 1920 it consisted of a great many small, lightly built corrugated steel sheds spaced 200 yards apart in open ground unprotected by blast walls or traverses. No comprehensive scheme of improvement was agreed, but it was recommended that traverses should be erected around the two most vulnerable buildings containing trench warfare ammunition and bulk gunpowder. A report issued in January, 1921, highlighted many grave deficiencies at Bramley, concluding that:

"No protection can be afforded from aerial attack or dropping bombs except by placing the depot underground, and the only effectual protection of a surface depot would be an efficient and adequate form of air defence."

The proceedings of these various inquiries were noted and put on file, but the mood of the time was not favourable to military expenditure on the grand scale. An incomplete list of potentially useful caverns and underground chambers was compiled, seemingly with little enthusiasm, but no further action was taken and the scheme was allowed to languish for nearly a decade.

The reasons for this apparent inertia were manifold. Within the Army Council the War Office members displayed the same conservatism that faced Lloyd George in 1914:

"The War Office was hampered by a traditional reactionism. Its policy seemed to be that of preparing, not for the next war, but for the last one or the last but one. Unfortunately, they only remembered the lessons which were better forgotten because they were inapplicable, and forgot all the experiences by which they ought to have profited because they were a foretaste of the methods of future warfare."

As late as 1937, following the disastrous military exercises of that year, the noted military commentator Captain B.H. Liddell Hart wrote in *The Times* of 27 September: "The ruling minds in the W.O. are still running on 1914 tram lines". Even Neville Chamberlain, certainly no Man of War, was to comment that, "The obstinacy of some of the Army heads in sticking to obsolete methods is incredible."

For a decade after the Armistice the keynote policy of successive Governments was one of increasingly radical disarmament. Throughout this period military expenditure was pared to the bone and orders for munitions dried to a mere dribble. The effect upon the ordnance factories was cataclysmic; plant was closed down and allowed to decay, skilled staff were laid off and, without the stimulus of healthy demand, research and development ceased almost completely.

TENTATIVE STEPS

The security of the Bramley depot was again brought into question at a War Office meeting in January, 1928, during the course of which attention was drawn to the large underground magazine then under construction by the Admiralty at Ernesettle, near Plymouth. The need for similar underground storage for Army reserves became apparent and it was decided that as a first step the Officers Commanding Area Commands should make preliminary investigations of the underground chambers listed in the file prepared by the Master General of Ordnance ten years earlier.

The inadequacy of this list was patent and on 6 July, 1928, Brigadier Wortham contacted J. Allen Howe, Assistant Director of the Geological Museum, requesting his co-operation in compiling a definitive list of all known underground chambers in the British Isles. The War Office received no reply for six months and felt obliged to prompt Allen Howe towards the beginning of January, 1929. The Assistant Director replied that his staff was having great difficulty collating the information and a list was not forwarded for a further six months, arriving at the War Office on 14 June, 1929. When studied, it proved to be very incomplete and limited in scope. However, Brigadier Wortham wrote to the GOC's Area Commands asking them each to send an investigative team to the mines and chambers suggested by Allen Howe:

> "I am commissioned by the Army Council to request that you will institute inquiries to ascertain the locality of any caves, unused tunnels and mines within your Command, which could be utilised for the underground storage of ammunition and explosives, and furnish a report giving information regarding present use, area, depth, approach by road or rail, atmospheric conditions and such other points as you may wish to emphasise."

Replies were received from the Commands well before the deadline of 31 March, 1930. Virtually all the locations were found to be gravely deficient regarding either size, safety, means of access, or proximity to nearest services. Southern Command submitted a list of eight sites: Tilly Whim, Acton and Herston caves in Dorset; Beer Quarry in Devon; Ridge Quarry in Corsham; Wren's Nest at Dudley in Staffordshire; and Hasley and Avening Quarries near Nailsworth.

By 23 May, 1930, the reports of all Area Commands had been scrutinized and a short list of five possible sites drawn up: Chislehurst Caves; Slate Mines in the vicinity of Blaenau; Scout Quarry in Rossendale; Meadowbank salt mine in Cheshire, and Ridge Quarry near Corsham. After careful consideration Ridge Quarry was chosen specifically for further investigation.

The Garrison Engineer, Exeter, reported that Ridge offered 12 acres of storage space, only half of which had been cleared and converted by the Ministry of Munitions for explosive storage during the 1914–18 War. A quarry tramway of 2'5½" gauge connected the mine with the GWR main line at Corsham station one and a half miles distant, where there was siding accommodation for twenty-one trucks in a loading platform specially adapted for ammunition wagons. Two-foot gauge decauville track existed in a good part of the workings serving raised stacking platforms, and a steam winding engine capable of lifting six tons was still in place at the top of the main entrance shaft.

THE 1934 TOUR OF INSPECTION

Unpopular in the Baldwin administration, and in 1931 excluded from the National Government, Winston Churchill argued tirelessly for re-armament and warned ceaselessly of the German threat. Churchill's advocacy of increased military expenditure, despite the financial crisis of 1931, earned the response from Chamberlain that—

> "If we were now to follow Winston's advice and sacrifice our commerce to the manufacture of arms, we would inflict a certain injury on our trade from which it would take generations to recover. We should destroy the confidence which now happily exists, and we should cripple the revenue."

But by 1933 events unrolled beyond the British shore in a manner to cast shades of doubt across all bar the most rose-visioned political mind. At the end of January Adolf Hitler acceded as Chancellor of Germany, next month the Reichstag burned, and just four weeks later Hitler was to assume full emergency powers over the German Nation: "the most numerous, most serviceable, ruthless, contradictory and ill-starred race in Europe."[1]

A few half-hearted gestures of consternation were made: in June,1934, the Standing Committee of the Disarmament Conference at Geneva was adjourned indefinitely and in Britain the 'ten year rule' on military expenditure was suspended.

At the level which concerns us some positive though painfully slow progress was achieved. Towards the end of 1934 all three Services were examining various underground sites. In November staff from the War Office returned to Ridge Quarry for a more thorough inspection. They were represented there by Major Minnis of the Royal Engineers, an able Officer and distinguished military engineer who was to play a continuing role in the efficient development of the project. At Corsham Minnis met Alan Pictor, managing director of the Bath & Portland Stone Co. since 1932, a man of vision who could perhaps see further than many of his contemporaries in the industry. Pictor fully understood Major Minnis' requirements and was quick to grasp the potential benefit of the War Office scheme to his company, which was in the doldrums with demand

[1] W.S. Churchill, *The Second World War* (Cassell & Co. 1948) Vol.1 p.55.

16

in decline. Throughout the 1930s Bath & Portland found itself paying dead-rents on many disused quarries and faced the prospect of laying off large sections of its skilled workforce through lack of trade. The sale of these otherwise unviable quarries to the government would be of immediate financial benefit to the company.

On 14 November, the day following Major Minnis' first inspection of Ridge Quarry, Alan Pictor visited the War Office where he met Colonel Stokes, Colonel Hunter and Captain Jennings. Pictor drew attention to the much larger Tunnel Quarry at Corsham, about two miles from Ridge and also owned by Bath & Portland. Next morning Colonel Stokes went down to Wiltshire to make a more detailed personal inspection of both Ridge and Tunnel quarries. The initial impression was favourable. During subsequent discussions it was agreed that the quarries at Corsham could accommodate filled shell and bulk explosives, the location being well situated to supply the new filling factory under construction near Hereford. Early in January, 1935, the War Office was granted permission to make a detailed survey of all the stone mines in the Box and Corsham area, but were warned that the Agaric Mushroom Company held a lease on Tunnel Quarry which had a further nine years to run. Stone quarrying had ceased at Tunnel some years earlier and the disused workings leased for mushroom cultivation. In 1928 the mushroom beds became infected with a fungal disease and the company, whilst retaining its lease as protection against possible competition, moved its operation to another disused quarry ten miles away at Westwood near Bradford-on-Avon.

Tunnel Quarry offered over forty-five acres of storage space, as opposed to a mere six acres at Ridge, and had the major advantage of being connected directly to the GWR main line by a branch entering a side tunnel at the eastern portal of Box tunnel. This branch led to a loading platform over half a mile inside the mine and one hundred feet below ground. Outline Treasury approval was granted on 15 August for the purchase of both Ridge and Tunnel for £35,000, with a further £1,000 required for the initial survey work.

A few weeks earlier, on 29 July, a meeting at Corsham was arranged between Major Minnis, Alan Pictor, Sturge Cotterell and representatives of the Great Western Railway to discuss the possibility of extending the siding accommodation at Corsham station. Sturge Cotterell noted that during the Great War Ridge Quarry, which had contained up to 16,000

17

tons of explosive, enjoyed exclusive use of the existing sidings from where it had despatched 500 tons of ammunition each day. The GWR traffic staff suggested that, as further extension of the Corsham sidings was not practicable, land at Thingley Junction a mile or so east of Corsham would be the nearest and most convenient site for the necessary assembly sidings.

On 10 December, 1935, Major Minnis again met Alan Pictor and Mr Chaffey of Bath & Portland to discuss the problems involved in increasing the ceiling height of the railway adit into Tunnel Quarry. During the course of the meeting Pictor showed Major Minnis plans of a quarry at Eastlays, close to Ridge. At the same time the War Office realized that still further underground accommodation would be required, following a prolonged debate to assess the relative costs of re-packing ammunition from wooden boxes into new steel boxes (which would take up 20% less space) and the cost of converting 20% more quarry space for storing ammunition in conventional wooden boxes. The Treasury finally decided, in February, 1936, that the cost of re-boxing ammunition (£110,000) was not acceptable and the cheaper option of adapting further quarry workings should be adopted, as a result of which the acquisition of Eastlays quarry was approved on 20 May. In the early summer of 1936 the War Office finally completed the purchase of all three quarries, Ridge, Tunnel and Eastlays, for £47,000.

The first cost estimate to convert Ridge and part of Tunnel Quarry to provide the necessary storage was £10,000. Increased requirements for anti-aircraft ammunition for the Air Defence of Great Britain and an agreement with the Air Ministry to store RAF bombs on their behalf rendered a further extension necessary, and consequently the purchase of another large quarry at Monkton Farleigh was sanctioned on 16 March, 1937. It was intended to adapt just thirty-eight acres to provide storage for 47,000 tons of anti-aircraft ammunition, together with 9,500 tons of RAF bombs. A further twenty-five acres were to be held in reserve to fulfil a probable storage requirement for another 20,000 tons of anti-aircraft ammunition, followed by a further 20,000 tons at a later date.

The future of the Monkton Farleigh project was in the balance during March due to a counter-proposal put forward by the Air Ministry, which was concerned that it would be at a tactical disadvantage if the bulk of their ammunition reserve was stored in the Southern counties (the underground magazines at Chilmark quarry having already been authorized), and politically they preferred not to be beholden to the War Office for storage accommodation. At the 65th meeting of the TISC on 5 March the Air Ministry spokesman, Mr Webster, argued in favour of their own proposal for a site at Acorn Bank in Cumberland, a recently decommissioned gypsum mine near Penrith which his department thought suitable for the storage of 6,500 tons of HE bombs. The conversion cost was estimated at about £16 per ton. Mr Lyons, for the War Office, suggested that accommodation could be provided at Monkton Farleigh for no more than £10–12 per ton. However, Mr Webster reminded the meeting that upon Mr Lyons' own admission none of the Corsham quarries would be ready before 1939, and Monkton Farleigh would not be completed until three years after its acquisition. The Air Ministry required storage space urgently for bombs scheduled for delivery in 1938 and they considered Acorn Bank the only site capable of providing it within that time.

The committee agreed that sanction should be given for the purchase of Acorn Bank and that the proposals for Monkton Farleigh should be considered again after a thorough assessment of the air-conditioning requirements had been made. Two weeks later Mr Lyons informed the committee that:

"Investigations have been made and the conclusion reached that atmospheric conditions in the quarries were not such as would involve extra expenditure if the quarries were adapted for the storage of ammunition."

Meanwhile the Acorn Bank scheme received a terminal setback when it was discovered that the mine extended under a number of important commercial properties, and was also liable to severe winter flooding. These factors finally induced the Treasury to agree the purchase of Monkton Farleigh Quarry with the proviso that the adaptation plans would be confined to the thirty-eight acres required for the storage of Air Ministry and War Office reserves as at present approved. By early April, 1938, with war now inevitable, it was imperative that ammunition should be stored in the Corsham quarries before the conversion work had been completed. To facilitate this and avoid unnecessary congestion of work authority was given for the adaptation of a further twenty-five acres of Monkton Farleigh as temporary storage.

The Terms of Reference

In 1934 the Army needed accommodation for filled shell and for bulk explosives awaiting transfer to the filling factories. The plan was to store £27,860,000 worth of filled shell plus £500,000 worth of anti-aircraft ammunition in a system of fifty-one separate but interconnected magazines totalling 316,578 square feet. This estimate related only to the storage of war reserves for the field forces, at a contact rate of 2,500 tons per day, on a basis of two months' expenditure of filled ammunition and six weeks supply of bulk explosives. The calculated requirement assumed that the existing magazine regulations would apply and that a maximum of 300,000 lbs of explosive would be stored in each magazine.

On 22 November, 1935, the Army Council confirmed that it was committed to underground storage at Corsham and stated that:

> "It is a programme which may cost £100,000 or £250,000, or £500,000 according to the amount of work which must be done. Whatever is the case it is not open to us to be content with anything less."

Filled ammunition currently available to the Army amounted to only 40,000 tons, but it was proposed to increase this to 134,000 tons. This was to be accommodated in the Corsham depot together with 19,000 tons of bulk explosive and 12,000 tons of RAF bombs. On 3 June, 1936, the first detailed estimates of both storage requirements and costs were drafted, based on three months' supply of each category and also taking account of home-defence anti-aircraft ammunition.

Following a superficial survey of the Corsham quarries, the War Office prepared a preliminary cost estimate for the proposed engineering works amounting to £430,000. It was emphasized that, as no such task had been attempted before and that access to much of the workings could not be gained until some 2,000,000 tons of waste stone had been removed, the prospective costs were very much guesswork. The estimate was later raised to £650,000 when the costs associated with the conversion of Eastlays quarry were added to the account. In December, 1936, just after preliminary clearing began, a serious roof slip occurred in Tunnel Quarry necessitating expensive remedial work and an immediate extra expenditure of £60,000.

20

STORAGE REQUIREMENTS

Description	Rounds	Tons
25 Pdr HE and smoke shell	2,535,450	56,600
18 Pdr HE smoke and Shrapnel	24,000	11,000
3.7" shell	52,380	720
4.5" shell	296,000	6,600
2 Pdr	778,450	2,170
3" and 3.7" tank rounds	93,500	2,100
3" 20 cwt A/A	1,500,000	16,700
Small Arms Ammunition	500,000,000	25,000
60 Pdr B.L.	8,800	235
6" Gun	12,690	560
6" Howitzer	32,425	8,925
8" Howitzer	13,440	1,200
9.2" Howitzer	22,260	2,800
Cordite charges for B.L. guns		960
Bulk Cordite		10,200
TNT and other nitrated explosives		7,000
Ammonium Nitrate		2,070

After the purchase of Monkton Farleigh in May, 1937, a revised estimate was prepared to include the entire cost of the underground storage scheme to date. This figure worked out at £2,000,000, the increase being due to a number of causes. Inflationary price increases had raised the cost of plant and machinery by over 30%, wage rates had risen by an average 15%, and the cost of building materials and general goods had risen proportionately. As work began on clearing debris from Monkton Farleigh mine it was discovered that the support pillars there were larger and more closely spaced than in the other quarries, making it necessary to convert a larger gross area in order to achieve the required storage capacity. In March, 1937, it was estimated that the conversion of Farleigh would cost £10–12 per ton of ammunition stored, a figure that proved eventually to be less than half the final cost.

In May, 1938, a further estimate was prepared to cover all requirements then known and the figure of £3,500,000 was reached. Progress in clearing debris disclosed that the different parts of the quarries varied greatly in their condition and that some would require much more expenditure than could possibly have been visualized. Ridge Quarry in particular was found to be in such an unsatisfactory state that the Royal Engineers stopped all work after only 4% of the area had been strengthened with concrete supports, pending sanction of the high cost involved.

On 12 April, 1938, it was revealed that air-conditioning would after all be necessary in all the Corsham quarries. Major-General Collins, representing the Army, stated that, with the scheme of conditioning envisaged, ammunition and propellant of all types could be stored underground undisturbed for at least ten years, but without air-conditioning its life would be less than three years. The Air Ministry was of the opinion that un-fused RAF bombs could be stored satisfactorily without air-conditioning, but anti-aircraft ammunition with powder fuses would deteriorate very quickly. At this stage the Treasury indicated alarm at the escalating cost and refused to sanction any expenditure on air-conditioning unless it could be proved that the running cost would be less than that which would be incurred by a programme of continuous ammunition maintenance. Eventually the War Office proved its case and in July, 1939, the necessary funds were made available.

The original development plan allowed a period of four years for construction, after which the Royal Ordnance Corps would take over the three sub-depots in the completed state. Unfortunately the accelerated rearmament programme made it necessary to speed up work on the project and to provide premature and temporary storage. The need had become so great that Ridge Quarry was brought into commission in a very unfinished state at the end of 1936 to store ammunition and explosives for the RAF and Ministry of Supply. Later the War Office ordered that Corsham was to commence receipts of Army ammunition from the factories on 1 July, 1938. District No.10 at Tunnel Quarry was nearing completion in May and extempore measures were devised using a second-hand steam winch to enable the first ammunition to be delivered on 13 July, 1938 – only two weeks behind schedule.

It was recognized that speeding up could only be done at the cost of extra plant and a relatively uneconomical increase in the labour force, and that the provision of premature storage must result in such a dislocation of the works programme as to seriously delay completion. This dislocation had to be faced at Tunnel and Eastlays, but to reduce the

22

disturbance to a minimum and to avoid its occurrence in the areas planned as permanent storage at Monkton Farleigh, it was decided temporarily to adapt certain spare areas there. These temporary storage areas were 'K' and 'L' Districts, later to be permanently incorporated in the sub-depot as Districts 19 and 20. In fact events overtook this scheme and Monkton Farleigh began receipts into No.12 District in March, 1940, two years before construction was finally completed. Only two of the eight storage districts at Farleigh were finished to the original standard, the others being prepared as semi-permanent storage and handed over to the RAOC in a somewhat incomplete state. At the time there was some debate as to whether the correct degree of permanence had been obtained to ensure low maintenance costs afterwards.

Doubt was expressed as to whether the new works could be contained within the £3½ million budget, and the estimate was carefully examined to see whether it was possible to reduce some of the items to meet the new requirements. Further work on Ridge Quarry was abandoned, as was the west end of Tunnel Quarry where conditions were particularly bad. Ridge was commissioned as a temporary store and the abandoned area at Tunnel, which was to have been No.1 District, was later utilized as a secure defence communications switching centre known as 'South West Control'. Full air-conditioning was to be installed only in Districts 21 and 22 at Eastlays, which were required for cordite storage.

The nett increases after this recasting come under the following heads:

(1)	Additional area at Monkton Farleigh required for temporary storage	£250,000
(2)	Heavy engineering	£500,000
(3)	Miscellaneous underground works	£150,000
(4)	Plant and temporary lighting	£70,000
(5)	Improved access	£70,000
(6)	Surface buildings	£70,000
(7)	Extra labour costs	£150,000
(8)	Heating for cordite storage	£60,000
(9)	Security fencing	£60,000
(10)	Provision of premature storage at Ridge, Eastlays and Tunnel quarries	£120,000
	TOTAL	£1,500,000

During the latter period of the project more stringent financial control was exercised and costs were to some extent brought under control. Nevertheless Major Parker had to report to a Cabinet Committee in November, 1941, when construction was nearly complete, that the final bill had worked out at £4,400,000, or £20 for every ton of ammunition stored.

3

THE CORSHAM QUARRIES BEFORE
THE COMING OF THE ROYAL ENGINEERS

Bath stone has been quarried on a large scale for building purposes since the first decades of the eighteenth century, although the stone reserves had been exploited in a small way since Roman times. The early development of the industry is attributed in great measure to the efforts of the eighteenth century entrepreneur and philanthropist Ralph Allan. The expansive scheme of rebuilding and development in Bath at that time gave Allan the opportunity to capitalize upon the vast reserves of oolitic limestone beneath his estate at Combe Down. The completion of the Avon Navigation in 1727, and of the Kennet and Avon canal in 1810, widened the market for Bath stone enormously and a great expansion of the industry followed. Another major impetus came with the construction of the two-mile-long Box tunnel for the Great Western Railway in 1838, which revealed the true extent of the stone reserves below Corsham Down. The coming of the railway further eased the transport problems that had dogged the stone industry, and stimulated the development of new quarries which hitherto had been too distant from suitable means of transport to make their working economical. The rate of expansion was such that by 1862 there was reputed to be over five miles of underground quarry roadways below Corsham Down.

Until about 1860 the Bath stone industry was monopolized by three large firms: Messrs Randall & Saunders who had quarries at Corsham, Monkton Farleigh, Westwood and Combe Down; Pictor & Sons of Box; and Sumsions with quarries at Combe Down and Monks Park. By 1885 there were at least twelve firms in fierce competition, which resulted in a price-cutting war that was of no benefit to any party. In 1887, under the guidance of the Pictor family, the seven major firms amalgamated to form the Bath Stone Firms Ltd, and by 1900 the combined firm was producing three million cubic feet of stone a year and boasted sixty miles of underground roadways in the Corsham area. The twentieth century has witnessed a gradual contraction of the quarrying industry with demand falling and the reserves exhausted or becoming too uneconomic to work. There were, however, at least seven mines still in production at the end of 1935.

The beds of building stone in the Bath and Corsham areas are over-lain by approximately 60–100 feet of inferior stone. Owing to the hilly nature of the surrounding countryside these beds of Oolitic limestone outcrop on the hillside in a number of places, where long surface quarries developed, followed by mines pursuing the beds under the hilltop capping. Where the beds did not outcrop it was necessary to sink shafts, normally inclined but in some instances vertical, through the inferior stone to the beds of building stone which lay below. At Corsham the stone was found to be at the same depth as the eastern portal of the newly constructed Box tunnel. Full advantage was taken of this by boring a parallel tunnel adjacent to the main line, by which a broad-gauge siding could enter directly into the heart of the stone workings. This tunnel proved to be of inestimable value to the War Department when they planned their underground complex at Corsham nearly one hundred years later.

The beds of workable limestone vary in thickness between ten and thirty feet. Above this is a stratum of ragstone and forest marble forms the roof of the workings. Below the building stone are beds of very hard corngrit which were not generally worked. Quarrying was carried out using only hand tools right up to the Second World War, the stone being sawn out in blocks weighing up to seven tons using picks and hand saws known as 'frig-bobs'. The quarrymen tended to follow the good stone, leaving pillars of the smallest possible size to support the roof safely, but leaving much larger pillars where the stone was faulted or of poor quality. Relatively straight roadways were cut for hauling blocks from the working faces to the slope shafts and thence to the surface. Haulage in the narrow underground tunnels was done by horses, pulling either ordinary wheeled wagons or in later days narrow-gauge railway trucks.

As work progressed inferior faulty stone and cutting waste was left behind in large quantities, packed into the quarried spaces and around pillars to within a foot or two of the ceiling. Millions of tons of this waste stone had to be removed by the Royal Engineers before the quarries could be developed for ammunition storage.

4

THE SURVEYORS START WORK

Examination of the old Bath & Portland Stone Company royalty plans indicated that they were only approximately correct, so a new survey was undertaken by a small detachment of surveyors under the command of Captain Terry, RE, and his subordinate, Sergeant-Major Kennedy. At each site a surface base line was prepared and from this a triangulation was extended to all the existing slope shafts, vertical air shafts and key points on the surface. From the inclined shafts theodolite traverses were taken into the underground areas. Below ground the surveyors were faced with hundreds of acres of old and often collapsed workings choked with waste stone backfill. The only lighting available was from acetylene hand lamps, and with these the men were able to plot routes over the debris by trial and error. The few existing clear haulageways were marked out for traverse work and, after much climbing, crawling and clearing, a sufficient number of traverse points were established to allow a full triangulation framework to be produced. The shape and position of all the existing pillars and underground features were now surveyed by means of offset measurements from the primary triangulation. The whole of this work was then plotted and drawn to a scale of 40 feet to an inch.

The surface area immediately above the underground workings was surveyed and contoured at five-foot intervals and plans prepared showing the correlation between surface and underground areas. The completed plans were passed to the War Office Tunnel Quarry Committee who were to decide upon the layout of the storage areas.

The layout was dictated largely by the shape of the existing workings and by the condition of the stone overburden. Certain parameters had already been set: the optimum height of ammunition stacks had been

28

established at nine feet and the total weight and mix of ammunition to be accommodated were forecast as detailed earlier. The quarries were divided into storage districts of five acres each, segregated from one another by concrete blast walls with ventilating and emergency escape corridors between. Calculations indicated that a total nett storage area of 112 acres would be required, together with a further 30% for service plant, ventilating and connecting tunnels, power stations, and offices. Study of the new surveys suggested that this area could be accommodated in the four quarries thus:

TUNNEL	44 Acres
RIDGE	6 Acres
EASTLAYS	24 Acres
MONKTON FARLEIGH	38 Acres

Ridge Quarry posed few problems, as virtually all the clearing work had been done by the Ministry of Munitions during the First World War. The gross area of the usable part amounted to nine and a half acres, of which three and a half acres consisted of support pillars, leaving six acres for storage.

It appeared that the twenty-four acres available at Eastlays could be divided into five more or less square districts, but as clearing progressed it was found necessary to abandon four acres in the south-east corner which were too wet. Hasty adaptations were made to compensate for this loss, as a result of which the quarry was divided into four, rather than five, main districts, the one furthest east being larger and more irregular in shape than the rest as it incorporated the rump of the abandoned area. For security reasons the powerhouse was to be constructed in the centre of the mine with an independent access shaft to the surface. To permit the required rate of movement of stores two further access shafts were needed, one serving the two districts to the west of the powerhouse, the other serving those to the east. To expedite flexible ammunition handling, a main access tunnel running the entire length of the northern extremity of the workings connected all the storage districts and slope shafts. To compensate for the four acres lost in the wet area 64,000 square feet to the north of the main haulage were adapted to provide a fifth district at Eastlays.

The layout of the storage areas at Tunnel Quarry was determined by

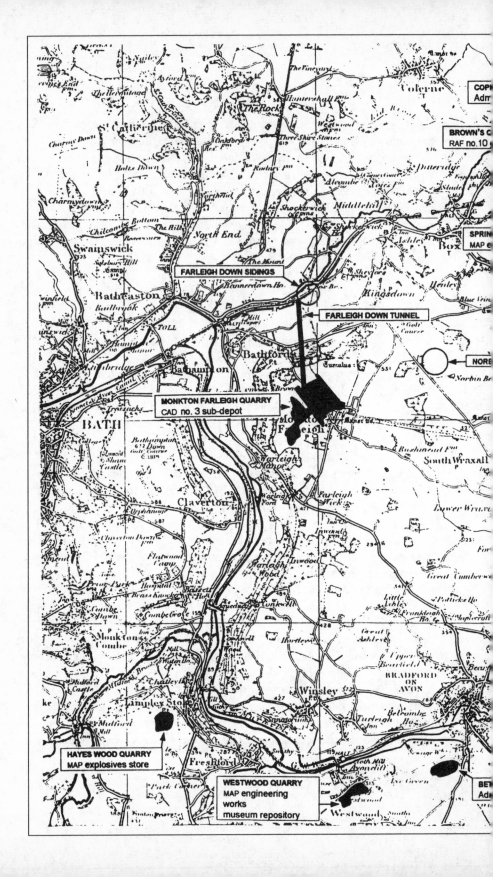

COPI
Adm

BROWN'S
RAF no.10

SPRIN
MAP e

FARLEIGH DOWN SIDINGS

FARLEIGH DOWN TUNNEL

NORE

MONKTON FARLEIGH QUARRY
CAD no. 3 sub-depot

HAYES WOOD QUARRY
MAP explosives store

WESTWOOD QUARRY
MAP engineering
works
museum repository

BE
Adm

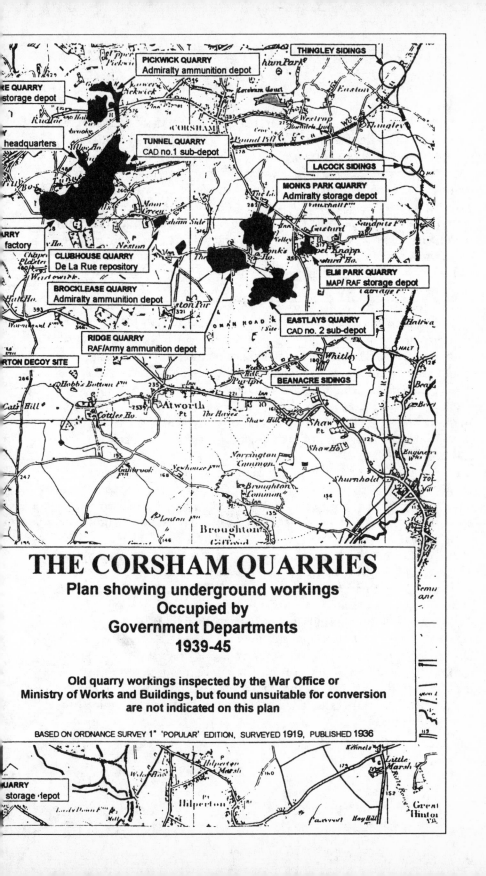

PICKWICK QUARRY
Admiralty ammunition depot

THINGLEY SIDINGS

RE QUARRY
storage depot

headquarters

TUNNEL QUARRY
CAD no.1 sub-depot

LACOCK SIDINGS

MONKS PARK QUARRY
Admiralty storage depot

ARRY
factory

CLUBHOUSE QUARRY
De La Rue repository

ELM PARK QUARRY
MAP/ RAF storage depot

BROCKLEASE QUARRY
Admiralty ammunition depot

EASTLAYS QUARRY
CAD no. 2 sub-depot

RIDGE QUARRY
RAF/Army ammunition depot

RTON DECOY SITE

BEANACRE SIDINGS

THE CORSHAM QUARRIES
Plan showing underground workings
Occupied by
Government Departments
1939-45

Old quarry workings inspected by the War Office or
Ministry of Works and Buildings, but found unsuitable for conversion
are not indicated on this plan

BASED ON ORDNANCE SURVEY 1" 'POPULAR' EDITION, SURVEYED 1919, PUBLISHED 1936

UARRY
storage depot

the wedge shape of the existing workings, by the presence of a standard gauge railway siding, and by the flooding during the winter of certain parts of the mine. The central position of the underground loading platform necessitated headings to the east and west communicating with the south end of each storage district. The position of the west haulageway was dictated by an agreement with the GWR not to store explosives within 100' of the main line railway tunnel. The alignment of the Main East haulageway was determined by the fact that during winter water rose regularly to a known level, with the consequence that the haulageway had to be sited across the dip of the strata above that level. When construction was complete the engineers were disappointed to find that during particularly adverse weather conditions the water still rose to an inch or two above rail level in the main adit.

The railway platform was designed to handle 2,000 tons of ammunition a day, but it was realized that any accidental stoppage at this point would paralyse the whole depot. Alternative means of ingress and egress were therefore provided with a capacity equalling that of the main loading platform, consisting of four slope-shafts and two vertical lift-shafts. This general layout was elaborated by the provision of a powerhouse, underground workshops, loco repair shop, offices, barracks and canteen facilities.

Clearance of debris at Tunnel revealed that at the extreme western end of the workings, which was destined to be No.1 storage District, there were two geological faults which made the stone very broken with a displacement in the strata of thirty feet. It was decided to abandon this area forthwith, with the consequential loss of four acres of storage space.

At Monkton Farleigh circumstances were somewhat different in that a substantially larger area of old mine workings was available than would be required for the finished storage depot. Farleigh Down is a broad hilltop site with a precipitous hillside to the west sloping steeply into the Avon Valley below. This hillside had been worked for stone for over 200 years by open quarrying and by innumerable mines tunnelling under the hilltop. Further to the east other quarry owners had sunk slope shafts through the overburden to win stone from underground. Over the years these many workings had run into one another with the result that by the 1930s the hillside was riddled with a network of tunnels extending over nearly 300 acres.

The western perimeter of the quarries is shallow and the overlying strata heavily fissured, allowing considerable volumes of water to percolate through in the winter. The eastern side was also subject to an ingress of water, probably caused by a disruption of the overlying clay. The area inside this belt amounted to about 150 acres, split in half by a major geological fault running north to south through the workings. The seventy acres to the east of the fault were quite dry, and it was considered that once cleared they would provide the required thirty-eight acres of storage space.

Several unique factors were involved in the layout of Monkton Farleigh which did not figure in the design parameters of the other depots. Firstly, Farleigh was positioned below a plateau some 450 feet above the valley in which ran the main line railway that was to be its principal source of supply. A radical plan was proposed to drive a mile-long tunnel from the heart of the workings terminating in an underground sorting yard built underneath the railway embankment in the valley below. This tunnel was designed to handle 1,000 tons of ammunition daily. As a safety precaution it was necessary to plan two auxiliary slope-shafts to the surface which would be able to cope with this turnover should a breakdown occur in the Farleigh Down tunnel. These shafts were positioned at the heads of two main haulageways running the length of the east and west extremities of the mine. The area between the Main East and Main West haulages was divided into seven equal districts of five acres each, with a haulageway through the middle of each district communicating with the main passages at each end.

Captain Terry's survey revealed that the pillars in Monkton Farleigh were unexpectedly larger and more closely spaced than in the other quarries, raising concern that the required nett storage area could not be obtained. The solution to this problem – later abandoned – was to remove all the existing natural pillars and build each district in concrete to a regular plan perfectly suited to operational requirements. As clearing progressed it was found that a large area at the northern end of the workings was in a poor state and subject to sudden roof falls. Six acres in this area had to be immediately abandoned, resulting in the loss of a complete district, so revised plans were prepared dividing the main area into six rather than seven storage districts.

In the meantime the accelerated munitions programme called for the emergency provision of temporary storage space at Monkton Farleigh, so hasty arrangements were made to develop two additional areas totalling fifteen acres to the west of the dividing fault. The design of these areas utilized the existing pillar arrangement to the fullest extent with the minimum of heavy engineering.

RIDGE QUARRY AND THE RAF RESERVE DEPOTS

Once sufficient manpower had been mobilized, construction began simultaneously at Ridge, Eastlays and Tunnel Quarry in July, 1936. The vast influx of men, materials and machinery was a source of some consternation to the small rural community of Corsham. Efforts were made to maintain an air of secrecy about the works there, and by way of subterfuge it was let slip that the Ministry of Food was building an emergency food dump. The shrewd Wiltshire folk, however, were not so easily deceived; Miss Berrett, a young Trowbridge schoolteacher, returning by bus from a shopping trip to Bath observed in her diary: "Wed. August 27th – Went to Corsham and saw the men at work on the munitions dump which stretches underground for a great distance."

It was made clear that Ridge Quarry must be ready to receive stocks of explosives by the end of December, 1936, and, given this precondition, there was an acceptance that further engineering works would necessarily be minimal. The mine had altered little since being vacated by the Ministry of Munitions in 1922, but it still proved necessary to remove a total of 96,000 tons of stone debris to provide sufficient storage space. All the raised stacking areas constructed in the Great War were removed and the floors rolled and levelled. The already comprehensive two-foot-gauge railway system was extended to serve all the storage bays, and the existing steam winch at the head of the access shaft was over-hauled and provided with a new boiler. Because the 1:3 gradient put a considerable load on the winding plant a standby electric hauling engine was installed in case of a breakdown of the primary set.

At the bottom of the main slope shaft the rails served a primary reception and marshalling area. Nearby an old vertical ventilation shaft was adapted for winding by the installation of a pair of counterbalanced electric lifts running in wooden guides. This was a primitive affair with a poor loading capacity, capable of handling only one third of the throughput of the slope shaft.

Underground, the mine is crossed by a major slip-fault, with the result that one half of the workings is about 20 feet lower than the other. Two sloping haulageways were driven to connect the upper and lower sections; to enable wagons to be drawn up these inclines two steam winches were installed, adapted to operate on compressed air supplied by compressors housed on the surface. Generally, however, loaded trucks were manoeuvred manually throughout the level areas of the quarry.

Some months after stacking had begun a construction programme was initiated, designed to produce a layout of storage areas more regular than the random pattern of existing pillars. It was planned to reinforce the stone pillars by corseting them with concrete, making them rectangular in section with straight haulageways between. Concreting began early in 1938 on fifteen pillars and a length of perimeter wall in the south-east corner of the quarry, but this operation was permanently suspended a few months later. The cost of the work and the quantity of materials consumed were much greater than anticipated and were out of proportion with the benefits obtained. The unfinished concrete reinforcing can still be seen in varying degrees of completion in the quarry today and illustrates the constructional techniques used in the larger and more sophisticated of the Corsham depots. It was during this period that the first fatal accident occurred, when, on 3 February, 1938, William Reed, a young married man from Pickwick, was crushed by a cage descending the lift-shaft at Ridge quarry. It appears that he was working at the shaft bottom and saw the cage descending, but as he stepped back to get out of the way he slipped and fell beneath it.

A second slope shaft, the steeply graded West Ridge incline, was reopened on 12 February, 1942, to improve access to the lower level of the mine and provide space for a further 1,500 tons of bombs. The underground access tunnel linking this shaft to the new storage bays passed through an area of treacherous roof formation that required substantial support to ensure safety.

Unlike the three other quarries that comprised the Corsham CAD, Ridge was never reclassified as permanent storage, and no further development was done underground after 1942. Surface buildings at Ridge were minimal. In line with War Office practice the first buildings to be erected were twenty-seven wooden huts to house military police personnel, built in two groups on open land between the quarry shafts and the lane to Corsham. The vertical lift shaft with its associated winding gear and compressor house was immediately between the two groups of police huts. The No.2 loading bay was the most substantial and is the only major building still surviving. During 1940 a buried emergency control room and defence point was built beneath an area of high ground east of the quarry, overlooking the whole site. A flight of iron rungs let into the wall gives access to a small observation post, pierced by narrow gun slits, which protrudes two feet above the top of the mound.

Although War Office property, Ridge quarry was initially allocated to the RAF for the storage of bombs and bulk explosives. To understand how this came about it is necessary to look in some detail at the history of RAF ammunition storage in the Second World War. During the inter-war years the minimal storage requirements of the RAF were adequately met by two surface depots at Altrincham and Pulham, both of which were essentially small-arms magazines and unsuitable for holding large stocks of bulk explosive or aerial bombs. Unlike the War Office, which had recognized the need for secure underground storage since before the 1918 Armistice, the RAF failed to address the problem until its first re-armament expansion programme was defined early in 1936. Treasury approval was then sought for a six-month war reserve of bombs, amounting to 98,000 tons, and for 16,000 tons of bulk TNT. No clear policy was reached at this stage regarding the types of storage accommodation required, and this lack of foresight was to hamper the Air Ministry throughout the war.

The inclination of the dilatory Governments of the mid-1930s had been to view the next war as one which would be fought and won quickly by overwhelming air power, so an extravagant proportion of the resources available for defence was directed to the RAF. From the early months of 1936 an accelerated programme of RAF ammunition manufacture was initiated, with a significant output scheduled to start flowing from September. Thus we see the RAF, supported by the Treasury, with huge stocks coming on-line shortly but with no suitable storage space available, while the War Office, with carefully developed plans for reserve storage depots, had no modern weapons to store in them and only grudging government financial backing.

As an interim measure the War Office was approached with the request that some of the quarry space under development at Corsham should be temporarily allocated to the RAF until the new Army weapons programme got properly under way. The outcome was that in November, 1936, the RAF was granted the exclusive use of Ridge Quarry, which was then approaching completion. Some time later a substantial part of Eastlays Quarry was also seconded to the RAF to supplement the Ridge holding.

Meanwhile the Air Ministry continued to search for suitable sites of its own. Most of the possible locations had already been taken over by the War Office, or else were rejected for the same reasons that the War Office enquiry rejected them in May, 1930. Two sites were eventually found: in June, 1936, limestone quarries at Chilmark, near Salisbury, were purchased to provide storage for 20,000 tons, and early the following year 450,000 square feet of disused gypsum workings adjacent to Peter Ford's plaster works at Fauld in Derbyshire were also acquired.

No other suitable mine was found, so the RAF fell back on its second option which was to build an 'artificial' underground depot. Sorrow Quarry, a disused open-cast limestone working at Harpur Hill near Buxton was purchased from ICI in the summer of 1938 to serve as the northern depot. The finished structure, built of reinforced concrete on the quarry floor, consisted of seven parallel, arched-roof bays running the length of the quarry with the abutments of the outermost arches sprung from the natural rock walls. The stone bed fell away at one side of the quarry floor allowing part of the depot to be built as a double-storey structure. A standard-gauge railway siding ran through the depot via tunnels that penetrated the sides of the quarry. After completion of the concrete work the quarry was filled with waste stone to a depth of forty-two feet over the crown of the arches to give protection against enemy bombs. The final cost of the project, which had capacity for 18,000 tons of High Explosive bombs with an additional 30,000 square feet set aside for Chemical Weapons storage, was just short of a million pounds. Stocking began at Harpur Hill in March, 1940; this was a little later than scheduled because when the first railway consignment arrived it was found much to the embarrassment of the Works Directorate that the tunnel portals had been built an inch lower than the height of railway box-vans.

On 18 August, 1939, the Air Ministry sought approval to acquire a disused slate quarry near Llanberis in North Wales, suitable for the storage of 18,000 tons of bombs. The purchase price was £20,000 and, in the absence of detailed estimates, the construction cost was expected to be about £460,000. Following the apparent success of the design employed at Harpur Hill the Air Ministry Works Directorate decided to use the same technique at Llanberis, but because of the great depth of the quarry the design was adapted to produce a structure with two floors throughout. The lower level had a conventional flat reinforced concrete ceiling which also formed the floor of the upper level, which had an arched roof like that at Harpur Hill. Standard and narrow-gauge railway lines entered the lower level of the depot through tunnels bored into the mountain, while three electric lifts transported bombs to the upper floor. Overhead protection was given by forty feet of broken slate. In response to pressure from the Treasury efforts were made to cheapen and accelerate construction at Llanberis, but unfortunately this cost-cutting had disastrous consequences only six months after the depot was officially opened.

The RAF storage requirement expanded enormously as the war progressed; the 98,000 ton estimate of 1936 growing to 632,300 tons by July of 1943. Current capacity amounted to only 158,000 tons, leaving a shortfall of nearly half a million tons, which was eventually catered for by a relaxation of the magazine regulations and by the provision of numerous open storage sites. In April, 1941, however, while the immediate problem was serious but not dire, a proposal was put forward to construct yet another underground depot in quarries at Linley, in Staffordshire. Within three months doubts about its viability were aroused following a series of serious roof falls, and in the following March construction was stopped and much of the site abandoned except for surface storage of obsolete bombs.

Overall the RAF venture into underground explosive storage was a tale of disaster and tragedy. Of the five Reserve Depots only Chilmark survived the war without a major catastrophe. Linley, as we have seen, was abandoned even before building work was completed. The main administration and storage depot at Fauld became the site of the largest explosion in the United Kingdom when, on 27 November, 1944, a total of 3,670 tons of bombs stored underground exploded en masse, leaving a crater half a mile across and one hundred feet deep. Sited directly above the crater, Upper Castle Hayes Farm, together with its occupants and cattle, completely disappeared in the blast which was heard a hundred miles away.

At Llanberis, too, the end came swiftly when, during the morning of Saturday 25 January, 1942, two-thirds of the structure collapsed within seconds under the weight of the overlying backfill, completely engulfing a train of twenty-seven wagons which was in the process of unloading. The collapse buried over 14,000 tons of bombs which at the time represented 14% of the total RAF stock. Most of the bombs were eventually recovered, the last being extricated on 22 October, 1942. Although the remains of the tunnels were eventually cleared of debris no ammunition was ever again stored underground at Llanberis. Air Ministry authority was obtained on 31 December to abandon the un-collapsed section and use the collapsed section for open storage of incendiaries. A Court of Inquiry concluded that faulty design was the principal cause of the failure: cracks were noticed in the structure as building neared completion but these were attributed to minor defects rather than to a major and fatal miscalculation.

Following the collapse of Llanberis concerns were raised regarding the stability of the tunnels at Harpur Hill, which were built on the same principle. An inspection revealed similar cracks developing there, and the level of disquiet was such that most of the protective overburden was removed immediately. On 12 February it was decided to fulfil all overseas issues from Harpur Hill in order to empty the depot as quickly as possible. By the end of March 5,634 tons were removed, the remaining 10,042 tons going by midday on 16 May. As the various bays were cleared of bombs action was taken by the Works Directorate to strengthen the tunnels by bricking up half of the arched openings in the concrete walls and shoring those which had to remain open with steel arches. The repairs were finally completed early in April, 1943, when the Air Ministry agreed that underground storage of HE bombs and small-arms ammunition could resume. Confidence in the structure had been severely shaken, however, and the storage of sensitive items such as Smith gun ammunition, boxed TNT, land-mines and chemical weapons was expressly excluded.

We can now look at the way in which the vacillating fortunes of the

Air Ministry reserve depots affected the running of the War Office works at Corsham. Ridge Quarry was allocated to the Air Ministry in November, 1936, under the command of Squadron Leader F.R. Lines, and was designated a sub-unit of the Altrincham small-arms depot. Control of ammunition and support supplies became the responsibility of RAF Maintenance Command following its formation in March, 1938, at which time Altrincham became No.2 Maintenance Unit (2MU) and Ridge Quarry No.2 Maintenance Sub-Unit (2MSU). The following spring separate Groups were formed within the Command for specific functions, ammunition, fuel and oxygen being the remit of No.42 Group.

Stacking and loading of bombs was carried out by a team of thirty civilian gangers, employed by the RAOC but under direct control of the RAF. The total capacity of Ridge Quarry was 13,000 tons, of which the RAF at first required about 5,000 tons to store 500 lb and 250 lb General Purpose (GP) bombs. By the outbreak of war RAF stocks at Ridge had expanded to 11,569 tons, including 4,000 tons of bulk TNT. At that time the RAOC retained a small area to store 2,000 tons of bulk explosive for Army use.

During the early months of the war Ridge Quarry was used as a temporary holding point for bulk explosives and as a long-term store for obsolete GP bombs returned from various active airfields via the Pulham depot. A typical week in September saw the receipt of twenty-two tons of raw TNT from the ICI works, and the despatch of four tons to the Thames Ammunition Company at Erith in Kent. The following month there began an appreciable increase in the inward flow of surplus bombs with 1,245 tons arriving in the first two weeks. A record 210 tons was transported underground in less than twelve hours on 7 November, but this continuous use overtaxed the aged steam winch which failed at 6 pm. Ninety minutes later the standby electric unit was coaxed into motion; this sufficed barely adequately until 8 pm when the more powerful steam winch was brought back into action following hasty repairs.

January, 1940, saw a reorganization of No.42 Group, resulting in the recently opened Chilmark reserve depot becoming parent to Ridge Quarry, which was re-designated No.11 MSU. Conditions underground were becoming congested due to the large influx of obsolete material which was accumulating with no immediate prospect of disposal; a problem made more acute by the RAOC insistence that they be allowed

41

to store rather more than the agreed amount of Army TNT in the quarry. The situation eased at the beginning of May when calling-forward instructions were received for a shipment of 5000 250 lb GP bombs destined for No.4 Base Ammunition Depot in the Middle East. The whole of this consignment was despatched from Ridge, where labourers were employed on overtime breaking down stacks and placing bombs on end beside the narrow-gauge railway ready for loading.

Large issues continued throughout July and the early part of August, the space vacated being filled by huge quantities of imported TNT from the United States and Canada, and eight tons of French manufacture and dubious nature hurriedly recovered from the continent. Administrative responsibility for all Air Ministry bulk explosives stored at Corsham was transferred to the RAOC in January, 1941, and independent accounts of receipts and issues disappear from the record book from that date.

The spring of 1941 saw increasing deliveries of munitions from the United States under the terms of the Lend Lease Act of 11 March. Turnover of bombs at Ridge Quarry increased dramatically and a two-shift system was introduced in an effort to increase the daily rate to 400 tons. Unfortunately the hectic work schedule was accompanied by a slackening of discipline resulting, on 11 March, in an accident that claimed the life of Mr Fall, a civilian labourer working underground. A Coroner's Inquest heard that a train of three trucks containing twelve 500 lb bombs was pushed into the slope shaft before being properly attached to the haulage rope. The wagons hurtled down the shaft, derailed at the bottom and crashed into a pillar, widely dispersing their bomb load. Mr Fall was struck by the flying debris and fatally injured. The inquest concluded that he died whilst trying to warn his workmates, and his death was recorded as accidental.

In preparation for the expected German invasion Ridge received 3,000 hand grenades from Tunnel Quarry on 22 August for issue to airfields and depots in the south-west within the next few days. Delivery also began at this time of tens of thousands of rounds for the Smith gun, a hastily cobbled together home defence weapon designed by a Mr Smith, chief engineer of the Trianco Engineering Company, makers of tinplate toys. The Smith gun was in service as a Home Guard and RAF airfield defence weapon by June, 1941, and quickly gained an unenviable reputation. Fuses fitted to the early batches of High Explosive shell were so sensitive and unreliable that even the official handbook was forced to admit that they had "a reputation for lack of safety". One Home Guard Officer went further, stating quite bluntly that the Smith gun had "a terrifying reputation for killing its crew".

Smith gun ammunition was stored in large quantities at Ridge Quarry, although it is unlikely that stocks were retained for long periods. 27,000 rounds were issued to airfields in the southern counties early in December, and further stocks were received early the following year, 1,750 practice rounds arriving from Chorley Ordnance Factory at the end of February, followed by 19,000 High Explosive rounds from Aycliffe on 10 March. The Air Ministry was undoubtedly wary of this ammunition, refusing, as we have seen, to accommodate it underground at Harpur Hill following completion of the strengthening work there, fearful that the slightest mishap could result in its detonation.

The whole of 1942 saw the Air Ministry sorely pressed for storage capacity and with its construction programme in turmoil following the failure to complete Linley. It was finding great difficulty in locating suitable sites for expansion, and on top of this it was suddenly confronted with the permanent loss of Llanberis and the concomitant temporary quarantine of Harpur Hill. The Air Ministry also faced pressure from the supply front; a memorandum from Maintenance Command to the Air Ministry in September noted that: "Owing to increases in deliveries of explosives from industry and overseas the storage position has become acute and will remain so until stabilised by completion of new units under construction."

Emergency measures were taken to help relieve the shortfall, such as increasing the authorized capacity of the Forward Ammunition Depots and airfield bomb stores, as well as pressing into use disused railway tunnels at Rowthorne in Nottinghamshire and Newlands in the Forest of Dean. Temporary surface dumps were established on the straggling slate tips at Llanberis, while a permanent surface High Explosives store was constructed nearby at Rhiwlas. A successful approach was also made to the War Office, resulting in the allocation of much of the Eastlays depot to the RAF.

Strenuous efforts were made to recover the bombs trapped in the un-collapsed section of the Llanberis depot. The task was overseen by Dr Rotter, Director of Explosives Research at Woolwich Arsenal, who was later to be awarded the George Medal for his participation in the infinitely more hazardous recovery operation following the Fauld explosion in 1944. Rails were laid in an old adit at the rear of the storage depot which led into an adjacent quarry, hitherto used only as an emergency escape route. The quarry into which it led was eighty feet deep and had no vehicular access, so as the 70,000 bombs were gradually extricated from the stricken depot they had to be manhandled through the escape passage and lifted individually by a crane set on temporary footings at the edge of the quarry. Evacuation began on 9 March and continued until 28 April when the last bomb was recovered. A total of 8,230 tons of ammunition was recovered in this exercise, nearly 2,000 tons of which was despatched to Ridge Quarry.

Between 30 March and 16 May a total of 15,676 tons of bombs and other ammunition was evacuated from Harpur Hill as a precautionary measure; of these just 650 tons was transferred to Ridge Quarry.

Once the abnormal activity resulting from the Llanberis accident had subsided, Ridge fell into a busy routine through the rest of 1942 and into the following summer. The average turnover amounted to balanced receipts and issues of about 2,000 tons each month. Receipts normally consisted of 500 lb bombs from the Risely and Swynnerton filling factories, 250 pdrs from Glascoed and a few 1,000 lb bombs from Ruddington.

ELM PARK QUARRY

Early in the war a small quarry a mile or so from Ridge was acquired by No.40 Group for the storage of lubricating oils and similar materials in drums, control of the site being exercised by RAF Quedgely in Gloucestershire. Conditions underground were far from suitable for the type of storage required by the Group, and on 1 March, 1941, Elm Park was transferred to No.42 Group as a satellite of No.11 MSU Ridge Quarry, under the command of Flying Officer G.N.R. Saltmarsh.

Elm Park was another of the small quarries acquired by the MAP to store aircraft engines built in the Spring Quarry factory, but subsequently abandoned. Little was done to improve conditions underground other than install a few electric lights in the main haulageway and to hide away two insalubrious bucket latrines for the convenience of the gangers. Haulage underground was performed by horses owned by Bath & Portland Stone, but the 350-yard-long entrance adit which, unlike those

44

at other quarries in the area had only a very gentle slope, was fitted with a modern electric winch. The ease of access that this adit afforded prompted staff at Elm Park to undertake a trial receipt of eighteen 1,000 lb bombs recently evacuated from Harpur Hill. The experiment was conducted on 22 March and was entirely successful.

Although Elm Park quarry fulfilled an immediate requirement, its inadequacies soon came to the fore, and within a year the Air Ministry was plotting its disposal. The final receipts, amounting to 111 tons, were made during January, 1943; stocks then remained dormant until early June when a rash of heavy issues presaged the final closure. Residual stocks were transferred to Ridge Quarry on 30 July. Three months later the quarry was transferred to the Admiralty to supplement the small Navy ammunition storage capacity at Pickwick and Brocklease quarries. Since 5 April, 1942, a heading at the innermost end of the quarry was let to the University of Bristol for the storage of archives and other material. This use continued throughout the Admiralty tenure until the end of the war.

During the early months of 1944 stock levels increased at Ridge to a peak of 31,563 tons, and in March preparations for the invasion of Europe began. During April and May the RAF dropped more than 200,000 tons of bombs as a direct preliminary to Operation 'Overlord'. The contribution to this effort made by Ridge Quarry amounted to 7,744 tons in April and a massive 14,294 tons in May.

The end of the war in Europe saw vast surpluses of ammunition accumulated by all three services. By May, 1945, Maintenance Command estimated that it would have to find storage for 15,000 tons of new bombs every week for the next three months, emanating from existing contracts with the Ordnance Factories. The Command also faced the tasks of de-stocking operational airfields of redundant explosives and absorbing the estimated 100,000 tons of bombs in unprotected roadside storage.

In June Ridge Quarry reported a vacant capacity of 15,000 tons, but 42 Group had reservations about using the Corsham depots due to the fact that they were only really suitable for bombs of 500 lb or less and that the inclined shafts limited turnover to a maximum of 400 tons per day. The limited potential of Ridge Quarry for storage over extended peacetime periods, deficient as it was in ventilation or air-conditioning equipment, had been questioned a year earlier following an inspection by the Air Ministry Director General of Equipment. Noting the poor condition there of a large stock of bulk TNT packed in wooden cases, he commented that:

"Storage conditions at that unit appear to be unsuitable for the prolonged storage of wooden items. Destruction of 2,000 boxes was recently recommended in view of an advanced state of decomposition due to wet-rot peculiar to the storage conditions at Corsham."

In February, 1945, a further inspection revealed that 6000 500 lb bombs of US manufacture stored in the lower section of Ridge were in a very unstable condition and that the wooden dunnage upon which they were stacked was rotting away. It was feared that the dunnage could collapse and initiate an explosion. The most dangerous of these bombs were removed to the Pembrey filling factory to be broken down over the next five months.

A number of airfields, redundant following the end of hostilities, were absorbed by 42 Group as concentration points for surplus bombs from active airfields, pending arrangements for disposal. Charlton Horethorne in Somerset was one such airfield, which acted as an overflow for 11MU Chilmark until the end of 1947. Long Newnton airfield in Gloucestershire was also absorbed by 42 Group, being taken under the wing of Chilmark in July, 1945. Stocks earmarked for disposal at Ridge Quarry were regularly sent by lorry to Long Newnton; over 100 tons of bombs being despatched at the end of May, 1948, followed by a further 445 bombs a week later. Most were eventually deep-sea dumped via Barry Docks.

The remaining stock of 7,249 tons of High Explosive bombs, together with a small inventory of non-explosive items such as bomb-tails, parachutes and packing cases, was finally struck off charge at Ridge Quarry and transferred to Chilmark on 4 January, 1949. The RAF did, however, maintain an interest in the quarry throughout the early 1950s during the evolution of its future weapons policy. For a while it was thought that an increased storage requirement for conventional ammunition would be needed, and in October, 1950, it was suggested that Ridge should be retained temporarily as the best subsidiary underground site until a viable alternative could be found.

By 1955 the centre of gravity of British defence policy had shifted toward the nuclear deterrent and large stocks of conventional weapons were seen as a luxury which the exchequer could not bear. Development of the 'V' bomber force was proceeding apace with the Valiant in service in 1955, the Vulcan in the following year and the Victor by the end of 1957. The coming of age of this new force and the apparent death knell of the conventional High Explosive bomb, occurred on 11 October, 1956, with the successful drop from a Valiant of the first British-built atomic bomb. The run-down of the large reserve depots paralleled these developments: the tunnels at Harpur Hill were emptied of HE bombs late in 1949, all functional stock was removed from Llanberis by March, 1955, and Fauld ceased holding High Explosives in 1958. Only Chilmark was retained, as a reserve depot for the replenishment of overseas stock. Ridge quarry was finally abandoned by the RAF in 1955.

The Army presence remained at Ridge until 1964 after which the site reverted to care and maintenance under the Ministry of Works and Buildings. This state of limbo continued for ten years until 1975 when Ridge Quarry was re-purchased by the Neston Estate which exercised its right of pre-emption. All the surface buildings were demolished except for the No.2 shaft transit shed, which has found a new agricultural use. Debris from surface demolition was bulldozed into the lift shaft and No.1 slope shaft which are now both completely blocked, although No.2 shaft is still accessible.

6

TUNNEL QUARRY

Some clearance had been undertaken at Tunnel Quarry with the consent of Bath & Portland Stone prior to July, 1935, to allow Captain Terry and his team of surveyors, together with the civilian consulting engineer Forster Brown, access to the remoter areas of the mine to compile their respective surveys.

In June, 1936, when the War Office drew up a preliminary schedule of works to be completed at Tunnel Quarry, it was thought desirable that as much as possible of the work should be done either by Royal Engineer detachments or by directly employed civilian labour. Certain specific tasks were, however, to be done by private contractors.

WORKS TO BE CARRIED OUT BY CONTRACT

(1) Clearing the main heading to the railway tunnel. To be completed by the Bath & Portland Stone Company on a 'cost plus profit' basis.

(2) Construction of inclined and vertical shafts.

(3) Erection of haulage gear including endless ropeways, lifts and haulage engines.

(4) Erection of power-house machinery.

(5) Provision of fireproof doors and fire-fighting apparatus.

(6) Provision of a telephone system. This was to be carried out by the GPO.

(7) Construction of dry walling around the concrete reinforcing packs.

(8) Alterations to the loading platform at Corsham station.

(9)   Supply of construction plant.
(10)   Construction of surface buildings.
(11)   Railway works at Thingley Junction and Corsham station.

WORKS TO BE CARRIED OUT BY DIRECTLY EMPLOYED LABOUR

(1)   Water supply and sanitation.
(2)   Temporary electric lighting in the quarries during
       construction.
(3)   Alterations to the portals of existing inclined shafts.
(4)   Construction of concrete packs and strengthening of weak
       pillars.
(5)   Laying concrete and macadam floors.
(6)   Permanent lighting throughout the quarry.
(7)   Construction work in the vicinity of the power-house.
(8)   Construction of the main underground loading platform.
(9)   Railway work inside Tunnel Quarry.
(10)   Laying track for endless ropeway systems above and below
       ground.
(11)   Provision of a lorry park and main surface loading platform.

Doubt was expressed about contracting the Great Western Railway to construct the marshalling yard at Thingley Junction, which was expected to cost £45,000. It was thought, however, that the importance of involving the railway company in building a major extension to its system, which would inevitably throw a heavy burden of increased traffic on to its main line, was an overriding consideration. The War Office considered it probable, in any case, that the GWR would insist that they carried out the work themselves as their engines and rolling stock were to use the track.

Until October, 1936, no surface building existed on the Corsham site except for a wooden hut at the side of Pockeridge Drive which served as a shelter for the Pay Officer on paying-out days. The only access to the quarry was via a standard-gauge railway tunnel adjacent to the eastern portal of Box tunnel built by the quarrying firm of Randall & Saunders in 1844. A vertical ladder leading down to the mouth of the tunnel was the route used by all workers to get underground. At the beginning of a

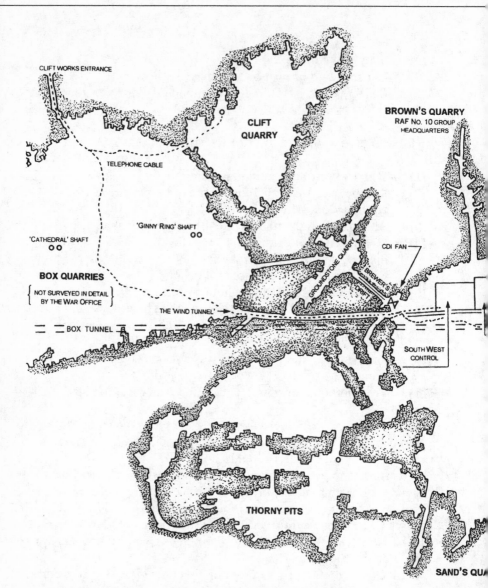

CLIFT WORKS ENTRANCE

CLIFT
QUARRY

BROWN'S QUARRY
RAF No. 10 GROUP
HEADQUARTERS

TELEPHONE CABLE

'GINNY RING' SHAFT
OO

'CATHEDRAL' SHAFT
OO

GROUNDSTONE QUARRY

BREWER'S

CDI FAN

BOX QUARRIES

{ NOT SURVEYED IN DETAIL
BY THE WAR OFFICE }

THE 'WIND TUNNEL'

≡ ≡ BOX TUNNEL ≡ ≡

SOUTH WEST
CONTROL

THORNY PITS

SAND'S QUA

CORSHAM QUARRIES – LAYOUT PLAN

Showing disposition of War Department Tunnel Quarry and
Box railway tunnel

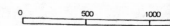

0   500   1000

SLOPE S

NOTE: REPRESENTATIONS OF INDIVIDUAL PILLARS ARE OMITTED FROM THIS PLAN FOR CLARITY

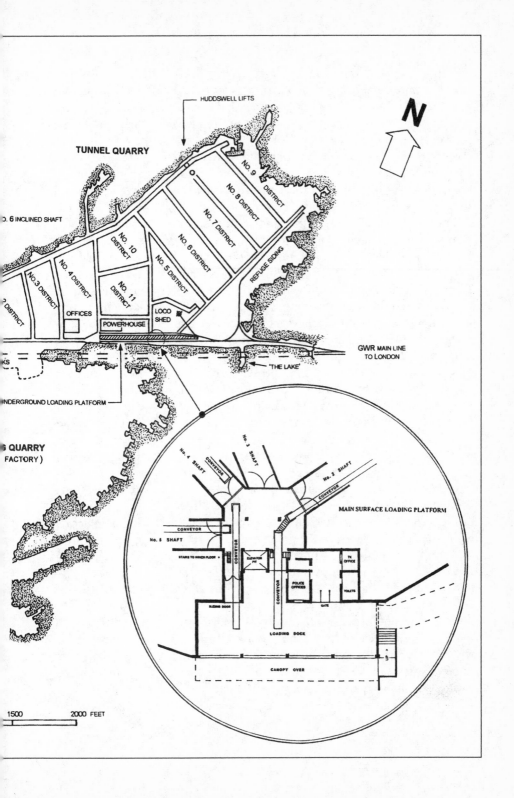

HUDDSWELL LIFTS

TUNNEL QUARRY

NO. 9 DISTRICT

NO. 8 DISTRICT

NO. 7 DISTRICT

NO. 6 DISTRICT

NO. 10 DISTRICT

NO. 5 DISTRICT

REFUGE SIDING

.O. 6 INCLINED SHAFT

NO.3 DISTRICT

NO. 4 DISTRICT

NO. 11 DISTRICT

? DISTRICT

OFFICES

POWERHOUSE

LOCO SHED

GWR MAIN LINE TO LONDON

'THE LAKE'

KS

INDERGROUND LOADING PLATFORM

KS

S QUARRY
(FACTORY)

No. 4 SHAFT

CONVEYOR

No. 3 SHAFT

No. 2 SHAFT

CONVEYOR

MAIN SURFACE LOADING PLATFORM

CONVEYOR

No. 5 SHAFT

STAIRS TO WINCH FLOOR

CONVEYOR

ELEVATOR PIT

TN OFFICE

POLICE OFFICES

CONVEYOR

TOILETS

SLIDING DOOR

GATE

LOADING DOCK

CANOPY OVER

1500   2000 FEET

shift the timekeeper called each man's name as he descended the ladder and checked them off before they ascended at the end of the shift. This system seemed satisfactory until it became apparent that some of the men had discovered that they could walk right through the workings and return to the surface via the long-abandoned No.7 or 'Strenic' slope shaft. In the early days there were cases of civilian labourers taking up second jobs in this way. Strenic shaft, which was too inconveniently sited to be of use in the finished depot, was blocked-up in 1941.

The task of clearing an estimated two million tons of stone debris was started from the area near the middle of the mine that was to become Nos. 5 and 6 Districts. Temporary two-foot gauge tracks were laid from the underground loading platform out into the old quarry roadways. Debris was manhandled into one cubic yard tipping trucks hauled by diminutive 20 hp diesel locomotives. As clearance proceeded the system was extended into the farthest extremities of the workings until ultimately over 500 tipper wagons and fifty-four locomotives were fully employed. The tipping trucks were emptied into standard-gauge GWR 10-ton wagons which were then formed into trains at the tunnel mouth and hauled away by main line locomotives. The bulk of the debris was tipped three miles away at Thingley Junction where it was used as landfill on the site of the assembly sidings being built to service the ammunition depots. In this way about 600 tons were removed every day by shifts of 150 men. Progress was held back by the multiple handling from narrow to standard gauge trucks, and in December, 1936, a 400-yard-long endless-belt conveyor was installed to overcome this bottleneck, positioned so that debris spilled directly into the main line trucks. Secondary belts radiating from the main conveyor enabled debris from the farthest areas to be transported to the loading point with a minimum of handling. Throughout 1936 and the early months of 1937 the only lighting underground was by means of dissolved acetylene flares, but the situation had improved by March with the installation of temporary electric lighting in most areas.

Teams of roof inspectors followed the clearing gangs. As they encountered areas of bad roof they either inserted temporary wooden props, or where necessary brought down all the loose stone to reveal the more secure stratum above. At first men more familiar with colliery techniques worked as safety men, but following an early fatal accident only Bath stone quarrymen were so employed. The accident occurred on Saturday

8 October at Eastlays Quarry, when two men were crushed to death by a roof-fall while erecting temporary supports. Witnesses described how they were unaware of any problem until they were thrown into darkness when their carbide lamps were blown out by the rush of air created by the falling stone. Evidence brought forward at the inquest by Mr Chaffey, the Bath & Portland works superintendent, indicated that the act of forcing in a wooden prop to support a thirty-foot expanse of roof which was thinner than expected caused the slab to fracture, culminating in its collapse. Mr Coombes, the roof-tester responsible for that area, stated that the roof seemed safe when he examined it a few hours before the incident, but when questioned he admitted that he had only worked at Corsham for seventeen months and conditions there were somewhat different from his previous experience in the coalfields. The inquest jury brought a verdict of Accidental Death, holding no one to blame, but recommended that the War Department should engage only Bath stone quarrymen to examine the ceilings in the quarries. Experienced quarrymen could determine the condition of the roof by tapping with a long bar or 'jadding iron'; a dull hollow thud would indicate that the ceiling bed was not securely attached to the upper bed and would need to be brought down.

While heavy work was under way in the congested eastern section of the mine the old mushroom beds in what was to become Nos. 10 and 11 Districts were also being cleared. This was a self-contained area of about fourteen acres, enclosed by dry stone walls, in which the floors had been made level and which still retained the light railway system installed by the Agaric Company ten years earlier.

Mushrooms were grown in a malodorous compost on raised wooden drills and long rows of these rotting structures had to be removed. It was said that when in full production over 20 tons of mushrooms were harvested each week. Officers superintending work in the mushroom area were disconcerted to find that one local entrepreneur had made clandestine use of the workings since the Agaric Company moved out in 1928. Concealed in a remote corner they discovered a die-press together with a considerable stock of counterfeit half-crown coins. Arrests were subsequently made and successful prosecutions brought, but the affair was not widely publicized at the time, as to do so may well have prejudiced the security of the project. Later it was revealed that on 9 January, 1937, three local people had been arrested in Bromsgrove for attempting to pass forged half-crowns at the Midland Cafe. At the subsequent court case one of the defendants claimed he had purchased a bag containing forty coins for £1 from an unknown drunken Irishman he met by chance on Bristol Bridge. All three were found guilty and sentenced to six months' imprisonment.

This small section of the quarry had obviously escaped the attention of the independent consulting engineer Mr Forster Brown, who had been commissioned by the War Office to report on conditions at the mine. There is evidence to suggest that Forster Brown's report was based solely upon his assessment of the relatively easily accessed parts of the mushroom area, and that insufficient evidence was obtained elsewhere. Of the mushroom area he reported that:

> "It is evident that this quarry has been worked to the utmost limit that was safe. I calculate, upon the assumption that 65 to 70% of the gross weight overlying the Quarry is operative, that the total weight acting over the 14.2 acres worked is equivalent to approximately 5 tons per square foot. The area of pillars is equivalent to 20% of the whole. Taking the figure at 20%, the pressure acting upon the pillars is about 25 tons per square foot if they were evenly sized and spaced. The safe working load on the pillars in their solid conditions would, I estimate, be about 40 tons per square foot, so that had the pillars been evenly spaced and sized probably no sign of crushing would have taken place.
>
> "The actual conditions, however, are that many of the pillars have been left of inadequate size and have had to carry areas of roof which have made the pressure acting upon them greater than their safe load, with the result that many of them have cracked, thus reducing their load capacity and throwing extra load upon neighbouring pillars."

Mining had been carried out on a haphazard 'pillar and stall' system, following no regularly planned distribution of roof support but dictated solely by the run of stone fit for sale. All the stone worth taking was extracted, with the result that where the quality of stone was exceptionally good the pillars left as roof supports were robbed to an unsafe extent, but where the quality was poor larger pillars were left. The effect of leaving irregularly sized pillars resulted in the uneven distribution of roof support noted by Forster Brown, and caused uneven settlement and crushing of the pillars. As clearance progressed it became obvious that to the east and west of the mushroom area the pillars were much more irregularly spaced than was expected with the consequence that the number of broken pillars per acre was much greater than anticipated.

The strengthening work necessary at Tunnel Quarry consisted of the repair of existing pillars and the provision of further permanent works to ensure that the overhead cover was adequately supported. It was considered at the time that the roof was so sound and the overhead cover so deep that there was no danger of it breaking up under bombing attack, but there was some doubt that it was sufficiently supported as a mass. Colonel Minnis noted to the War Office Tunnel Quarry Committee that:

> "There is no doubt that with the passage of time some part of the overburden which rests on crushed pillars will, if left, subside by its own weight, and some pillars are so nearly loaded to their ultimate capacity that vibration of the mass of the overburden by bombing would, in my opinion, be likely to start a movement which we may be unable to resist."

Forster Brown's report disclosed evidence of movement of the overburden along the dip of the strata towards Box Tunnel, which, he suggested, could be arrested by the provision of three heavy support packs, each about 150 feet square, consisting of concrete perimeter walls filled with packed stone debris. When, by November, 1936, work on clearing debris and excavation for the foundations of these packs was well advanced it was noticed that a number of small pillars between the GWR tunnel and the quarry railway heading were failing. This indicated that the south-easterly movement of the overburden had been accelerated by removal of such support as had been afforded by the debris excavated. Colonel Minnis immediately suspended all excavation and built about 500 feet of the twenty-foot thick concrete cut-off wall between the GWR tunnel and the quarry heading, incorporating within it the small pillars which were failing. This prompt action arrested the movement. The subsequent completion of the three packs, strengthening of weak pillars in Districts 10 & 11 and the building of boundary walls around the districts finally removed all danger of further movement in the central area of the quarry.

55

Overloaded pillars showed the symptoms of stress normal in blocks of material subject to compression. The first indications are irregular cracks starting at the top or bottom and curving inwards towards mid-height. The method of dealing with pillars showing signs of bursting was to bind them together with reinforced concrete corsets, incorporating sufficient steel in horizontal rings to take up the tensile stress.

By the spring of 1937 large areas had been cleared of debris and construction was well in hand. The labour force had greatly increased and the awkward vertical ladder leading to the tunnel mouth was replaced by a covered stairway, pedestrian access underground being maintained in the meantime via the old No.7 incline. Another inclined shaft, known as '6 shaft', was re-opened at the western end of the quarry and re-graded from its old steep gradient to one easier for traffic. Plant, equipment and building materials were arriving daily, delivered by train via the underground branch line that had recently been re-sleepered.

Some of the stone waste was retained in the quarry and used to build up the floor to the required level, which was then rolled and consolidated using five Aveling Barford diesel road rollers of 3 and 5 ton capacity. Vast quantities of Bath stone waste were also consumed underground to make concrete, which was not of the usual type but was a mixture of Portland cement and crushed stone. The resulting conglomerate had a greater crushing strain than Bath stone and was thought quite suitable for the job in hand. Stone crushing plant installed underground supplied the whole of the aggregate and sand.

The method of building concrete supports was similar, whether for reinforcing existing pillars, building new pillars, or constructing division walls. First, excavations were taken down through the floor filling to the solid rock below. This was usually done by hand, sometimes using tiered staging so that debris was thrown up from platform to platform. As soon as solid rock was reached the foundations were filled to floor level with concrete. The pillar, wall or column was concreted up to the roof using a system of recoverable steel shutters, consisting of light-gauge steel panels strengthened by slotted steel flanges which could be securely locked together using tapered steel pins. After the forms had reached a suitable height and the concrete had set, the lower ones could be removed and used higher up after cleaning. When concrete walls and pillars reached the roof, after a certain amount of time had elapsed to allow for shrinkage to take place, two-inch diameter diagonal holes were bored through the wall to include the joint between the top of the concrete and the roof. High-pressure grout was then forced in until no more could be taken in order to form a perfect joint. Progress was greatly accelerated by the use of Blaw Knox concrete pumps, which could deliver successfully through a 700-foot run of six-inch pipe against a forty-foot head, and were placed in carefully selected sites to be central for several jobs.

Where it was necessary to excavate large quantities of virgin stone a number of machines were employed to expedite the work. Up to this time all commercial stone extraction in the Bath quarries had been done using hand saws or 'frig bobs', wedges and jump bars. The War Office, acting on the advice of colliery managers drafted in to work on the scheme, introduced modified coal-cutting machines which proved so successful that they were universally adopted by the quarry owners when some of the quarries were de-requisitioned after the war. Three types of machine were used: the Samson chain cutter and Hardiax and Siskol rotary percussion drills.

The Samson coal cutters, built by Mavor and Coulson of Glasgow, were large machines weighing several tons, mounted on caterpillar tracks and powered by 50 hp electric motors. At the front of the superstructure was a geared universal drive head carrying a large chain saw on a jib about seven feet long which could be raised, lowered, slewed to any angle and rotated through 360 degrees. The chain carried hardened steel cutters which were capable of cutting very rapidly through stone to a depth of six or seven feet.

The Hardiax and Siskol arc-shearing machines were much smaller, being similar in appearance to the pneumatic drills used by roadmen today. The Hardiax was the preferred type and was powered by compressed air, whilst the Siskol was electrically driven. Both of these arc shearers were much slower than the chain cutters but were very successful in constricted locations which were inaccessible to the Samsons.

By the midsummer of 1937 the heavily faulted west end of the quarry had been abandoned and effort was now concentrated on the loading platforms and the eastern end of the workings. Consideration was also being given to improving the main railway adit which had been a cause for concern since the winter of 1935. The problem was that the tunnel had been built with only sufficient headroom to accommodate low-sided

57

10-ton stone wagons. On 10 December Colonel Minnis met Messrs Pictor and Chaffey of Bath & Portland Stone to discuss the possibility of clearing the main tunnel heading to fifteen feet in height by taking down the roof. Careful inspection revealed that, except for short lengths where about nine inches of height could be gained, it would be extremely difficult to increase headroom in this way. The Bath & Portland representatives felt it would be impractical to interfere with the roof, but suggested that if it had to be done then the cost would be in the region of £7–10,000. No action was taken at that time, although the War Office was aware that something would have to be done because, as things stood, the loading gauge was insufficient to allow covered ammunition wagons access to the underground loading platforms.

The question was finally resolved in March, 1938, at a specially convened meeting of the Tunnel Quarry Committee. General Hill suggested that the easiest option would be to lower the floor of the adit by five feet, but Major Minnis pointed out that such a course would run the line at about the high-water level within the quarry, would mean very steep run-outs from the storage districts, and would require the Main East haulage to dip below water level at one point. The locomotive repair shop would have to be abandoned as it would be impossible to give a grade into it of less than 1:45 off the lower level of the adit, and very costly recasting of the half-completed concrete loading platform would be required. Major works would also be needed outside the quarry to re-grade the cutting approaching Box Tunnel and to construct a retaining wall to support the GWR main line. The rise of 1:150 would necessitate the use of larger and more powerful locomotives and all trains would have to be braked when standing for loading. It was decided that the option to increase the height of the roof was the most satisfactory and least expensive, even though that was now expected to cost at least £50,000, very much more than originally estimated by Bath & Portland.

Progress was also being made with the underground platform, the surface loading platform and the Hudswell lift shafts. The crude rubble platform built by Randall & Saunders was reconstructed in concrete to the standard GWR loading gauge and a new heading driven to provide space for a second siding along its north face. At the west end, where No.5 slope shaft descended from the surface to touch the quarry floor between the west ends of the two loading platforms, it was important that access should not be obstructed by roof support pillars and that the

58

connection to Main West haulage should be left clear. In order to leave the floor space unencumbered yet provide adequate support for the broad expanse of roof a massive concrete skew arch with a span of some twenty feet was constructed. Lengths of old railway track and scaffold tubes, bent to the rough shape of the arch, were used as makeshift re-inforcement. The platforms were completed and handed over to the RAOC in October, 1939.

A pair of old vertical winding shafts in the north-east corner of the depot once gave access to Hudswell Quarry. In the summer of 1937 work began on lining them with rapid hardening concrete in preparation for the installation of electric ammunition lifts. Excavations had also started on construction of the Hudswell drift, a tunnel 1,750 feet long connecting the extreme northern sections of all the storage districts and terminating at the Hudswell lifts. Some old workings to the north of the Hudswell area were sealed off at this time with four-foot concrete walls, but as work was nearing completion it was realized, much to the Engineers' dismay, that a five-ton diesel roller was marooned behind them.

By May, 1938, Nos. 10 and 11 Districts were almost finished; the floors were graded, rolled and surfaced with an inch-thick layer of special spark-proof tarmac; concrete walls were built around each district and air-lock emergency doors were provided to give access to the adjoining ventilation and escape passages. It had been intended from the beginning that these two districts should be air-conditioned and used to store the types of ammunition most sensitive to moisture, particularly pyrotechnics and cordite. A particular feature of these magazines is that they were provided with two additional shafts that were normally sealed at the top, but in the event of a fire underground would open in the manner of safety valves to release smoke and combustion gases.

Hudswell lift shafts were completed in June but the electric lifts would not be available for a further eighteen months. In the meantime the War Office had ordered that the depot should commence receipts of ammunition from the factories on 1 July. At the time it seemed impossible that this could be accomplished, so labour was withdrawn from the works at Eastlays and Ridge and concentrated at Tunnel Quarry to meet the deadline. Hudswell No.1 lift shaft was hurriedly fitted with a second-hand steam winch and makeshift lift cages, and on 13 July, 1938, within thirteen days of the scheduled date, ammunition started to arrive.

Construction work next began on the Main Surface Loading Platform (MSLP), situated off Hudswell Drive near the east portal of Box tunnel. The War Office stipulated that alternative entrances should be available to handle the maximum load of the depot in the event of a total breakdown of the railway system. Calculations indicated that this could be accommodated by four slope shafts rising from diverse areas of the mine, working in conjunction with the limited capacity of the Hudswell lifts. An additional requirement was that for safety reasons the 'Smoke' and 'BLC' (Breech Loading Cartridge) Districts (Nos. 10 & 11) should have independent access to the surface. The scheme adopted at Tunnel Quarry was somewhat different from those at the other sub-depots in that all four slope shafts were to surface at the same loading platform. Construction of the MSLP and its associated shafts was a major undertaking and was not completed until 1941. The substantial reinforced concrete structure was built partly into the sloping hillside and covered by an earth bank. Behind the platform is an impressive hexagonal inner chamber with four slope shafts radiating from it.

An area between the boundary wall of the GWR tunnel and the ammunition magazines was allocated to various service installations, including the power-house and locomotive repair shop. When the depot was operational three War Department Hunslet diesel locomotives were used to shunt main line trains within the quarry. Because of the vulnerability of railway installations to aerial attack it was imperative that stabling and repair facilities for the locomotives should be provided underground, so a three-bay 'roundhouse' style locomotive shed, complete with a twelve-foot turntable, was built immediately west of the haulage and as near as possible to the loading platform. Providing access to the engine shed entailed boring a curved approach tunnel and the construction of a steel girder bridge carrying a spur from the platform line over the east haulageway.

The question of a secure electricity supply was first raised at a meeting of the Treasury Inter-services Committee on 6 July, 1936. The Army argued that an emergency generating station within the mine was absolutely essential; without it, disruption of the external grid supply by enemy action would paralyse the depot. The Treasury initially refused to sanction construction on the grounds of cost, estimated at £16,000, but by the end of the month the War Office had argued its case with sufficient persuasion and tentative approval was given. The matter rested inconclusively until early in 1939, when the need arose to finalize plans for the permanent electrical system in the mine. On 19 February Colonel Minnis reported to the Treasury Committee that:

"Our present scheme is to take the whole of our requirement from the Grid and to have small underground power stations sufficient to supply in emergency our requirements for reduced lighting and haulage, but not air-conditioning. We shall have one station at Tunnel and one at Monkton Farleigh and we have not yet made up our minds whether to have a very small plant at Eastlays or to connect that quarry with the plant at Tunnel."

A Treasury official responded that the cost of the Corsham project had now reached £3.5 million, and that the power station scheme could not possibly be sanctioned as further expenditure was now envisaged with the urgent need to provide air-conditioning in all the sub-depots. By this time, however, the Treasury was losing control and within a few weeks the firm of Kennedy and Donkin was appointed to oversee construction of the power station. By June the engineers had prepared detailed plans for the entire installation and a contract to supply diesel generator sets was let to Messrs Ruston & Hornsby of Lincoln. The shell of the power-house was completed by the end of December, 1940, and, on receipt of detail drawings of the plant, foundations were prepared by the civilian direct labour force. The 150' long power-house has a minimum ceiling height of twenty feet, dictated by the requirement to install an overhead travelling crane for maintenance purposes. The tender specifications stated that the contractor's first task should be to install the crane as this would be needed to erect the rest of the plant. The extra headroom was obtained by lowering the floor level by ten feet, and for this reason access to the power station is via a flight of wide concrete steps.

The initial plan envisaged two generators in the power-house, but before construction began questions were raised regarding emergency power for the Fighter Command No.10 Group control centre in nearby Brown's Quarry. The RAF considered establishing an independent power-house within its own precinct, but in January, 1942, agreed instead to finance the cost of placing a third alternator set in the Tunnel Quarry power-house. Foundations, cable trenches and exhaust pipe ducts were provided for all three units but due to a lack of funds the third set was never installed. After some delay, caused by the rigorous pre-delivery test procedures insisted upon by the War Department, two 650-hp 400kVA generator sets, each weighing sixty tons, were delivered on site towards the middle of 1942. No.1 plant was first run on 16 September and the second set was commissioned on 18 February, 1943.

Farther to the west, between Main West haulage and No.10 District, an office complex was built to accommodate a telephone exchange, teleprinter room, medical rooms, chaplain's office, etc. Communication between these offices was provided by Lampson Tube, the system once common in large department stores, whereby documents are transferred from place to place in cylindrical carriers propelled by compressed air, rather like loose pistons, through three-inch diameter tubes.

Seepage water was generally not a problem but where this did occur it was absorbed by the soakaway formed by the stone rubble beneath the floor. Drainage water from the railway platform area and from the nearby Ministry of Aircraft Production underground factory at Spring Quarry flowed into a large natural watercourse underneath Box railway tunnel. This watercourse, known as 'the lake', was regularly patrolled by a man in a small dinghy who looked after the various valves and sluices.

By the autumn of 1941 most of the storage areas were complete, except for No.9 District which was at the far end of the Main East haulageway. Covering 5¼ acres, this was the largest district in Tunnel Quarry. A novel form of construction was implemented here, similar to that employed with disastrous results at Monkton Farleigh a year earlier. Instead of strengthening the existing roof supports, a series of parallel concrete walls were built, spaced about twenty feet apart, and all the natural stone remaining between them removed, leaving a series of standard-sized rectangular 'rooms'. Following the experience encountered with this technique at Monkton Farleigh the plan was abandoned at Tunnel when less than half the district was complete. The remainder was finished in the conventional manner and the district handed over to the RAOC on 6 July, 1942.

The end of 1942 saw the standard-gauge railway system and all the major underground building work completed; the power-house was operational and all ten storage districts were in use by the Ordnance Corps. Giving an overview of the previous year, the Royal Engineers Commander at Corsham wrote in the War Diary for January, 1943:

62

"The year 1942 can be said to mark the completion of the original Corsham project . . . No.9 District at Tunnel was completed in July 1942 and provides a further 15,000 tons of storage. This is the last District to be completed and brings the total storage at Tunnel to 100,000 tons."

BARRACKS, WORKSHOPS & COMMUNICATIONS

Following the decision not to proceed with the development of No.1 District the space became available to the Royal Engineers, allowing No.6 slope shaft, which enters the quarry at this point, to be fitted with rails and a winch for maintenance purposes. Old workings south of the main haulage were converted into workshops and stores and a number of machine tools installed to enable light repairs and alterations to be undertaken there.

In view of the invasion threat of 1940 it was decided that underground barracks should be provided for the men working in the Corsham quarries and at Tunnel an area near the workshops was adapted for this purpose. The barracks, for 300 soldiers, were fitted out with comfortable dormitories, central heating and extensive canteen facilities. It was accepted from the outset that underground billeting was not really satisfactory and the barracks were rarely occupied except by WAAF's working in Brown's Quarry and South West Control, although a special RAOC Christmas dinner was served in the canteen in 1942. The barrack area finally fell into disuse early in 1943, but the facilities remained intact until the early 1980s. Access to the workshops and barracks was gained directly from the end of Main West haulage via a pair of reinforced steel blast doors, beyond which a military police contraband point was established to control personnel movements in and out of the magazine areas.

'SOUTH WEST CONTROL' AND BROWN'S QUARRY

Early in 1940 Brown's Quarry, a small independent quarry north of the barracks, connected to the western workings by a long narrow heading, was converted at great expense into a secure underground Command Centre for No.10 Group, RAF Fighter Command. Its most prominent feature was a wood-panelled hexagonal operations room with a plotting table at ground level overlooked by two mezzanine floors accommodating the controllers and radio operators.

Brown's Quarry was considered by Mr F.W. Allan, the engineer in charge, as the most exacting and difficult of all the construction tasks undertaken at Corsham. The project was overseen by the Royal Engineers in close co-operation with the RAF and GPO, the latter being responsible for installing the cabling and technical equipment. Plans for the operations room called for a single chamber fifty feet square and forty-five feet high, unobstructed by any sort of roof support. Drawings were prepared by Mr John Bell, a civilian mining surveyor from Lanarkshire, and implemented under the direction of Mr Allan. The first construction task was to excavate just sufficient space for two massive concrete side walls, each four feet thick and over forty feet high, using the conventional blow-form shuttering technique. Heavy-gauge rails were then secured to the top of each wall and well greased. Work next began on cutting and removing the stone still in place between the walls until there was sufficient space to allow a series of steel girders, each twenty inches deep in the web, to be hoisted up level with the top of the walls, where their ends rested on the greased rails. Sections of stone were next cut away at roof level so that the girders, which would eventually support the weight of the roof, could be gradually forced along the rails by hydraulic power until they were all in their correct positions. The remaining stone could then be removed below the girders and the floor graded and concreted.

The walls of the operations room were finished with a special paint scheme specified by the RAF, consisting of Goblin Green on the lower sections graduating slowly into Primrose Yellow on the upper parts, the idea being to produce a background which would not distract the girls operating the plotting table.

The main heading in Brown's Quarry extends for some distance to the north beyond the area occupied by the RAF, and it was suggested that this should be further extended by several hundred yards to a point beneath the surface camp at Rudloe Manor, where a lift shaft would be sunk. Although a little exploratory work was started the scheme was soon abandoned because its cost was calculated to far outweigh the operational benefit. Access to Brown's Quarry is via an electric lift. There is a story (probably apocryphal) that this was requisitioned from Harrods in Knightsbridge when it was found that a new one could not be acquired from the manufacturer at short notice. Unlike all the other surface structures at Corsham, the lift-head building for Brown's Quarry was built using the shuttered concrete technique used underground. There was doubt at the time as to whether this method would allow construction to proceed quickly enough, but by using the blow-form panels in double lifts entirely satisfactory progress was made.

Officers from No.10 Group first arrived at Rudloe Manor mansion on 1 June, 1940, and found few facilities awaiting them. The airmen were housed in temporary tents for some weeks, although the Officers took over the house on the 8th, by which time work had begun on the permanent buildings. Control was at first exercised from a temporary operations room in one of the huts until, at 12.30 pm on 15 January, 1941, the underground operations block was opened. Although falling into disuse soon after the war, the control room remained unchanged until the mid 1980s when major alterations were undertaken for the Controller, Defence Communications Network. Personnel working here during the war years have said that conditions were excellent: "You wouldn't know you were underground, except that it was warm and there were no winter draughts."

The other RAF site, adjacent to the barracks, was constructed under very difficult geological conditions to provide a secure defence communication centre known as 'South West Control'. The 30,000 square foot complex housed an important military telephone exchange and teleprinter centre. As at Brown's Quarry, access was by electric lift, installed in May, 1943, at a cost of £7,500. Most of the telephone cables running into South West Control were taken underground some distance to the west of the depot through an airshaft in a long-abandoned section of the old stone workings. Although these cables were removed many years ago, empty concrete ducts and long runs of steel wall brackets can still be seen in the mine workings under Box Hill.

TRANSPORT ARRANGEMENTS IN TUNNEL QUARRY

It was proposed in 1936 that Tunnel Quarry should store a varied range of filled ammunition, while Ridge and Eastlays would take bulk stocks of TNT, cordite and other High Explosives. Consequently, heavier and more complex materials handling equipment would be required at Tunnel to manoeuvre heavy shells such as those for the 18" howitzer, which could weigh over a ton each. Each district was originally designed with a central haulageway equipped with a two-foot gauge rope-hauled railway system connecting with a similar system in the main haulageway. Electric winches at the head of each slope-shaft would haul ammunition to the surface.

As the first storage districts were completed this type of equipment *was* installed; the Hudswell Drift, for example, was fitted with a continuous overhead rope haulage system which delivered loaded wagons directly into the lift cages. This ropeway remained in use until the closure of the depot in the late 1960s, but a similar system set up in District No.10 in 1938 was replaced when the first experimental conveyors were installed a couple of years later. In the interim, and in response to the need for premature storage from 1938 onwards, a simpler system was adopted using hand-propelled trucks running on decauville track laid directly on the tarmac floor.

From the outset the RAOC was unhappy with narrow gauge railways, and especially with the overhead rope system which they considered cumbersome and dangerous. Trucks had a habit of becoming detached from the haulage rope, often with disastrous consequences, particularly when working up or down slope-shafts. Handling experiments indicated that the method best suited to the underground depots was one ensuring a steady, constant flow of material, a situation for which the continuous belt conveyor was ideal. Following pressure from the Commanding Ordnance Officer at Corsham, appraisal orders were made with leading conveyor manufacturers. Equipment supplied by Richard Sutcliffe & Co was found most suitable and this company was subsequently awarded a contract to supply a total of fifty-seven units varying in length from eighteen feet to 2,400 feet. The pattern adopted was the standard surface type modified to run with a twenty-six-inch-wide flat belt. It was necessary for the belts to run bi-directionally and great care was needed by the maintenance men in tracking the rollers accurately to achieve this. The decision to utilize belt conveyors was met with universal delight by the RAOC. The saving in labour was immense, and receipts and issues continued smoothly and efficiently without the danger, inconvenience and nerve-racking din caused by lines of trucks grinding their way over temporary tracks and points.

Installation of the conveyors began in the late summer of 1942; eight were completed and running by Christmas and the remainder were finished during the following two months. A single conveyor ran through the middle of each storage district terminating at either the Main East or Main West haulage. These main routes were each provided with two parallel conveyors, known as the 'High' and 'Low' belts. The low belt ran closest to the district conveyor and was fixed directly to the floor. The high belt was mounted on piers which increased in height as it approached a district conveyor, allowing a bridging unit to span the low belt. Using two belts ensured that receipts and issues could be made simultaneously from adjacent districts without interference.

After some early mishaps it was found essential that there should be central control over the main haulage conveyors so an elevated control room was built on a gantry high above the middle of the underground loading platform, housing remote control apparatus for all the conveyors in two groups, one for the Main East belts, the other for those in Main West. The control apparatus consisted of control panels with 'start' and 'stop' buttons for each belt, together with red lights to indicate which were running. Above the control panels were layout diagrams and indicators like those found in old hotels, with a bell and 'flags' which vibrated to show which belt the incoming 'start' and 'stop' signals referred to. These signals were transmitted from push buttons mounted at intervals along the belts.

Provision had to be made for moving the largest shells, which could not be put on the belts, in the event of a breakdown of the Hudswell lifts or the underground railway platforms. To this end No.5 slope shaft was adapted for winching ammunition wagons as well as being fitted with a conveyor. A second floor was provided over the hexagonal rear chamber of the MSLP to house the winding engine and unloading platform, and a short elevator was installed to lower ammunition into the lorry-loading bays below.

The northern ends of the district conveyors terminated at the Hudswell drift, and thus provided an alternative route for receipts and issues via the Hudswell lifts. These lifts were installed by Herbert Morris & Co in December, 1940, and consisted of two pairs of 30 cwt double car units. The two-foot gauge wagons used in the drift were fitted with castor steering mechanism and draw-bars at one end, enabling them to be connected 'mane & tail' like conventional trucks when used on the rails, while also allowing them to function as trailers when pulled around by electric tractors. Wide wheels with rubber-covered flanges were fitted to prevent damage to the tarmac floors in the storage areas. Several of the wagons were fitted with wooden cradles and wrought-iron securing hoops to carry 18" howitzer shell; a train of these huge projectiles trundling through the narrow confines of the Hudswell drift no doubt presented an awesome sight. Six Ransomes Sims & Jeffries 2-ton battery-electric tractors were supplied to the depot for hauling the trucks around the storage areas.

Steam locomotives were not allowed into the ammunition depot for obvious reasons, so the War department acquired three large Hunslet 0-6-0 diesel shunters to transfer main line trains between the underground station and the reception sidings at Thingley Junction. These locomotives (WD Nos. 855, 856 & 857) were maintained in the underground locomotive shed, but were transferred to the Royal Engineers' main railway workshops at Bicester for major overhauls.

BASIL HILL BARRACKS & THINGLEY SIDINGS

The development of the surface facilities at Tunnel Quarry followed the guidelines, intended to improve the soldier's lot, proposed by Hore Belisha during his fraught tenure as Secretary of State at the War Office. A large part of the Pockeredge estate was purchased in 1936 to provide for the spacious layout of Basil Hill Barracks, Pockeredge House itself being adapted as a rather elegant RAOC Officers' Mess.

The ornamental lake which the house overlooked was drained, dredged, lined with concrete and used to supply emergency fire-fighting water for the entire depot. Many years later, after the depot had closed and Basil Hill barracks were used by the Army School of Preliminary Training, British Railways complained that water was seeping through the brick lining at the east end of Box tunnel. The lake is situated directly over the tunnel at this point and it was erroneously suspected that the lining had cracked and this was the source of the seepage. Rather grudgingly the army agreed to drain the lake to inspect the bottom. No cracks were found, but as the water level dropped no less than seventeen bicycles were discovered in the mud. An inquiry revealed that they were dumped there by young soldiers from Basil Hill who, after a night out in Corsham, rather than walk home from the pubs, chose to 'borrow' some of the many bicycles left about town by the rather too trusting art students then resident at Lord Methuen's Corsham Court.

A two storey barrack block was built of local stone by Hoskins &

68

Pond of Newbury in a style to complement the old mansion, and a Sergeants' Mess was constructed nearby in a similar style. Both have mellowed well, given a head start, it is recorded, by liberal applications of cow dung and soot slurry which accelerated the growth of lichen, thus aiding the camouflage. The extreme west end of the site had from the earliest days been the province of the Royal Engineers, where over a period of years their various huts, workshops and stores had accreted in a haphazard manner around the top of No.6 slope shaft. The vulnerability of these closely spaced wooden buildings was brought home when on the night of 24 June, 1939, the RE stores was gutted by a fire which destroyed over £2,000 worth of paint and other materials. Another serious fire on 30 November, 1942, destroyed the "Attery" block at Basil Hill Barracks which was at that time used as ATS quarters.

Shortly after the depot was commissioned it was deemed unsafe to perform many of the laboratory functions, such as dismantling and repairing ammunition, in the underground areas. There *were* special bays in each district, known as 'permitted areas', where random sampling of the ammunition stock was routinely undertaken by members of the Ammunition Inspectorate, but this only amounted to external examination and low-risk tasks such as removing fuses to inspect the gaines of HE shell.

Large-scale ammunition examination was undertaken in a remote compound above ground, outside the maximum safety distance from inhabited property, 500 yards south-east of the Police quarters at Pockeredge Farm. The buildings were designed with the post-war development of the depot in mind, with all the facilities required for peacetime procedures and standards. In order to test-fire certain classes of ammunition a two-cell proof yard was established in an isolated compound to the west of the laboratory complex. Work started early in 1946 on the erection of a large Marston shed which was to contain equipment to mechanically scrape, repaint and stencil shells. This was particularly important in the immediate postwar years when millions of rounds were being returned from temporary stores and depots in the various theatres of war. Although much of this stock was redundant and was disposed of by deep-sea dumping or demolition, huge quantities were overhauled at Pockeredge and prepared for long-term storage.

Throughout the war a staff of nearly 300 men and women were

69

employed in the Hudswell laboratories, including Ammunition Inspectors, RAOC storemen, ATS storewomen, REME artisans and Pioneer Corps 'humpers'. Inside the repair sheds the Ammunition Inspectors wore thick felt overboots and loose-fitting white felt suits without pockets, buttons or turn-ups.

The laboratory site overlooked Pockeredge Drive, a private road that was once the rear approach to Pockeredge House, which for over half its length runs along the very edge of a precipitous cutting through which the Great Western main line approaches Box tunnel. Extensive works were under way down in the cutting during the spring of 1938. As we have already seen, there had been until that time a low tunnel portal with ornate carved Bath stone facing, to the right of the main-line tunnel, which gave access to the stone quarry. Unfortunately increasing the tunnel loading gauge involved the destruction of the original portal and its replacement by a massively constructed reinforced concrete edifice, secured by huge steel gates. Incoming trains were taken over by the War Department diesels outside the tunnel near the GWR ground-frame, at which point the GWR locomotive could be detached and run back onto the up main line. War Office locomotives normally did not go beyond a ground-signal protecting the trailing connection near the tramway bridge.

Three miles east of the depot Thingley sidings was the most important of the railway facilities constructed for the Corsham Ammunition Depot. Rail movements from the underground loading platform, Farleigh Down sidings and the sidings at Beanacre were all controlled from here, and full train loads of outward-bound ammunition were assembled at Thingley for despatch to the ports. Under normal circumstances inbound trains from the factories and docks were broken up here for distribution to the appropriate sub-depot. Provision was also made for the transhipment of ammunition to road vehicles should the local railway system be unable to cope or be put out of action for any reason.

A few temporary buildings were erected at Thingley Junction including offices for a GWR despatcher and an RAOC movement controller who was responsible for all War Office and RAF stores. This office was in teleprinter contact with each sub-depot and also had a direct line to the War Office.

AIR-CONDITIONING

During the First War the Ministry of Munitions utilized quarries at Ridge and Chislehurst to store bulk explosives with no apparent ill effect, though it is probable that the rapid turnover of stock meant that batches of explosives were despatched before they had been in store long enough to be affected by the unfavourable environment. The only problem foreseen at Corsham was that of providing an ambient temperature above 45°F, the freezing point of cordite, which is not a thoroughly stable substance and slowly but continuously decays from the day it is produced.

Under natural conditions the temperature in the quarries is stable throughout the year at about 50°F, but the air is very nearly saturated. The permeability of the rock overburden allows a continuous inflow of surface water which, although not sufficient to cause flooding, does create a source of free water that can evaporate into the air. During the summer months very warm air with a high moisture content passes into the workings and, on being cooled to the ambient temperature, promptly precipitates its excess moisture content as condensation.

In a well-ventilated mine the most favourable conditions for storage purposes obtain during the winter months when the air can hold only a small absolute amount of moisture even when saturated. It was unfortunate that the first measurements of humidity were taken in isolation at Tunnel Quarry in March, 1937, at a time when atmospheric conditions underground would have been at their best, inevitably giving rise to erroneous conclusions.

By early 1938 the War Office had been in control of the quarry for over a year and those in charge of operations were becoming increasingly concerned about the extensive seasonal fluctuations in humidity levels. In March an isolated area of No. 11 District was utilized for a small-scale experiment in air-conditioning, making use of an old boiler on the surface in conjunction with steam radiators underground. The results were sufficiently encouraging to justify the installation of a full-scale system serving the whole of Districts 10 and 11, the areas destined to contain stocks of cordite and smoke shell. It was considered at this time that adequate ventilation would provide sufficiently stable conditions for the other types of ammunition stored in the remaining districts.

A 144" axial flow fan in the main ventilating passage blew air through

71

a bank of radiators via ducts into the storage districts. Steam was provided by a pair of Cochran vertical boilers, delivered new in May, 1938, and set on their footings in a purpose-built underground boiler-house near the barrack area a few weeks later. After the boilers were delivered to Corsham there was some doubt whether the only cranes on site were capable of lowering them down the one-hundred-foot-deep vertical boilerhouse shaft, and the resident engineer decided that it would be safer to erect sheerlegs and pulleys over the shaft and, by using all the available manpower, lower the boilers slowly by hand.

Although the first air-conditioning system worked after a fashion, it was obvious by the summer of 1939 that a much more comprehensive installation would be required if the depot was to function properly. As storage districts in the various depots were completed and stock receipts began, the problems associated with high humidity became apparent. Condensation caused corrosion of steel shell bodies and ammunition boxes, and, in combination with lime leached from the stone ceiling, began to affect copper driving bands and brass fuses. Wooden ammunition boxes and organic packing materials also fared badly in the damp atmosphere. The greatest fear was for the safety of powder-filled Shrapnel shell and composition time fuses, which would be rendered useless if the fine gunpowder in the timing rings became even slightly damp.

Meetings were held throughout 1938 and the early months of the following year to consider the air-conditioning problems at the Corsham depots. It was realized from the outset that fully refrigerated air-conditioning would be ideal, but that the cost of applying such a system to an area as huge and as difficult as the Corsham complex would probably prove prohibitive. A phased scheme was therefore developed, with each stage being implemented only if the previous one failed to achieve its objective.

The first phase incorporated only forced ventilation using extraction and pressure fans to create a rapid flow of air through the magazines, producing an effect rather like that of a brisk breeze on a washing line. Phase two included air heating in conjunction with induction and exhaust fans. The final phase consisted of full refrigerated de-humidification, air heating and controlled distribution. In July, 1939, detailed specifications were drawn up and advice sought from plant manufacturers and other experts in the field.

By 1942 the depot had been operational for nearly four years but nothing had been done to reduce the humidity. Storage conditions were very unsatisfactory and in August it was noted that the recently completed No.9 District was particular damp. A report on the situation concluded that natural ventilation by itself was totally ineffective, so the following January exhaust fans were fitted to the outlet shafts of each district, but this had little effect on the humidity underground.

Fresh air entered the depot through a 500-yard-long tunnel blasted many years previously by the quarry company to connect Spring Quarry with Clift workings. This passageway, known to local cavers as the 'wind-tunnel', was segregated from the ammunition depot by massive iron security grilles. Work began on the adaptation of the tunnel as part of the natural ventilation system during 1941, but the plans had to be altered almost immediately due to security problems associated with the development of Spring Quarry by the Ministry of Aircraft Production. The inbye end was sealed with a concrete wall, while Brewer's Drift, a haulageway to the north of the wind-tunnel, was enlarged to enable air to be drawn into Tunnel Quarry from other parts of the old workings.

In March, 1943, it was decided to go ahead with phase two of the scheme in a modified form, with completion expected in the spring of the following year. A compromise was made between the simple heating system first envisaged for phase two and the hugely more complex refrigerated dehumidification proposals embodied in phase three. Full advantage was taken of the several hundred acres of disused mine workings, contiguous with the depot, which could be utilized as a 'cold-sink' from which air was drawn for ventilation. Outside air drawn through the relatively cold mine workings would deposit most of its moisture content in the sink before reaching the depot, and by then warming it up a suitable degree of dryness and temperature could be obtained. This system proved to be only modestly efficient, but enjoyed the twin benefits of cheapness and simplicity.

At the far west end of the quarry a large chamber was walled off and prepared to house the huge 160" Corsham Depot Inlet (CDI) fan, the largest installed in the Corsham complex, with a capacity of 400,000 cubic feet of air per minute. To reduce vibration its concrete foundations were laid on a four-inch-thick cork membrane. The fan drew air into the depot through the wind-tunnel and Brewer's Drift which was increased in cross section and streamlined to improve the air flow. The outlet side of the fan chamber communicated with the main ventilating passageway which ran parallel with and to the south of the Main West haulageway. Concrete overcast ducts connected the airway to subsidiary fans and heater batteries at the south end of each district.

By February, 1944, all the district extract fans were in place and the CDI fan was installed and running. The engineers were optimistic that an average humidity of 80% could be achieved within a short time, but by July conditions had only marginally improved and depressing reports spoke of at least another year before the district would be dried out adequately.

Whatever its shortcomings, the newly air-conditioned No.2 District offered the most satisfactory storage in Tunnel Quarry, and in November, 1943, 1,500 tons of the worst damp-effected ammunition from other areas were transferred there as a remedial measure. The situation had become so bad that the depot's entire holding of 40mm Bofors ammunition had to be sent to the surface to be re-boxed due to deterioration of the original packing, and millions of 12 bore cartridges had to be dried out in the Hudswell laboratories. In June an inspection had shown that stocks of 3.7" and 4.5" anti-aircraft shells were in particularly bad condition, showing serious deterioration of fuses and primers. The 3.7" ammunition was relegated to practice usage, but the 4.5" rounds, which were overstocked in any case, were returned to the factories and broken down.

Work started in the autumn on a new surface boilerhouse to replace the inadequate underground plant, but by March, 1944, little had been achieved and Major Minnis had to advise the War Office that construction was progressing slowly due to the poor quality of labour then available, but he hoped that building would be finished by July. It was not, however, until the new year that the system was fully commissioned. Operation of the plant was semi-automatic, coal being delivered direct to the furnace hoppers by a Priestman coal-grab running on rails which extended from the coal-yard over the boilerhouse roof.

Three Lancashire boilers were installed, although only two were ever in steam at one time, thus allowing for a programme of preventative maintenance. Throughout the war there had always been a shortfall in the supply of new boilers caused by a shortage of skilled boilermakers, most of whom had been drafted into the shipyards in the early war years.

The War Office was not immune from this shortage and all the boilers at the Corsham Ammunition Depot (except those purchased in 1938 for the underground boilerhouse) were second-hand, from various manufacturers and of mixed vintage.

7

MONKTON FARLEIGH MINE

Prior to its purchase by the War Office Monkton Farleigh mine had been abandoned for many years. The old adits in Farleigh Down Plantation were collapsed and choked with debris, while saplings and more impenetrable undergrowth were rapidly encroaching on the old tramways and stacking grounds. All around the hillside edge, overlooking the village of Bathford, deep ravines bore witness to the centuries of stone extraction from the surface outcrops which predated the intensive underground quarrying that became predominant during the middle years of Victoria's reign.

On the Kingsdown side of the Bathford to Farleigh Wick road a rutted, unmetalled track led across the fields to a more recent slope-shaft entrance, sunk just before the turn of the century. No buildings remained on the site, but a substantial mound of waste stone indicated the extent of the underground workings. The plans prepared by Captain Terry and his survey team incorporated this slope shaft, later known as 'Main East', as part of the storage development. As this was the only serviceable entrance to the network of galleries under Farleigh Down, the Royal Engineers' preliminary works were concentrated at this point.

The planned layout of the depot envisaged six rectangular storage districts, each 1,420' long and 180' wide, with central haulageways built adjacent to one another but separated by four-foot-wide pedestrian escape passages on each side. These haulageways and escape passages were known as 'laterals' and were numbered consecutively 1–12 from north to south. The eastern end of each lateral was to connect with a main haulageway leading to the existing Main East shaft, the western ends with a parallel main haulage that was to surface via a newly excavated slope-shaft to be known appropriately as 'Main West' entrance.

Little development work was possible underground during the latter part of 1937. A small single shift was engaged on clearing the Main East slope-shaft and laying temporary two-foot gauge track in the shaft and in the underground roadways radiating from it. During the winter a new road was laid to Main East and progress was being made on the erection of engineers' workshops and a large corrugated iron shed for the fabrication of steel girders. There were no mains services available on the site, although the Wessex Electricity Company was extending its Bathford feeder cable towards Main East, and a pumping station was under construction to supply water from Box Brook.

By February progress was such that three shifts of thirty men could be engaged underground on clearance and construction work, a task that was to continue uninterrupted around the clock for over four years. During the early months debris was loaded into narrow-gauge tipper trucks and pushed to the bottom of the slope-shaft by hand. As it had not yet been possible to install a winch the Royal Engineers had improvised a system for raising the loaded trucks to the surface. A straight run of railway track was laid on the surface equal in length to Main East shaft, on which ran an old petrol-paraffin locomotive. With the aid of a long wire hawser this locomotive was able to haul laden wagons up the slope.

Conditions had improved by April. Electricity was now available, allowing temporary lighting to be installed in the busiest parts of the workings, replacing the cumbersome acetylene flares used previously. An electric winch was installed at Main East, and seven 3-ton 20 hp Ruston & Hornsby diesel locomotives were put to work underground, dramatically increasing the efficiency of the clearing gangs. A few weeks later another eleven similar locomotives and 300 tipper trucks were delivered from the Hudson-Hunslet works. Clearing was concentrated near the east end of No. 12 District and in the area where Main West slope-shaft was to be driven, and stone cutting was in progress along the route of No.1 lateral using two Hardiax arc-shearing machines.

Early summer saw work opened up over a much broader front with 100 men on each shift. Cutting was in progress in Main East and Main West headings, and in Nos. 1, 2 and 4 laterals. The Hardiax cutters were

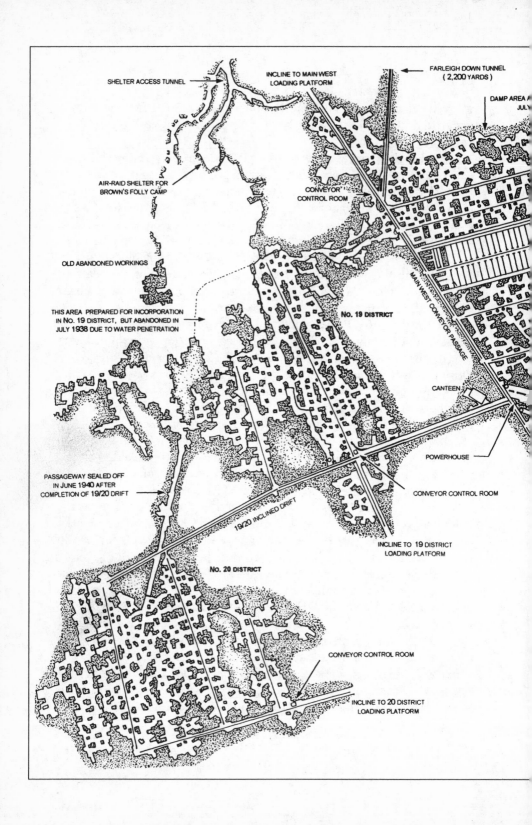

SHELTER ACCESS TUNNEL

INCLINE TO MAIN WEST
LOADING PLATFORM

FARLEIGH DOWN TUNNEL
(2,200 YARDS)

DAMP AREA A
JULY

AIR-RAID SHELTER FOR
BROWN'S FOLLY CAMP

CONVEYOR
CONTROL ROOM

OLD ABANDONED WORKINGS

THIS AREA PREPARED FOR INCORPORATION
IN No. 19 DISTRICT, BUT ABANDONED IN
JULY 1938 DUE TO WATER PENETRATION

No. 19 DISTRICT

MAIN WEST CONVEYOR PASSAGE

CANTEEN

PASSAGEWAY SEALED OFF
IN JUNE 1940 AFTER
COMPLETION OF 19/20 DRIFT

POWERHOUSE

CONVEYOR CONTROL ROOM

19/20 INCLINED DRIFT

INCLINE TO 19 DISTRICT
LOADING PLATFORM

No. 20 DISTRICT

CONVEYOR CONTROL ROOM

INCLINE TO 20 DISTRICT
LOADING PLATFORM

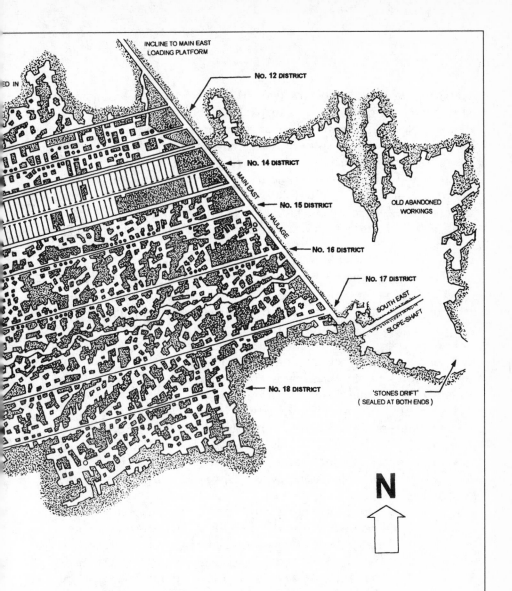

INCLINE TO MAIN EAST
LOADING PLATFORM

No. 12 DISTRICT

No. 14 DISTRICT

MAIN EAST HAULAGE

No. 15 DISTRICT

OLD ABANDONED
WORKINGS

No. 16 DISTRICT

No. 17 DISTRICT

SOUTH EAST
SLOPE SHAFT

No. 18 DISTRICT

'STONES DRIFT'
(SEALED AT BOTH ENDS)

N

MONKTON FARLEIGH QUARRY

LAYOUT OF STORAGE DISTRICTS PRIOR
TO ALTERATIONS FOR
AIR CONDITIONING SYSTEM
1943

0   100   200   300   400   500   600   700   800   900   1000 feet

augmented by a total of twenty-two Siskol electric arc-shearers, which were found to be quicker and more manoeuvrable than the compressed-air machines in the cramped conditions encountered at Monkton Farleigh. Meanwhile a space was cleared near the middle of No.14 District for a stone crushing plant in preparation for the concreting that was soon to begin. Until this time the only concrete work undertaken had been a short length of wall built to stabilize the site of Main West slope shaft. Materials were mixed by hand, the water having been brought in drums via a tortuous route from a well a mile away in No.20 District.

The Cementation Company could now start work on Main West slope-shaft, and within eleven weeks the tunnel was 'holed through' underground. By the time the slope-shaft was sufficiently developed a good length of Main West heading had been cleared, making it possible to install a trough-belt conveyor running the full length of the heading and up the shaft to the surface. This discharged onto a second 1,200-foot-long conveyor which deposited debris at the rate of 400 tons per shift into old open-cast workings behind Brown's Folly. This system released Main East shaft to be used as an access point for the vast amounts of material required for construction underground. More labourers were drafted onto the site during August and September, 1938, bringing the total employed to over 2,000. To speed up work, waste was dumped in the wet, abandoned areas of the mine to the north and east of the storage areas as well as being spilled on the surface.

The construction gangs started work late in the summer of 1938. Small or weak pillars were corseted with steel reinforced concrete, and those which were irregular in shape were built up to a rectangular section with mass concrete using steel shuttering panels. Where there was insufficient roof support octagonal columns were designed to give the necessary stability and to carry the network of steel beams.

Late in June the first intimations were heard from the War Office that alterations might have to be made to the original plan. Storage space was urgently required for an extra 40,000 tons of anti-aircraft ammunition, which was to be provided at Monkton Farleigh. It was hoped that this could be done without disrupting progress on the main works by adapting certain spare areas on a temporary basis. A survey of the old workings between the main area and the outcrop edge indicated that the additional storage space could be found there. The surveyors marked out two districts, designated 'K' and 'L', each with a nett area of approximately six acres. Only one narrow underground roadway connected 'K', or No. 19 District, with the main area, passing across the Farleigh fault. To the west there were a number of old adits opening on to the hillside which could have been used for access, but their remoteness made this impracticable. 'L', or No. 20 District, had originally been an isolated quarry with no independent access to the surface, its only link with the outside world being a two-hundred-yard-long tunnel connecting it with the larger mine workings to the north.

THE TEMPORARY STORAGE AREAS

Development started in 'K' area at the beginning of July, labour being withdrawn from other parts of the quarry to facilitate this. Most of the locomotives and skips were concentrated in this area for several months and a great deal of temporary track laid. Approximately 2,000 tons of debris was cleared every day, most of it being sent to the surface via the Main West conveyor, the rest transported in skips to the outer perimeter of the workings and stowed there. The surface arrangements for dealing with the debris were altered during the final months of 1938. The open quarries behind Brown's Folly were full to capacity, so it was decided to re-route the conveyor, extending it over the village road to spill the waste on the fields directly above the main storage area. A Cletrac excavator was used first to scrape off the topsoil, then the waste was levelled to a depth of eight feet and the topsoil replaced. Hay seed was then planted to camouflage it as much as possible.

The Cementation Co, which was already working on the ventilation shafts for the main area, was also contracted to drive two new inclined access shafts in the temporary districts. Construction of the perimeter walls was well in hand by the start of the new year, but as debris was removed from the north-west corner of 'K' District a number of serious roof collapses occurred, so all further work was abandoned in that area, resulting in the loss of 20% of the planned storage capacity. A limited amount of steel-work was put in place to support the roof, but as 'K' area was classified as only temporary storage extensive use was made of creosoted wooden props, over 520 of which were erected. By March heavy construction in 'K' area was complete and the slope shaft lined with concrete. It was decided to leave the floor with a consolidated Bath

81

stone surface, dispensing with the spark-proof flooring used in the permanent districts.

Other gangs were busy on the surface erecting the corrugated-iron transit shed for No. 19 District. Ammunition transport within the district was to be by overhead endless rope haulage, although the system was not ideally suited to working on steep inclines as the weight of the rope tended to make it drag on the ground and cut into the front of laden wagons ascending the shaft. To prevent excessive wear steel rollers were fitted between the rails to support the rope, and the ends of the trucks were fitted with notched steel guides to prevent the rope damaging the wooden bodies. Following the installation of the haulage system No. 19 District was handed over to the RAOC and inward movements of ammunition began on 1 May, 1939.

As No.19 District neared completion, attention was focused on 'L' area or No.20 District, which was now required with even greater urgency. Until completion of the slope shaft the only route along which materials could be brought in was the narrow heading that connected this area to the old workings at the front of the hill. Debris was at first stowed in the abandoned workings near the outcrop edge, but after completion of the slope shaft a trough belt conveyor was installed to bring it to the surface, from where it was hauled away by locomotives and spread above the underground workings to a depth of four feet.

Just at the time construction work in No. 20 District was coming to a close, agitation from the RAOC in favour of belt conveyors for ammunition transport was having some success. By way of experiment, the trough belt conveyor installed in the slope-shaft for waste disposal was converted to a flat belt to carry ammunition. Three additional Mecco conveyors from the batch purchased for assessment trials were installed in the district in time for the hand-over in September, 1939.

THE AERIAL ROPEWAY

Before the depot could be commissioned an efficient means was needed to bring in ammunition from the main-line railway at Farleigh Down sidings. The sidings were just over a mile from the depot as the crow flies but more than four miles by road, along steep and tortuous country lanes.

In November, 1937, the GWR was contracted to lay the sidings and build a one-thousand-foot-long raised loading platform complete with the narrow-gauge track that was to carry the ammunition wagons. Outline plans had already been prepared for the construction of a mile-long tunnel from the sidings to the depot, but this was not scheduled for completion for another three years. In the meantime work started on a 2,000 yard mono-cable aerial ropeway which was to stretch in a straight line from the sidings, up over the brow of Farleigh Down to a transfer station near No.20 District loading platform. The Farleigh Down terminal was a huge, inelegant structure spanning the full width of the loading platform and both main-line sidings. Two counterweighted electric lifts raised ammunition from the narrow-gauge trucks in specially shaped skips which were then slid into carriers attached to the rope. A similar arrangement existed near No.20 district, though built at ground level. Two conveyors connected 19 and 20 District loading platforms with the ropeway transit shed, the belt from No.19 District passing under the main site access road by means of a reinforced concrete tunnel terminating just inside the transit shed.

The wire rope was supported throughout its length by fifteen-foot-high steel lattice pylons spaced at 350 foot intervals. The system was quite efficient, handling a maximum of sixty tons per hour, but soon gained notoriety for shedding its load whilst traversing the steep and heavily overgrown section of the route through Ashley Wood. Patrols were regularly despatched to recover damaged boxes of ammunition which had fallen from the rope, and until quite recently it was possible to find odd rounds which had spilled from broken boxes. In later years spotlights were fixed to the pylons to ease the task of search and recovery.

A modification of the original plan called for a permanent underground link between the temporary districts and the main depot. A tunnel was to be driven from Main West haulageway to connect with the south end of No.19 District, continuing on to join the northern extremities of the haulageways running through District 20. When completed this would allow secure underground communication between the so-called temporary storage areas and the Farleigh Down tunnel. Excavations began during the last week of December, 1938, and immediately ran into difficulties. Digging had progressed only fifty yards when the nature of the ground changed abruptly. The stone became very broken and turned into a mass of loose waterlogged gravel which formed a break between the good stone and a vertical band of strong blue clay.

This clay exerted a terrific pressure, causing 4" × 3" section steel arch girders to buckle.

Driving the tunnel at its full dimension would be a dangerous undertaking so it was decided to bore a four-foot-square pilot tunnel first, supporting this with a box section structure of 12" × 8" railway sleepers. Many of these timbers were broken by the pressure of the clay and several layers were required to provide adequate resistance. The pilot tunnel was gradually increased to its full dimension by supporting short sections with RSJs carried by double props, thus forming a steel box to which a grid of reinforcing bars was attached, the whole then being encased in two feet of concrete.

A further geological fault existed between Districts 19 and 20 where the strata had slipped by thirty feet. Because of this change in levels the last section of the drift had to be cut to a gradient of about 1:20 for the last 200 yards. Following the completion of the drift the old narrow haulageway which had served as the only communication with 20 District was sealed off, and the new connection handed over to the RAOC in June, 1940.

THE PERMANENT STORAGE DISTRICTS

With the temporary districts now in use the labour force could again be concentrated in the main area of the depot, where work had continued at a reduced rate. As work progressed from west to east through District 12 the heavy construction gangs were followed by groups of men who completed the detail work. Electricians fitted permanent lighting and contractors 'gunited' all the exposed steel-work to protect against corrosion. The floors were graded, rolled and then covered with a two-inch layer of 'Colas' spark-proof asphalt. Meanwhile other gangs were preparing the access to the main area so that stocking could begin in No.12 District as soon as possible. A start had been made on the foundations for Main West loading platform and work was in hand on the section of the drift between No.12 District and the slope-shaft.

Although the slope-shaft was finished it was likely that Main West would be required for the evacuation of debris for at least another twelve months, so temporary means similar to those employed at Tunnel Quarry were adopted to get ammunition into the storage districts. A vertical ventilation shaft at the west side of No.12 District was fitted out as a winding shaft, with a small engine-house on the surface to house a

84

1. A typical underground view of Tunnel Quarry in 1943 showing stacks of 6"
   howitzer shell being broken down for issue. Approximately ten thousand
   rounds are visible in this photograph, with a gross weight of some 385 tons.

2. 'Already scurrying blobs of khaki have piled it high with war stores.' Five hundred tons of 6" howitzer shell awaiting despatch during the build-up to the
   Normandy invasion.

3. A diminutive Ruston diesel locomotive and Hudson tipper used to remove debris from the old workings. Virtually all the loading was done by hand following an unsuccessful attempt to use electrically powered mechanical excavators.

4. A Samson coal cutter at work in Tunnel Quarry in 1936. Note the rotating head slewed horizontally to undercut a large stone block.

5. A superb view of Hudswell drift as seen from the lift bottom just after completion in 1938.

6. Tunnel Quarry No.5 slope-shaft just after completion, looking up into the Main Surface Loading Platform with the belt conveyor to the left of the steps and the runway for winch-hauled trucks on the right.

7. Tunnel Quarry Main Surface Loading Platform. Smoke in the background is from the boilerhouse chimney, which is directly behind the MSLP.

8. Tunnel Quarry switchroom, with transformers in the background and indicator panels on the left.

9. Tunnel powerhouse. One of a pair of Ruston Hornsby VLB5 alternator sets, identical to the single unit installed at Monkton Farleigh.

10. ATS Corporal Edna Bullen operating the underground private branch exchange at Tunnel Quarry in 1943.

11. The underground kitchen at Tunnel Quarry. Completed in 1940, these facilities were little used.

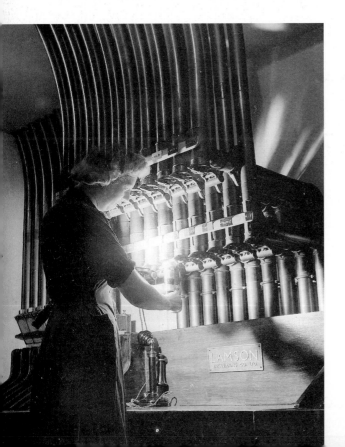

12. A young WAAF operating the Lamson tube terminus in South-West Control in 1943.

13. Fighter Command No. 10 Group HQ, RAF Rudloe Manor underground control room, 1943.

14. A large issue of anti-tank mine fuses being entrained from the south face of the underground loading platform at Tunnel Quarry in 1943. The portable gravity runways are linked to the belt conveyor on the platform.

15. No. 10 District haulageway in 1938, showing the newly installed rope-haulage system under test. Note the special quick-release clip connecting the haulage chain to the rope.

16. Hudswell North lifts nearing completion, with the temporary cages in use. The left-hand cage can be seen on the lower landing. This view, taken from the drift, shows the winding motor for the overhead rope-haulage working the drift behind the camera position. Tracks in the background serve Districts 8 & 9.

17. Shell for the 18" railway gun stacked in No 2 District. Each round weighs over one ton and manoeuvring in such cramped conditions involved some personal danger.

18. One of the War Office Hudson-Hunslet locomotives undergoing scheduled maintenance in the underground engine shed at Tunnel Quarry during 1943.

19. Tunnel Quarry. A train of ammunition wagons is drawn into the depot by one of the WD Hudson-Hunslet 0-6-0 diesel shunters, which can be seen just inside the tunnel mouth.

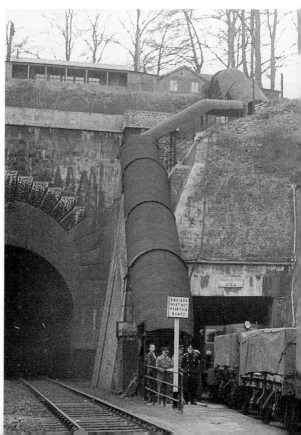

20. A unique view of the aerial ropeway at Monkton Farleigh, taken from inside the transit shed at No. 20 District. Several skips are approaching on the right, and No.19 loading platform is visible in the left background.

21. No. 14 District main haulageway, "...a great bomb-proof cloister carved from the living rock". Storage bays nearly one hundred feet deep stretch back from each side of this passage.

22. Unloading 155mm propellant charges at Farleigh Down in the autumn of 1943. Virtually all movements were now done via the tunnel belt and the aerial ropeway saw only intermittent use. Note the trucks adapted with end plates for work on the tram-creeper.

23. Farleigh Down Sidings, with the aerial ropeway in operation during the summer of 1941. The pit in the foreground is the unfinished motor-room for the tunnel tram-creeper. After completion of the tunnel, the handrails were replaced by an open-fronted corrugated iron shed.

24. A superb view of No. 5 District haulageway, stacked to the roof with ammunition of all types.

25. The bottom of No. 5 slope-shaft showing the shaft conveyor on the right and boxes of 25 pdr rounds travelling under the skew arch towards the north railway platform.

26. Construction nears completion at Eastlays. Floors are being graded with small stones prior to rolling and tarmac laying. Note the temporary cables festooning the walls.

27. Pioneer Corps gangers breaking down a stack of RAF 1100 lb bombs ready for despatch from the Eastlays bomb store in 1943.

28. The disastrous result of a runaway on No 2 slope-shaft at Eastlays on 8 May, 1944.

29. An interior view of Monkton Farleigh Main West building during a receipt of 6" howitzer shell in November 1943.

30. Lend-lease TNT from the Atlas Powder Company stacked in No. 23 District at Eastlays in the summer of 1942.

boiler and steam winding gear. The shaft surfaced near the route of the aerial ropeway connecting No.20 District to the Farleigh Down sidings, so a second transit station was constructed under the ropeway, similar to that at No.20 District. A covered concrete platform carrying twin narrow-gauge tracks connected the transit shed to the shaft-head building.

No.12 District was painted and ready for occupation by late November, 1939, but delays in completing the lifts and the decision to install another of the experimental Mecco conveyors in the haulageway resulted in its hand-over to the RAOC being deferred until March, 1940. Within a short time the district was full to capacity, with 15,000 tons of mainly obsolete shell hurriedly transferred from Bramley.

Following the withdrawal of the British Expeditionary Force from France in the spring of 1940, and from the ill-fated incursion into Norway in June, large quantities of ammunition were shipped back to England. The bulk of this stock, which in the first instance found its way to No.12 District at Monkton Farleigh, had been hastily despatched and was found upon receipt to be in a very mixed state, badly packed and in poor condition. Included among the returns were several tons of gas shells of French and British manufacture. As this ragbag assortment of bullets and shell was sorted and cleaned, the ammunition inspectors found that many of the boxes had been stuffed with letters to relatives and loved ones by soldiers of the BEF who feared they would never return home.

After completion of No.12 District in November most of the labour force was concentrated in No.14 District. It was calculated that all the stone debris remaining in the quarry would be consumed in making concrete. As a consequence Main West shaft was no longer required for the evacuation of debris, allowing construction of the surface loading platform to proceed unhindered. Buoyed by the success of the symmetrical layout achieved in No.12 District, an even more radical concept was proposed for No.14, resulting in the theoretically brilliant but technically flawed scheme to remove all the stone pillars in the five-acre area and replace them with a series of regularly spaced concrete walls. This was the largest underpinning task ever accomplished in Europe, probably in the world. Although the scheme was eventually completed, it was accompanied by a number of disastrous mishaps which at one point threatened the failure of the whole project.

The plan was to replace the existing random support pillars with a series of sixty-eight four-foot-thick concrete walls each 180' long running across the district and spaced at 21' 9" centres. Each wall was to have seven semi-circular arched openings eight feet in diameter, the centre archway being on the line of the lateral running from east to west. The haunches of the outermost arches were to be monolithic with the boundary walls of the district. The wide expanses of ceiling would be supported by roof beams carried by the walls at five-foot centres. The load on these beams was calculated to be about one ton per foot run. In order to save steel, consideration had been given to the use of standard reinforced concrete beams, but this was ruled out on account of their size and weight. Major Withers, who was at that time DCRE to Colonel Minnis, suggested that the use of pre-stressed concrete should be investigated, and after gaining agreement from Minnis, Major Withers approached Dr Mautner of the Building Research Board, to whose design some pre-stressed beams were made for test purposes. These were a complete success, being half the weight of reinforced concrete and consuming only a fraction of the steel otherwise needed. The experiments were conducted in the presence of the Chief Engineer of the Ministry of Transport and representatives from the Ministry of Works, and their success was such that the Ministry of Transport immediately arranged for the casting of a large stock of standard beams which were stored at strategic locations to make emergency repairs to bomb damaged bridges. A contract was given to the specially incorporated Pre-stressed Concrete Co. Ltd to cast the beams on site at Monkton Farleigh. These beams are significant in that they represent the very first use of pre-stressed reinforced concrete in the United Kingdom.

Starting in December, 1939, 2,000 men were set to work on the underpinning of No.14 District. Four concrete pumps were strategically placed along the southern edge of the district and a large number of Hardiax cutters held in readiness. The task was divided into four stages: first the line of each wall was cleared by cutting away stone pillars which obstructed the route; secondly the foundations were excavated to solid stone and filled with concrete to floor level; next the walls were built up to ceiling height, archways formed and steel corbels inserted to hold the roof beams; finally all the stone remaining between the walls was cut away, roof beams inserted and floors graded. Every third wall – nos 1,4,7, etc, – was to be completed from west to east before starting from the west again with walls 2,5,8, etc. In this way congestion of labour was largely avoided, and it was hoped that the risk of leaving large areas of roof temporarily unsupported would be obviated.

Construction proceeded favourably with the first series of walls, but late in April, 1940, as excavation was under way for the second and subsequent series, disaster struck. A serious roof fall occurred in the area of walls 12–15, followed by further collapses nearer the east end of the district. Many of the completed walls were badly crushed and the roof was seen to have dropped several inches. All further work was immediately suspended and an inquiry instituted. On 7 May an inspection was conducted by Mr Whitehouse of the Fortifications and Works Directorate and a report prepared for the War Office. It appears that, whilst the first series of walls were constructed satisfactorily, excavations and pillar removal for the intervening walls was pushed on too rapidly, the work getting so far ahead of the building that a much larger roof area than ever contemplated was left unsupported and its weight consequently thrown upon the completed walls. In a number of cases these were unable to take the stress and were badly crushed and pushed out of alignment. It was estimated that, whereas the original plan allowed for 15% of the roof to be taken up with concrete walls, the total roof support in the collapsed area, including the crushed walls, fell to only 5%.

Instructions were given that no further pillar extraction should be undertaken until those walls already started were completed and that all the arched openings except those adjacent to the external walls and the central ones on the haulage should be blocked up. Mr Whitehouse criticized an earlier decision to reduce the thickness of the walls from five feet to four feet and recommended that supplementary walls should be erected where necessary to give lateral support. In compliance with this advice buttresses were built along the line of the central haulageway. In view of what had happened, it was decided that the scheme should be modified and that some sacrifice of storage space should be made in the interest of safety. Where sound pillars were encountered they were to be left intact. In several instances this procedure did not seriously affect the storage space available since the areas cleared for the building of walls were used for storage and the existing pillars left to afford the necessary support.

At the east end of the district the situation was particularly acute where the badly faulted roof exacerbated the problem. Here eight walls at various stages of completion were written off, the area being filled with rubble, sealed up and abandoned. It was considered that the plan adopted for No.14 District, whilst theoretically attractive, should not be continued in the rest of the depot and that the policy adopted for No.12 District should be reverted to. Because of the reduction in manpower available due to the call-up, and with the urgent need for more storage space, even this plan was aborted and the remaining areas were completed to only the semi-permanent standard of Districts 19 and 20.

Only 1,265 of the 1,770 pre-stressed beams cast for No.14 District were used. Most of the remainder still exist, gradually breaking up in the winter frosts in a neglected overgrown heap behind the rusting shell of Main East entrance building. Notwithstanding the difficulties encountered, No.14 District was completed within twelve months. A team of Sutcliffe's men were employed for eight weeks in the early winter fitting and testing a 440-yard-long conveyor in the district, which was finally handed over to the RAOC in January, 1941.

The decision to remove all the stone pillars from No.14 District meant that a great deal more debris was arising than had originally been foreseen and means had to be found to dispose of it. It was doubted for a while that Monkton Farleigh mine would ever be completed, and, with this in mind, all the stone removed from No.14 District, and the small amount still to be cleared from Nos.15 and 16, was dumped at the south end of the mine in the area destined to be Districts 17 and 18, as it was considered unlikely that work would proceed there.

Fear of aerial bombardment in 1941 resulted in No.14 District being equipped as a temporary barrack sleeping 300 soldiers who hitherto had lived in miserable tented accommodation on the surface. At the same time one of the original mine adits in the copse behind Brown's Folly was heavily timbered throughout its length and fitted out as a permanent air-raid shelter for the civilian surface workers.

By the spring of 1941 the temporary districts had been in use for nearly two years, but these were remote from the main area underground, and by virtue of the aerial ropeway link to Farleigh Down sidings their operation was unhampered by the construction going on apace elsewhere. In the main area District 12 was also in use, but could only receive or despatch stores in inconvenient half-ton parcels via the temporary lift shaft. No.14 District, although finished, functioned only as an improvised barrack-come-air-raid shelter until completion of the umbilical conveyor connecting it to the surface at Main West.

During April the War Office decided it was imperative that the full storage capacity of the CAD should be maintained and issued orders that all the planned districts, including Nos. 17 & 18 at Monkton Farleigh, should be completed, albeit in a modified fashion. Districts 15 and 16 were to be prepared as semi-permanent magazines to the standard of 'K' and 'L' areas. In the interests of economy it was decided to dispense altogether with physical barriers between the two districts. These changes alone saved the cost of placing nearly 40,000 cubic yards of concrete. District 15/16 was handed over to the RAOC at the end of April, although reservations were felt by both the Ordnance Corps and the Royal Engineers regarding their ultimate suitability. The Engineers were concerned that the correct degree of permanence had been attained to ensure low maintenance costs in the future, while the RAOC feared that the Magazine Regulations regarding safety distances and maximum stockholdings could not be adhered to in such a large area.

A number of problems arose following the decision to proceed with the conversion of Districts 17 and 18. The original concept of identical rectangular districts called for the excavation of 60,000 cubic yards of virgin stone, weighing well over 100,000 tons, from the south-east corner of the quarry. The sensible decision was taken to avoid the unquarried area and instead adapt the whole extent of the existing, irregularly shaped old workings to the south. This created a net storage area equal to the original specification but avoided the need for any major new excavation.

Removing the huge volume of stone debris from Districts 17 and 18 proved an immensely difficult task. Over a quarter of a million tons of 'gob' stacked haphazardly by the Victorian quarrymen had been overlaid by a further 200,000 tons recently transferred from Districts 15 and 16. With all the old roadways blocked, the Engineers were faced with a very narrow front from which to start removing the debris.

It had been expected that the debris arising from No.14 District via Main West towards the end of October, 1939, would be the last that was brought to the surface for tipping and all the surface arrangements for transporting and camouflaging the waste stone were dismantled. By mid-1941 it was impossible to recommence tipping in the locations previously used and the problem was compounded by the fact that Main East and Main West inclines were now fully utilized for more important purposes. The solution was to sink a new slope-shaft as near as possible to No.18 District and concentrate all the remaining building work in that area. A point was chosen twenty-five yards south of No.17 District haulage where the difference in level between quarry floor and surface was only thirty-three feet. The new south-east shaft was excavated, lined with concrete and brought into service within six weeks. About 25% of the waste was dumped on land directly above No.17 District adjoining the old tip, but to save time the bulk of the debris was spilled to a depth of twenty feet on land immediately adjacent to the shaft top.

By the end of April, 1942, No.17 haulageway and the area on its north side were complete, and the conveyor was installed from Main West to a point eighty yards from the east end early in June. This allowed a service track from Main East to be maintained, enabling the south side of the lateral and No.18 District to be completed, while the RAOC was given occupation of the two acres of storage north of the conveyor. The outstanding work was finished during the following two months and in August No. 17 District conveyor was extended to Main East. The whole area was available for ammunition storage in October.

Progress in Main East corridor was less rapid because the slope shaft and haulageway had been in constant use since the earliest days for evacuating debris and bringing in materials. Following the introduction of conveyors as the primary haulage the need for a second main access point became less imperative. Early in July, 1942, handling trials conducted at Tunnel Quarry to assess the ability of the conveyors to transport ammunition for the new 7.2" howitzer proved satisfactory provided that a minimum spacing of nine feet was maintained between rounds. This gave relief to the Ordnance Staff, who foresaw the ability to move these shells only by rope-haulage as a bottleneck that would severely inhibit the efficient working of the depots.

Rounds for the 7.2" gun and for the 25-pounder became the predominant field artillery ammunition stored at the CAD during the latter half of the war, and in the weeks following D-day the Farleigh Down belt was issuing 25-pounder rounds at the rate of forty tons an hour, while both Main East and Main West were issuing constant streams of 7.2" shell and bag-charges. Between D-day and VE day 159,898 rounds of 7.2" ammunition were despatched to the 21st Army Group alone. Sustained issues at this rate would have been impossible had it been necessary to manhandle all the projectiles on and off the rope-haulage.

Although nearly complete, work at Main East was suspended until the late spring of 1942 while plans were made to transfer the redundant rope haulage system from No.19 District into Main East haulage. The transfer was completed in September and the finished loading platform handed over to the RAOC on 19 January, 1943. To the dismay of the operating staff it was decided at the last moment that, having equipped Main East with a railway-based system, it would be sensible to extend this into the east ends of the storage districts. Much disruption was consequently caused to the storage arrangements in the affected areas because thousands of tons of stock had to be moved temporarily while the rails were laid. With Districts 17 and 18 fully commissioned and rapidly filling with ammunition of all kinds in the summer of 1942, construction of the magazines at Monkton Farleigh was complete and the depot could now hold its maximum allocation of 120,000 tons of ammunition.

On the surface a range of temporary laboratories was erected to avoid having to transport suspect ammunition to the Hudswell laboratories at Corsham for repair. Items too dangerous for repair were destroyed in demolition pits in a field, previously laid out as the Camp football ground, near Farleigh Down plantation south-west of No.20 District.

After the war, during a brief optimistic period when it was thought that Monkton Farleigh had a secure future, the laboratory site was completely redeveloped. The temporary buildings were swept away and two large ammunition repair sheds built, together with four modern centrally heated laboratories. The main task of the staff working there was to oversee the inspection and maintenance of stores returning from Korea, and later to dispose of the residues left as the depot was progressively run down.

FARLEIGH DOWN TUNNEL

A tunnel to the railway sidings at Shockerwick was a key feature of Monkton Farleigh mine, offering a secure route invisible to aerial reconnaissance. The tunnel terminated at a loading platform thirty feet below ground level at a right angle to the main-line platform. The design was finalized in December, 1938, and by the end of the following year the upper terminus was completed. Boring the one-and-a-quarter-mile-long tunnel was a specialist task completed under contract by the Cementation Company. The tunnel runs from quarry floor level near

Main West to the underground loading platform near the main line railway at a constant gradient of 1:8½. Deep tunnelling was required for the top half of the route whilst the lower half is at or just below ground level and was constructed by the 'cut and cover' method. A depth of 180 feet was reached near the edge of the Farleigh Down escarpment.

Work on the entire length of the tunnel started simultaneously, and to facilitate this two deep shafts were sunk at 800 foot intervals. A further shallow opening was made just below the Kingsdown road from which point a broad trench was opened out across the fields in preparation for construction of the 'cut and cover' section. Drilling equipment and head-gear was erected at the site of the two deep shafts from where tunnelling continued until the summer of 1940. Waste from the top shaft was carried by rail across the village road and dumped in the quarries behind Brown's Folly. Waste from the shaft in Ashley Woods was distributed among the trees where the dense overgrowth provided adequate camouflage.

Lining the rough excavation started in July and took a further year to finish. The upper half of the seven-foot-wide tunnel was completed with a semi-circular brick-arched roof having a maximum headroom of 6' 9". On the lower section of the tunnel a much simpler, eight-foot-square reinforced concrete box-section was employed, built in a trench of varying depth in order to maintain the specified gradient. At some points, depending upon the undulation of the land, the box was completely buried, but for much of its length it was hardly below ground at all and had to be disguised by forming a gently sloping earth bank over it. By May, 1941, almost half of the length was completed and the floor and side walls of the remainder were in place, as were the main walls of the underground sorting yard.

A thirty-foot deep slope-shaft was sunk at the west end of the loading platform to communicate with the underground sorting yard. Trucks were controlled on the slope by a Head-Wrightson tram creeper-retarder, the mechanism of which consisted of two heavy-duty roller-chains driven by vertical motorized sprockets. Each link carried a steel 'dog' which projected upwards and engaged an axle of any truck pushed over it, and thus either propelled it to the surface or lowered it slowly underground.

In November, 1941, engineers from Richard Sutcliffe Ltd started assembling the tunnel conveyors, completing the task by the following

April. Because of the heavy load carried against the gradient when on receipt, it was necessary to use two separate units running in tandem and linked by gravity rollers. The upper conveyor was 2,171' long and the lower one 2,372'. Although the majority of the belts in the depot were twenty-six inches wide running at seventy-five feet per minute, those specified for the tunnel were heavy-duty type MU25, using thirty-inch belts running at 350' per minute. Initially Sutcliffes suggested the best results would be obtained by spacing the belt support rollers at eighteen-inch intervals throughout the length of the conveyor, but in practice this spacing caused certain types of ammunition boxes to bounce uncontrollably and fall off. Eventually it was found that the most satisfactory results were obtained by using a regular progression of roller spacing, from nine inches to three feet and back again, along the whole length of the belt. The tendency to bounce was further reduced by increasing the tension on the belt to three and a half times that for which the machine was designed, and by reducing the speed from 350' to 250' per minute. It was expected that these alterations would put an excessive load on the existing gearboxes and this proved to be the case. Within nine months the teeth of the large spur gears were worn wafer thin and the main drive shafts had collapsed twice in quick succession, putting the tunnel out of action for several days.

Great vigilance was required to ensure that correct spacing of the shells or boxes was maintained in order to prevent congestion at the top of the tunnel where the ammunition was transferred to the much slower S15 belts in Main West corridor. Men were stationed at intervals along the conveyor charged with the unutterably boring task of keeping watch over the thousands of ammunition boxes as they trundled past in the cold miserable gloom, checking that none slipped off or jammed. Pulling an emergency stop wire attached to the side of the conveyor immediately stopped both belts simultaneously from any point in the tunnel by breaking the control circuits of the motors, which could then only be re-started from the switching station near Main West. Spotters indicated that the belt was clear by flashing the tunnel lights, which were provided with strategically placed switches for this purpose. Following the instal-lation of conveyors in Main West a signal-box was built at the junction of Main West and the tunnel to control all the main haulage conveyors and the two tunnel belts.

With the tunnel in service the temporary lifts in No. 12 District exhaust shaft were no longer required so all the equipment together with the nearby aerial ropeway station were removed in March, 1943. However, the ropeway link to No.20 District was maintained intact as a standby in case of a failure of the tunnel belt. It was used for a while in January, 1944, following a breakdown of the Farleigh Down tram-creeper. Later, approaching D-day, the tunnel belt and overhead rope were used simultaneously for the enormous issues of ammunition required for the invasion of Europe.

THE POWER-HOUSE

Work proceeded steadily throughout 1940 on the underground power-house. Ducts were built into the floor for the various exhaust and water cooling pipes needed for the two alternator sets, the exhaust duct also acting as a seepage water drain, terminating in a thirty-foot deep sump below the power-house air shaft. This shaft was divided for its full height by a brickwork mid-feather wall to provide separate inlet and exhaust ducts which separated at the surface. Normally engine aspiration air and air for the engine coolers was drawn through galvanized trunking from the inlet side of the shaft, but dampers would allow all or part of the supply to be taken from the engine room when needed for ventilation purposes. Waste air from the coolers was ducted up the outlet side, which also carried the exhaust pipe to the surface. This complex arrangement ensured that in the event of enemy gas attack the power-house could function safely, with personnel in the engine room isolated from outside air.

To guarantee a continuity of electricity supply the depot was connected to two independent 11,000 volt sources, provided by different generating companies and approaching the site from opposite directions. The primary supply was taken from the Bath Corporation Electricity Company's Bathford feeder, while the reserve supply was provided by the Wessex Electricity Company, which entered the mine at No.19 District loading platform having travelled overhead from the company's Winsley sub-station. The switchgear and transformers were brought into use in January, 1941, but the generator hall remained unfinished until the No.1 alternator set was installed in the autumn of 1942, the foundation plinth having been prepared earlier in the spring. The seventy-seven-cubic-yard concrete bed was placed in one pour, thus avoiding the risk of lack of adhesion between layers that may have occurred if a built-up technique had been used.

The generating plant was ordered under the same contract as that at Tunnel Quarry. There were a number of special conditions to the contract which are interesting to recall, bearing in mind that the contractor was only being asked to supply their standard product. Only British workmen were to be allowed to work on the manufacture and installation of the plant, and only British or Empire materials were to be used. No duplicates of any drawings were to be produced, and all annotations describing the function of the various parts were to be erased, even on drawings issued to sub-contractors. Final assembly of the complete equipment was to be undertaken in a corner of the factory securely screened off from the rest of the works.

By the time the War Office was ready to take delivery, the development programme at Monkton Farleigh had been curtailed and it was decided to install only one of the two alternator sets in the first instance. Under-floor duct-work existed to take service pipes and cables for the second unit, should this ever be required, and the necessary control gear had been installed in the switch room a year earlier. The option to install the second unit was reviewed regularly and was not abandoned until 1946.

The plant was delivered to the site by road in March, 1942, and was taken underground via Main East. The parts were transported through the unfinished No.17 District on temporary rails, to be stored for several months in a bay at the west end. Towards the end of July the bed-plate was bolted down and levelled, and over the following two months the engine and its associated equipment were built up. Installation was completed in September when the series of service tests began. These lasted eight days and were trouble free, the plant being accepted by the Royal Engineers on 6 November. The power-house was finished to a high standard, with suspended ceilings throughout, painted white with black wood beading. An attractive almond-green paint was used on the walls, which contrasted well with the red quarry-tiled floor and dado. Fixing the tiles was the last job undertaken and was completed in the middle of January, 1943. 25,000 gallons of fuel, sufficient for 120 days' continuous operation, were stored underground in two welded steel tanks located near the powerhouse.

FIGHTING THE ELEMENTS

By the summer of 1942 Monkton Farleigh contained 60,000 tons of ammunition, nearly half its design capacity, but efforts were only just now being made to improve the manifestly unsatisfactory humidity levels there in parallel with the three-stage programme currently being implemented at Tunnel Quarry. District No.19, the most badly affected area, was fitted with an Aeroto exhaust fan just before Christmas, and within two months the difference was noticeable but not encouraging. Early the following year two belt-driven 84" Davidson fans, surplus to requirement at Tunnel Quarry, were transferred from Corsham and installed in 17 & 18 exhaust shafts, which were then nearing completion and were specially adapted to accept them. Extract fans for the remaining districts were purchased from the Airscrew Fan Co of Weybridge and installed in the existing shafts during the summer. Once the lifts in No.12 District airshaft were dismantled in April, 1943, the shaft head was rebuilt as a conventional turnover-top and the last fan installed there later in the year.

Because the construction programme at Farleigh was running two years behind Tunnel Quarry, the failure of phase one of the air-conditioning was recognized even before the building of all the magazines was completed, allowing immediate modifications to be made for the implementation of phase two. It was planned that each district should have a heating plant and circulating fan near the bottom of its inlet air shaft, but as a result of the decision to complete Districts 15–18 to only temporary standard the original scheme was applied only to Districts 12 and 14. The combined area of Districts 15–18 was provided with one huge fan, identical to the CDI fan at Tunnel Quarry, which ventilated the whole twenty-acre area via several miles of steel trunking, the erection of which was still not complete at the end of the war. Throughout the relatively short life of this plant adequate air supply on the inlet side proved a continuous problem, making the fan difficult to start and causing the motor to draw an unacceptably high current.

It was hoped that the surface boilerhouse would be completed by June, 1944, although there was some difficulty in finding suitable boilers. The furnaces were first fired on 9 August, the boilers then being run on low steam for six weeks to dry out the footings. Steam was turned on to the 12 and 14 District heater batteries early in October. The system was fully operational by the end of 1945, and there were great hopes that it would justify its expense through the following summer. It was estimated that the capital investment and running costs would be recouped in five years by savings in manpower otherwise required for ammunition maintenance, but by the summer of 1950 it was obvious that the system did not work, for humidity levels were as bad as in 1943. The anticipated cost savings had not been achieved and over 25,000 tons of coal had been burned to negligible effect. Despite the prospective cost, implementation of stage three was now inevitable.

Stage two could only be justified by redesignating all the hitherto 'Temporary Districts' as permanent. This had been first proposed in July, 1943, although nothing substantial could be done until the wartime pressures were relieved. Early in 1945 a works programme was developed calling for the replacement of 1,977 wooden props in the six temporary districts with 645 new concrete pillars and 131 tons of steel roof beams. The estimated cost of £56,568 was approved and work began simultaneously in Districts 15 and 20 in July. A year later less than half of No.15 and only one third of No.20 District was complete, but the project was already over budget. A revised estimate produced in October, 1946, amounted to £166,300, with a further three years needed for completion.

The finished works were impressive but fatally flawed. Of the new concrete pillars, all except a handful were built on shallow grouted foundations in the backfill. Conditions created by stage three of the air-conditioning scheme soon exposed the weakness of this form of construction and necessitated remedial work costing several times the original expenditure.

In January, 1951, the Chief Engineer of the Salisbury Plain District was instructed to investigate the performance of the air-conditioning system at Eastlays as a basis for the design of the new plant at Monkton Farleigh. The Eastlays plant, which had been commissioned in 1940, was designed in accordance with the best American practice and had performed better than expected; this result was not, however, achieved economically and many improvements were intended in the equipment planned for Monkton Farleigh. The detailed design work took eighteen months to complete, after which a contract specification was issued to selected firms in July, 1952.

The specification called for four dehumidifiers underground and three new air-shafts. All the existing inlet shafts on the Main East side of the main area were to be abandoned and sealed, as were two of the exhaust shafts. Districts 12 and 14 were to be supplied with conditioned air from a plant built around a new shaft in the middle of the twin lateral separating the two districts, the existing induction fans for these districts being repositioned. A similar arrangement of plant was devised to serve Districts 15/18, with a new shaft midway along 15/18 lateral and two new fans, each of 180,000 cfm capacity and twelve feet in diameter, at this location. The old 160" fan was to be scrapped.

A major finding of the Eastlays report was that steam heating was not the most efficient means of maintaining the required temperature underground. A low-pressure hot water system was therefore proposed for Monkton Farleigh. Two of the original boilers were to be retained, derated to provide the hot water, while the remaining pair would be scrapped. Detailed specifications were issued for the surface refrigeration machinery which it was proposed to house in a matching brick extension to the west side of the boilerhouse. Three sets of refrigeration equipment were specified, each capable of independent operation, consisting of diesel-driven ammonia compressors, shell and tube condensers, and multi-tube evaporators. A forced-draught timber cooling tower was to be provided to process hot water from the condensers and compressor cooling jackets.

Arthur Scull & Son Ltd of Bristol submitted a tender of £188,963 for the main electrical and mechanical work which was accepted on 24 March, 1953. Installation was scheduled for completion in July, 1955, followed by a three-month test period during which conditions underground would be most demanding on the new equipment.

The contractors selected York Shipley four-cylinder in-line compressors powered by National R4AU6 six-cylinder diesel engines as the most suitable to fulfil the rather demanding requirements. These sets were larger than anticipated in the original estimate and it was impossible to fit them into the intended boilerhouse extension. Ground conditions and the presence of the power-house air-shaft limited the space available for extension west of the boilerhouse to only twenty feet, which was quite insufficient, so it was necessary to design a completely new 5,000 square foot plant house nearby.

Some of the plant selected for the underground air-washer stations was also larger than anticipated, requiring more extensive excavations than had been allowed for in the estimated budget. Installation could not in any case begin until all the building work was completed by the Direct Labour gangs, and here numerous unforeseen difficulties were encountered. The consequent delays during the summer of 1954 prompted an inquiry by Southern Command headquarters, and it fell to Colonel Amers, Chief Engineer of the Salisbury Plain District, to explain the shortcomings. On 19 July he replied with a summary of progress to date, together with an unwelcome revised costing, showing an increase of £36,000. By this time the new air-shafts were finished but less than 5% of the electrical and mechanical contract had been completed. Sculls were confident, however, that if the factors beyond their control ran smoothly then the job would be finished on time and within budget.

Colonel Amers drew attention to the delay in letting the building contract for the new plant house, which was now holding up progress on the main contract and threatening serious repercussions. He pointed out that July, August and September were the only months when the weather was suitable for full-scale tests, and that the contract had been scheduled for completion in July, 1955, to allow tests to be completed during the following three months. He stated that:-

"Allowing five months for installation of plant after completion of the plant house and six months for building the plant house, the target date can only be achieved if the plant house contract is let by 1st September 1954, which is only six weeks from the present date. If there is any delay beyond this, the target date for testing would be put back a year and certain portions of the E&M contract will have to be stopped in order that ventilation of the workings underground may continue during the winter months, as is essential for the stored ammunition. This may lead to contractual difficulties."

It was not possible to begin work on the new plant room within the time specified and the year's delay became inevitable. The tests were finally completed during the summer of 1956 and the plant accepted in September of that year.

From May to October the refrigeration machinery was operated according to the moisture removal requirement in the underground workings. Air in the quarry was recirculated in a closed system, the only fresh air entering by infiltration from the main adits. The amount of moisture removed was dependent on the volume of air passing through the dehumidifiers, controlled by modulating dampers operated by humidity meters positioned in the return air ducts at each station. The amount of heat required was directly proportional to the amount of refrigeration being utilized, so it was necessary to run one, two or three hot water circulating pumps depending upon the number of refrigeration sets in operation. Control of the radiator temperature was effected by manual adjustment of the automatic boiler stokers. During the winter period the refrigeration machinery was entirely shut down, the modulating dampers on the air washer inlets closed and the bypass dampers opened. The extract fans were run continuously with both the inlet and exhaust dampers operated by the master controller in the main return air duct.

Full air-conditioning should have ended the recurring difficulties at Monkton Farleigh, allowing the depot to settle into an easy and none too hectic post-war routine. This, however, was not to be, for within two years a new and greater problem directly attributable to the air-conditioning installation was to render untenable the entire future of the depot. Dangerous structural faults started to appear which required urgent attention and were to cost over £200,000 to rectify.

The cause of the problem was summed up by the civilian Garrison Engineer, Mr F.W. Allan, in a report prepared in October, 1959. After a brief introduction explaining how, due to wartime pressures, much of the depot was finished hurriedly to austerity standards, Allan continues:-

"Prior to 1956 ventilation of the storage areas was by a system of force and exhaust fans with necessary heaters provided on the inlet side. After this date dehumidification plant was installed which served to give a lower relative humidity and improve ammunition storage conditions. However, this drier air has had the adverse effect of extracting moisture from the natural rock, causing this to become more friable, and also affecting the clay-filled vertical fissures, thereby loosening these with resultant loss of cohesion between adjacent masses of stone, the combination of which producing an overall deterioration in the safe condition of roof and walls."

Of the 1,010 stone pillars in the 'temporary' districts, 244 needed urgent strengthening and numerous concrete pillars built without sufficient foundation required underpinning. The Ordnance Corps was faced with a virtually insoluble dilemma, or at least a dilemma which could be solved only by digging inordinately deep into the public purse. Without air-conditioning ammunition stocks were subject to rapid deterioration; with air-conditioning came the imminent risk of structural collapse.

The developing weaknesses first became apparent within a year of the system being commissioned, when cracks were noticed in some of the arches in No.14 District. Little importance was attached to this at first as there had been similar occurrences earlier, attributed to gradual settlement following the collapse during construction in 1940. Elsewhere the problem was more severe, with large slabs of concrete falling from the walls and splits appearing in concrete pillars. In No.18 District and at the west side of No.20 District there were minor roof falls and widespread evidence of roof settlement. A survey indicating which concrete pillars were founded on solid rock, which were on backfill and which incorporated steel reinforcement was completed in March, 1959. Stone pillars in need of urgent strengthening were also identified, together with others expected to require attention within three years. It was apparent that the best solution with regard to the faulty stone pillars was to excavate the backfill around their bases down to solid rock and encase them in shuttered concrete 'corsets' to a thickness of two feet. Daunted by the prospective cost of this task, the engineers experimented with alternative techniques to find a cheaper way to make the necessary repairs.

The experiments were not successful and in February, 1960, it was concluded that in most cases only the most expensive solution – concrete corsets – would be satisfactory. Mr Allan's opinion was that the local force of directly employed labour was inadequate to cope with the task, and that it would be necessary to undertake the task by contract spread over a period of two or three years depending upon the rate at which the RAOC could clear areas of ammunition in order to allow repairs to proceed unhindered.

By this time political events were overtaking the engineering problems at the Corsham depots, and towards the end of the year it was obvious that closure was imminent. News of this came as a relief to the maintenance staff at Monkton Farleigh who were becoming overwhelmed by

101

the magnitude of the task ahead of them. The depot stayed open for a further four years while stocks were run down, but only minimal remedial work was undertaken and no major reconstruction contracts were made. Many hundreds of tons of building materials were laboriously transported into No.19 District for use by the residual direct labour gang, but very little was consumed. Most of it still remains thirty-five years later, long forgotten under gradually accumulating layers of soot and stone dust.

8

EASTLAYS

Construction began at Eastlays in July, 1936. Development of this site and the nearby Ridge Quarry was intended to progress in parallel with that at Tunnel Quarry, but the urgent need for premature storage disrupted this plan at an early stage. Most of the labour force was withdrawn in the autumn and concentrated at Ridge Quarry which had to be completed to a minimum standard by December. Urgent work was also needed at Tunnel Quarry to finish the first storage district there by July, 1938, to meet a War Office deadline, resulting in a further transfer of labour and equipment from Eastlays.

Although it was originally intended that Eastlays should store a mixed inventory of Army field ammunition similar to those at Tunnel Quarry and Monkton Farleigh, agreements reached with the Ministry of Supply in 1939 and with the RAF in 1940 resulted in a radical change of plan. The RAOC agreed to act as agent for the MOS, managing a substantial holding of bulk TNT and cordite on their behalf which was eventually destined for the shell-filling factories.

In October, 1940, Wing Commander Lines, representing 42 Group RAF, visited Corsham to discuss the storage of Air Ministry bulk explosives, and was subsequently granted the use of one complete district at Eastlays for this purpose. Later the RAF occupied a second district as a bomb store to supplement its existing holding at Ridge Quarry. It was agreed that non-phosphorous incendiaries could be stored underground safely and that all such stocks would be transferred from the Altrincham depot, as would surplus stocks from the RAF reserve depots at Fauld, Chilmark and Harpur Hill.

Eastlays quarry lies midway between Melksham and Corsham below

103

land belonging to the Monk's Park estate. After some difficult nego-tiations, the War Office purchased the land directly above the workings from Alice Goldney Robinson of Monk's Park House, who was most unwilling to sell, despite the War Office having a warrant for compul-sory purchase at a price of £2,500 agreed by the local Valuation Officer. At the end of January, 1937, the War Office was compelled to apply to the County Court for possession of the land under Section 19 of the 1842 Defence of the Realm Act, the first occasion that DORA had been used for this purpose.

Prior to its purchase by the War Office only one slope-shaft gave access to the workings; this was very steep and not suited to the movement of ammunition without considerable modification. Moreover, it was not well positioned, as it terminated in the middle of the mine near the loca-tion destined for the underground power-house and barracks. Ultimately the existing shaft was used only for the evacuation of debris and later for engineering services. Two new permanent access shafts were sunk, one serving the storage districts west of the power-house, the other serving those to the east.

An accurate survey showed the quarry ceiling to be much more badly fissured, and the stone more deeply bedded and excavated to a greater depth than expected, with the extra depth later filled with rubble back-fill. Clearing the unexpectedly large quantities of waste was made more difficult because no provision had been made to dispose of it discreetly, as had been done at the other quarries. The land surrounding Eastlays was flat and open; there were no old quarries to fill or woodland for cover, and no convenient railway line to carry the debris away. Eventually the War Office had no option but to create huge new spoil-heaps (depressingly obvious to aerial reconnaissance) which grew rapidly on the western and southern boundaries of the site.

As clearance progressed through the summer of 1939 the full extent of the 'pillar robbing' by the quarrymen became apparent. It was clear that every pillar would require reinforcement and that this would have to be taken down to a solid stone foundation. During reconstruction of the pillars every effort was made to align the walls as evenly as possible to create the most efficient storage space. The volume of concrete required due to the poor condition of the pillars was much greater than the initial quantity survey had allowed for, resulting in a considerable increase in material costs and delay before completion. These adverse factors were exacerbated by the need to support the badly faulted roof with closely spaced steel girders of large cross section. Such beams were required at Eastlays in far greater quantity than in any other of the War Office quarries.

Building work in No.21 District was not finished until the late autumn of 1939, and until that time TNT scheduled for storage at Eastlays was held under less than ideal conditions at Ridge Quarry. The first stocks were accepted into Eastlays early in January, 1940, at which time the RAOC agreed to transfer all of its remaining storage space at Ridge to the RAF. Heavy inward movements of explosive and delays in the completion of No.22 District meant that the Army was unable to keep to this agreement, and on 15 January the Commanding Ordnance Officer (COO) requested space for a further 1,000 tons of TNT at Ridge. The RAF complained about the monopolization of the Ridge Quarry winding shaft by the RAOC, which was engaged in an urgent shipment of TNT to Bombay. Meanwhile the temporary inability of the RAF to receive stock at Ridge created congestion farther down the supply chain and within two days thirty-two truck loads of obsolete bombs despatched from the overstocked and unsuitable RAF small-arms depot at Pulham had accumulated at Thingley sidings and more were on their way.

These problems were compounded by the worst weather conditions experienced in North Wiltshire for many years. Snow and ice, high winds and freezing temperatures brought down trees and blocked the narrow roads around Corsham, while illness brought down over a quarter of the workforce. By 30 January, 1940, telephone communication was cut and the electricity supply was failing. The following day all road and rail traffic from Thingley was stopped. At 3.30 pm on the 31st the electricity failed and those labourers who *had* managed to reach the site were sent home. Although conditions improved gradually, normal operation did not resume until 14 February.

As the conversion of No.22 District neared completion a major modification was made to the construction procedure in the light of experience gained at Monkton Farleigh. A policy of minimal engineering was adopted, which had the twin advantages of cheapness and speed of construction, with only a negligible sacrifice of storage space and operational efficiency. No.22 District was handed over to the RAOC in May, 1940, and stocking began immediately with Ministry of Supply cordite.

EASTLAYS QUARRY

C.A.D SUB-DEPOT No.2

PLAN SHOWING LAYOUT
OF
STORAGE AREAS AND VENTILATION AIRWAYS

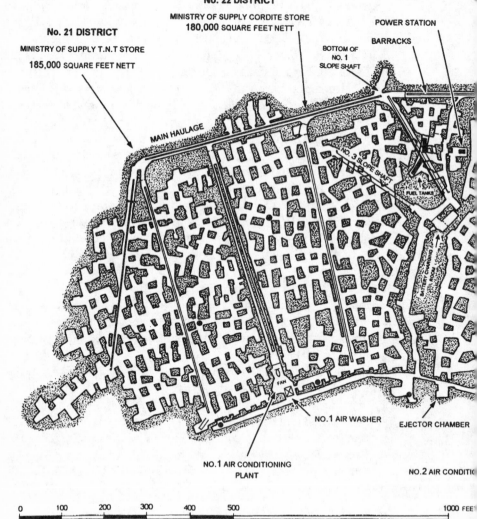

No. 25
MINISTRY OF S
64,000 SQ

No. 23 DISTRICT
MINISTRY OF SUPPLY & RAF T.N.T STOR
156,000 SQUARE FEET NETT

No. 22 DISTRICT
MINISTRY OF SUPPLY CORDITE STORE
180,000 SQUARE FEET NETT

No. 21 DISTRICT
MINISTRY OF SUPPLY T.N.T STORE
185,000 SQUARE FEET NETT

POWER STATION

BARRACKS

BOTTOM OF
NO. 1
SLOPE SHAFT

MAIN HAULAGE

NO. 3 SLOPE SHAFT

FUEL TANKS

BATTERY CHARGING

FAN

NO.1 AIR WASHER

EJECTOR CHAMBER

NO.1 AIR CONDITIONING
PLANT

NO.2 AIR CONDITIO

0   100   200   300   400   500   1000 FEET

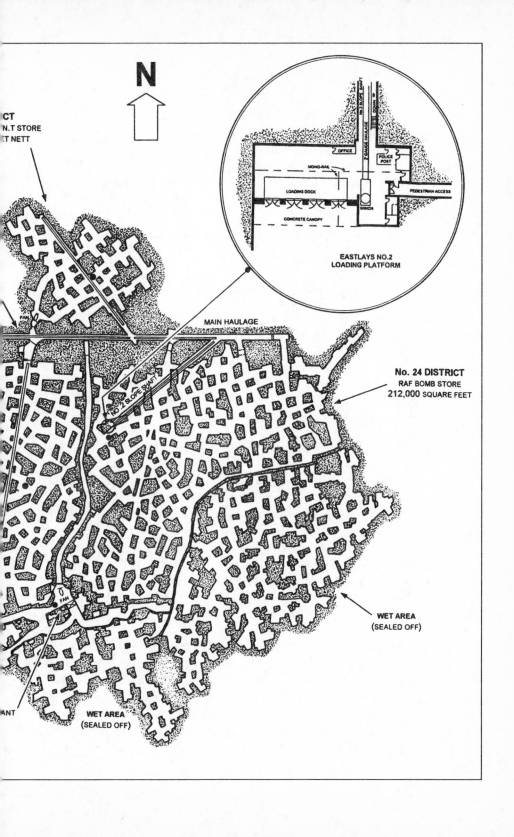

N

EASTLAYS NO.2
LOADING PLATFORM

OFFICE

POLICE
POST

MONO-RAIL

LOADING DOCK

PEDESTRIAN ACCESS

CONCRETE CANOPY

WINCH

CT
N.T STORE
T NETT

FAN

MAIN HAULAGE

NO. 2 SLOPE SHAFT

No. 24 DISTRICT
RAF BOMB STORE
212,000 SQUARE FEET

FAN

WET AREA
(SEALED OFF)

ANT

WET AREA
(SEALED OFF)

The need for air-conditioning at Eastlays was an important consideration from the earliest days, ever since its prime role as a cordite and TNT magazine had been established. Free of financial restraint, the War Office would have preferred to fully condition the whole depot, but, following a difficult meeting of the TISC in April, 1938, a more limited scheme was approved. This amounted to full-scale refrigerated air-conditioning of only one district, at a capital cost of £70,000. The running cost of this modest scheme was estimated at £35,000 per year.

Erection of the surface and underground plant was expected to be complete by early August, 1939, just as construction work in No.21 District was drawing to a close. Initial results after the first test run in January, 1940, were encouraging, aided by the fact that ambient conditions at that time were favourable, the freezing external temperatures experienced that winter maintaining a consistently low relative humidity in the incoming air. Experience indicated that the estimated running cost had been greatly exaggerated, and that the equipment had sufficient capacity to condition twice the area that was originally envisaged. Plans were therefore prepared to extend the system to No.22 District and permission sought to spend a further £9,000 on the necessary equipment.

The surface refrigeration plant was coal-fired, using a Bellis & Morcom compound steam engine as prime mover, and was not of the most modern design. Primary steam was supplied by a pair of hand-fired ex-marine horizontal boilers of French manufacture, already very old when installed at Eastlays, having recently been removed from an obsolete French destroyer. The boilerhouse was built near the top of the inlet shaft for No.22 District, which emerged underground close to the main fan-chamber and was utilized as a duct for the steam and chilled water pipes. Two horribly vertiginous eighty-foot vertical steel ladders scaled the shaft to provide the maintenance fitters with a quick route between the underground and surface machinery rooms. Most preferred the half-mile walk via No.3 slope shaft.

The compressors which provided control air for the underground fan chambers also worked two Shone ejectors set in a pit at the shaft bottom, used to pump sewage and seepage water from the mine. Early in 1942 a new treatment works was opened at government expense a couple of miles away in the Ladbrook valley just north of Gastard. Built principally to cope with effluent from the Spring Quarry factory and its associated hostel sites, an improved public sewage system was later linked to the Ladbrook works, much to the delight of local residents for whom sewage disposal had previously been a primitive affair, muttered about darkly.

THE BOMB STORE

By the spring of 1940 Districts 21 and 22 were turning over 2,000 tons of bulk explosive weekly. Meanwhile development of the remaining area was progressing well although conditions in the south-east corner of the mine had proved too difficult to make conversion viable, resulting in the abandonment of about four acres and substantial redesigning of the east end of the depot. Development of No.23 District progressed quickly, despite the fact that there was no reduction in the extent or standard of pillar corseting. This course of action ultimately resulted in a very strong structure which surpassed that of all the other sub-depots, prompting the RAOC Commanding Officer, Colonel A.H. Allen, to comment that "When Eastlays is fully air-conditioned it should offer the best storage in the Corsham complex."

When completed in October, 1940, No.23 District was handed over to the RAF under an agreement to store Air Ministry TNT negotiated a few weeks earlier. Two months later the newly completed No.24 District was also allocated to the RAF to store high-explosive and incendiary bombs. The first stock receipts were made on 15 January when 50,000 incendiary bombs were received from the reserve depots at Altrincham and Chilmark. Coincident with the construction of the bomb store an area of old workings north of the main haulage was converted to minimum standards to provide a fifth storage district, No.25, to compensate for the space lost in the damp part of the main area.

For transportation underground the Air Ministry preferred Ransome-Rapier electric tractors, similar to those used to move heavy shells at Tunnel Quarry, in combination with castor-steering dual-purpose trucks suitable for use on both smooth surfaces and narrow-gauge tracks. Trucks full of bombs were lowered down the No.2 slope shaft by an electric winch in trains of three to be picked up at the bottom by the electric tractors.

The massively proportioned No.2 surface loading platform was completed in February, 1941. A four-ton electric winch was positioned clear of the shaft top, arranged so that its hand-brake was mechanically interlocked with detent dogs at the top of the slope in such a way that the dogs were raised when the drum was not under the control of the operator. This system was supposed to prevent wagons being accidentally jolted into the shaft while loading, which it accomplished quite successfully, but it could not prevent trucks breaking away from the winch cable once they were in the shaft. This is exactly what happened during the afternoon of Monday, 8 May, 1944. Three trucks loaded with 500 lb bombs became detached near the top of the shaft, careered down the incline, scraped around the corner at the bottom and continued at great speed for a further twenty-five yards before smashing through the reinforced blast doors into No.24 District. Many of the bombs were thrown a further thirty feet into the bomb stacks, disrupting these and creating more havoc. Surprisingly, no bombs were seriously damaged and there were no injuries, but the district doors were buckled beyond repair.

THE SERVICE AREA AND POWERHOUSE

Although it was intended from the start to incorporate an independent powerhouse in the Eastlays sub-depot, the Royal Engineers wavered in their resolve under pressure from the Treasury, and in February, 1939, Colonel Minnis admitted to the TISC that "we have not yet made up our minds whether to have a very small plant at Eastlays or to connect that Quarry with plant at Tunnel". The necessity to maintain a continuity of supply to the air-conditioning plant then under construction finally forced the decision.

Specifications issued in June, 1939, called for one 235 kilowatt diesel-driven alternator to back up the single 11Kv grid supply. Building work in the service area was well advanced by the late summer of 1939, but, due to delays caused by the demands of more urgent work upon a rapidly depleting workforce, erection of the plant was not completed until November, 1942. Kennedy & Donkin wished to equip all three sub-depots with Ruston & Hornsby class VLB diesel engines to simplify spare-part stock-keeping and maintenance procedures. The Ruston engines were of a simple, conventional design and well-tried in practice, but unfortunately an engine of suitable size to meet the Eastlays specification was not available. The engine and alternator combination eventually accepted was of a far from conventional design, consisting of a Blackstone Brush type 8.M9.P eight-cylinder diesel unit with two banks of four horizontally opposed cylinders, driving a 357 kVA Mather & Platt alternator. The engine was supercharged by a centrifugal blower belt-driven from a pulley on the alternator shaft.

THE DEPOT IN OPERATION – 1939 TO D-DAY

Although Eastlays was designed for operation as an integrated whole with loading and transport arrangements planned for utmost flexibility, this was not the case for most of the war years. There were effectively two separate users with distinctly different material handling and storage requirements. The differences were such that should a breakdown occur in the No.2 slope-shaft which was dedicated to movement of heavy RAF bombs then there was no viable alternative means of access, the No.1 slope shaft operated by the RAOC being equipped with conveyors and quite unsuitable for such bulky loads.

Notwithstanding these difficulties, the depot muddled along reasonably well under joint masters until 1944. During the early days of the war receipts of British-manufactured TNT into No.21 District amounted to only about twenty tons per week, but by the spring of the following year this increased enormously due to the flow of imports from Canada and consignments from the United States, now freely available following the repeal of the Neutrality Act in November. Within a year the depot held over 12,000 tons of TNT on behalf of the Ministry of Supply in Nos. 21 & 25 Districts, and a further 4,000 tons of TNT on Air Ministry account in No.23 District. Meanwhile receipts of cordite for both the Air Ministry and War Office had started in No.22 District, the first consignment arriving from the British Manufacturing & Research Company of Grantham on 28 August.

Management of the increased capacity now available to the Air Ministry required more RAF inspection and clerical personnel than their hard-pressed resources could offer. These difficulties were resolved towards the end of January, 1941, when it was agreed that the RAOC would henceforth vouch for all RAF explosives held at Ridge and Eastlays, and a month later, on 24 February, the RAOC Inspection Ordnance Officer agreed to supervise inspection of all RAF ammunition in the Corsham depots, all the necessary gauges being transferred on 14 March. The rationalization was completed in May when the COO Corsham took responsibility for the entire RAF inventory held in the CAD.

The monthly turnover of high explosive bombs was in excess of 2,000

111

tons until July when it dropped temporarily to about half that volume. A provisional allocation of storage capacity was made at this time which allowed the RAF to maintain 21,000 tons of assorted bombs at Ridge and Eastlays, and not more than 4,000 tons of TNT in No.23 District. These limits were soon exceeded and by August, 1942, the total holding of Air Ministry TNT at the two depots was well over 43,000 tons, together with 28,000 tons of bombs.

The second half of 1942 was a period of intense activity at Eastlays, with a particularly heavy turnover of bulk TNT. At the beginning of July the total stock amounted to 39,000 tons and this was increasing daily due to the huge imports of Lend-Lease material from the United States. During just four days ending 16 July 693 tons of American TNT was received by rail via the Beanacre sidings. Three weeks later, following unprecedented demands from the filling factories, there were very large issues of explosives from Nos.21 & 22 District and the Ordnance staff reported that there was now plenty of spare room in these districts. The influx of bulk explosive accelerated again in November when the first 7,000 packages of Canadian TNT arrived. Large imports from this source continued throughout November and December, and by Christmas the depot was nearing capacity with space left for only 2,500 tons of TNT and 1,500 tons of Cordite.

While these heavy movements of explosives were stretching the capacity of No.1 slope-shaft, an equally prodigious weight of American 250 lb, 500 lb and 1,100 lb HE bombs was putting a similar strain on No.2 shaft. American made small-arms ammunition was also arriving in significant quantities. Most of this, along with some dubious home-produced ammunition for the notorious Smith gun, was stacked in the bomb store. Consolidation of the odd Air Ministry items currently stored in disparate sub-depots of the CAD was put in hand at this time, and to this end during October and November fifty lorry-loads of incendiary bombs were transferred to No.24 District from Monkton Farleigh, where they had lain in temporary surface accommodation since the start of the war.

Co-operation between the RAOC and RAF continued smoothly until the weeks approaching D-Day, when the increasing turnover of War Office stock proved too great to be dealt with without the full capacity of the Eastlays depot. It was resolved in April, 1944, that the Air Ministry would give up their Eastlays holding, although implementation of this decision was deferred for several weeks. Arrangements were accordingly made to transfer all RAF stock to other storage within No.42 Group, the labour and transport for this task being provided by the Army. On 19 June Eastlays was designated a shuttle depot for incoming War Office ammunition as Tunnel and Monkton Farleigh could no longer cope with the increased volume of traffic. The RAF vacated No.24 District and within ten days it was filled to capacity with 11,000 tons of 5.25" and 6" shell, thus easing congestion at Tunnel Quarry. From the beginning of June all issues of RAF bombs to Forward Ammunition Depots normally supplied by No. 11 MU were made from Eastlays, the small residual stock being transferred to Ridge Quarry on the 22nd.

A few weeks after the RAF relinquished the bomb store the Ministry of Supply gave up Districts 23 and 25, freeing space for a further 13,000 tons of field ammunition. In August Nos 21 and 22 Districts were also cleared of high explosives, increasing the storage capacity available to the RAOC to 45,000 tons. Alternative underground accommodation had been found for the 4,000 tons of MOS high explosives at yet another Bath-stone quarry at Hayes Wood, near the village of Limpley Stoke on the Wiltshire/Somerset border.

Seven acres of workings at this site had been requisitioned by the Ministry of Works in 1940 to provide temporary buffer accommodation for 600 Centaurus engines, built by the Bristol Aircraft Company at Spring Quarry, but a Parliamentary exposure of the scheme's extravagance led to its abandonment.

The quarry was forgotten about until the end of May, 1943, when it was inspected by Officers from 42 Group who wished to assess the feasibility of adapting space there for light metal storage. The workings did not meet their expectations and they noted, rather despondently, that, although some clearance had been done, work had obviously stopped at an early stage. Some months later the Treasury was asked to agree to a scheme proposed by the MOS to prepare Hayes Wood for the storage of 4,000 tons of TNT, as the location was thought suitable to serve the filling factories at Bridgend, Glascoed and Hereford. The revised estimate of expenditure was £48,000, which was cheaper than that for similar surface accommodation recently completed at Pontrilas. Following approval, work progressed quickly and by the spring of 1944 Hayes Wood quarry was ready to accept explosives from the CAD and elsewhere.

Hayes Wood quarry was abandoned shortly after the war and returned to its former owner. Most of the surface buildings still remain, although adapted for various agricultural uses. In 1984 quarrying resumed at Hayes Wood, which is now yielding stone of exceptional quality.

With the Ordnance Corps now enjoying exclusive occupancy of the entire Eastlays depot, air-conditioning was extended to all the remaining storage districts. No addition was required to the surface plant which already had a substantial excess capacity, but a second air-washer station was established underground at the south end of the lateral separating Districts 23 and 24.

BEANACRE SIDINGS

During the first year of operation all deliveries of bombs to Ridge Quarry were made by lorry from the small yard at Corsham railway station, but after the opening of Thingley sidings in 1937 rail interchange operations were concentrated there and Corsham fell into disuse. The prospect of a vastly increased volume of traffic between Thingley and the Ridge/Eastlays area following the opening of the Eastlays depot prompted the War Office to look for additional siding accommodation nearby. With the co-operation of the GWR a site was found just south of Beanacre Halt on the Thingley to Bradford Junction loop line, just a ten-minute lorry drive from Eastlays. Treasury consent to purchase the necessary six and a half acres of land was given on 6 September, 1938, and construction started soon after.

Squadron Leader Creighton from 42 Group Headquarters visited the sidings on 19 August, 1941, in company with Colonel Allen, COO at Corsham, to discuss the possibility of establishing an RAF component store on land adjacent to the yard. Accommodation was needed for fuses, strikers and bomb-pistols for which there was no suitable provision at Ridge or Eastlays, and which were accumulating in excessive quantities at Altrincham. Within three months a few temporary storage sheds were in use and construction of a permanent examination laboratory was nearing completion. Even while work was in hand on the component store the Air Ministry was gestating more expansive plans. Drawings were produced for a 10,000-ton pyrotechnic store on the site and a small amount of preliminary ground-work was completed, but in March, 1941, the scheme was abandoned and all work stopped. A little later the proposals were revived in the form of an even more grandiose scheme

114

for a 20,000-ton surface high explosive depot. These plans were abandoned in July, 1942, when the new RAF reserve depot at Longparish was opened.

As the RAF activity at Ridge and Eastlays wound down after the war the need for Beanacre sidings diminished. The small amount of Army traffic to and from the sub-depots was generally routed by road from Thingley Junction, rendering the sidings increasingly redundant. All the railway facilities were taken out of use on 15 March, 1948.

9

DEFENDED AND SECURE AGAINST ALL
POSSIBLE THREAT

Corsham Garrison encompassed a large part of north-west Wiltshire, its perimeter stretching from the Somerset boundary at Bathford to enclose all the Government-controlled quarries at Monkton Farleigh, Corsham and Gastard, together with the railway sidings at Thingley, Lacock and Beanacre, and the strategically important Widdenham pumping station in the Bybrook valley, which supplied water to most of the Government establishments.

Defensive measures were required to protect against three possible threats: aerial bombardment, fear of which was the depot's fundamental *raison d'être*; invasion by land or air, which was expected daily through the spring and summer of 1940; and sabotage by spies or fifth-columnists.

Only two attacks by enemy bombers are recorded; both were against Monkton Farleigh sub-depot in August, 1940, and were probably intended for the nearby Colerne airfield, as the depot did not appear on German target maps until the following November. At 5.45 on the afternoon of Wednesday the 4th a pair of JU88 A-1s of 1/LG1 flew low over the depot dropping eight 250 kilo bombs in the fields behind Main East loading platform. No damage was done, but the aircraft continued across the valley to drop more bombs on Colerne airfield which was at that time unfinished and used only by 39 Maintenance Unit for aircraft storage. The Headquarters Offices and civilian canteen were destroyed and two airmen lost their lives. Bombers from the same group went on to attack Hullavington airfield, causing considerable damage and killing four airmen. A few days later, early in the morning of 16 August, a lone

116

31. Deep excavation under way in the station area of Tunnel Quarry during 1936. Waste is thrown up from platform to platform to be loaded into the GWR 10-ton open truck parked at the end of the original underground siding.

32. A view of the aerial ropeway transfer station during a busy day at Farleigh Down in 1941. The steel shedding at the top of the structure protects the lift winding motors.

33. This view of the Main East haulageway at Tunnel Quarry shows boxes of contact mine fuses being despatched from No. 5 District onto the low-belt which will carry them to the north face of the underground railway platform.

34. 6" shell arriving at the bottom of No.2 shaft. The conveyor in the foreground is a short portable unit connected to the belt in No.5 District. Main East high and low belts are visible through the arch on the left.

35. One of the three boilers is manhandled after being lowered down an airshaft at Copenacre Quarry.`

36. `A view of the boilerhouse at Copenacre Quarry showing the three boilers in position.

37. Westwood Quarry. A view of the underground drawing office in the BSA factory.

38. Westwood Quarry. Typical view of one of the machine shops in the BSA factory.

39. Westwood, showing surface canteen on the left and the quarry entrance on the right.

40. One of the nine heavily protected lift-shaft buildings at Spring Quarry.

41. A section of the 'Power Egg Shop' at Spring Quarry.

42. An anti-gas 'butterfly' valve in a main underground ventilation airway at Spring Quarry. One of the 120" diameter induction fans can be seen in the background.

43. Looking up slope-shaft 'E' at Spring Quarry. This was the emergency exit route from the main operatives canteen area in the south-east section of the quarry.

44. Manod Quarry. A lorry loaded with pictures from the National Gallery at the quarry entrance, during the evacuation from the temporary surface store at Aberystwyth, 2 September, 1941.

45. Manod Quarry. Inside the main entrance tunnel leading to the underground repository. The brick building to the left houses the power station and switch-room, 2 September, 1941.

aircraft dropped four bombs near Main West building at Monkton Farleigh causing only negligible damage.

There was little concern about camouflage at Corsham until work got under way on the nearby Spring Quarry aircraft engine factory late in 1940. At first the War Office looked favourably upon the plan to put the factory railway sidings on the Thingley–Bradford Junction branch line because this would avoid congestion on the main line through Box and Corsham, which was already near capacity with priority ammunition traffic. However, the increasing complexity of the Spring Quarry proposals caused the COO at Corsham to voice his apprehension at a meeting with representatives of the MOWB, the GWR and the Ministry of Aircraft Production, on 4 September, 1941. His concern was that the widespread MOWB surface workings and the construction of extensive MAP sidings west of Thingley would attract the attention of enemy bombers to his nearby ammunition sidings.

At depths of nearly one hundred feet the quarries were beyond the penetration range of the largest German bomb, but the transhipment sidings at Beanacre, Farleigh Down and Thingley Junction were extremely vulnerable. Destruction of these would paralyse the depots, preventing the issue of vital ammunition and creating bottlenecks at junctions and assembly points back down the supply chain to the ports and factories. Railway sidings are difficult to disguise from above, but by the time the Corsham sidings were fully operational German daylight raids had virtually ceased, to some extent relieving the burden on the defenders.

Measures to protect against night raids developed from the decoy and deception plans first put forward at a Bomber Command meeting in September, 1939, convened to examine ways to protect vulnerable airfields by the use of decoy runway lighting to attract night bombers away from their true targets. Intended at first to represent only operational airfields the night decoys, or 'Q' sites, were later extended to protect armament factories, supply dumps, and important railway installations. Two distinct types of night decoy were developed: 'QF' or fire decoys, and 'QL' or lighting decoys, both of which were often built on the same site.

Effective operation of the 'QL' sites depended upon an efficient blackout of the genuine target. Following warning of an imminent attack, lighting would be turned on at the 'QL' site to simulate the pattern of lighting the enemy might expect at the real target. The lights would then be shut off after a slight delay, simulating an emergency blackout, but with a few small lights showing to represent faulty blackout, which would guide the bombers to their target. 'QF' sites operated in a similar manner to the larger 'Starfish' sites described below.

Two combined 'QL' and 'QF' sites were constructed to protect Thingley Junction and Farleigh Down Sidings respectively. The Thingley site was at Queenfield near the village of Lacock, in fields next to the long-disused Wilts and Berks canal (Grid reference ST922669). The Farleigh Down decoy spanned the turnpike road from Kingsdown to South Wraxall near Norbin Barton Farm (Grid reference ST823662). In January, 1942, this site was adapted to protect the airfield at Colerne as well.

Following the very heavy raid on Coventry on the night of 14 November, 1940, plans were drawn up for fire decoys on a much larger scale to protect centres of civilian population. The impulse for this decision was the discovery in June, 1940, by the Air Ministry Scientific Intelligence staff that the Luftwaffe was using a system of target location using intersecting radio beams. Unknown to the Germans, government code-breakers at Bletchley Park had broken the 'Enigma' code used to transmit the daily beam settings to bomber Gruppe KG100. Intelligence from this source was graded at the highest level of secrecy known as 'Ultra', and was limited to very restricted circulation. RAF No.80 Wing was set up under Wing Commander Addison to deal with the beam problem, and after some initial hiccups radio countermeasures were developed which jammed or deflected the beams to an extent, although the radical 'beam-bending' described in some accounts is something of an exaggeration. 'Ultra' intelligence regarding the beam settings, if it could be deciphered quickly enough, gave 80 Wing prior warning of targets, enabling defensive measures such as decoys, anti-aircraft guns and fighter cover to be effectively organized.

The larger fire decoys, referred to at first by the code-name 'Crashdec' and later as Special Fire (SF) or 'Starfish' sites, were under the direct control of No.80 Wing, for, unlike the locally administered 'Q' sites, they were intimately connected with the beam-jamming operations. Premature ignition of a Starfish site may have exposed the 'Ultra' secret. A directive issued from 80 Wing on 23 November, 1940, clearly illustrates the *modus operandi*:

"The use of dummy fires is to be co-ordinated with the beams used by KG100 and the Knickebeins. If for example the beam is on Birmingham all preparations should be made to enable a large extensive fire to be lit almost immediately after the first canister of incendiary bombs has been dropped by KG100 in the place where the fire will act as the most useful decoy. If for example a 'Y' message [decrypt] from KG100 discloses the fact that the beam from the Cherbourg peninsula has been bent to the west of Birmingham then it is obvious that a fire to the west of Birmingham would provide the best decoy."

Possible target cities were usually provided with three Starfish sites around their perimeters, each about four miles from the centre. Bath, however, had only two sites, the eastern one of which was formed by greatly expanding the Farleigh Down 'Q' site at Norbin Barton Farm. A second site to the west of the city was established in the Wellow valley, near the village of Hinton Charterhouse.

'QF' decoys employed a number of devices to simulate various classes of explosion and fire. Basket fires were designed to burn for an hour or so, and rows of them would give the impression of buildings well alight, whilst structures built of scaffold poles and asbestos covered in roofing felt burned with a rich flame and copious black smoke. Special equipment known as 'boiler-fires' produced spectacular explosive effects by allowing water to pour into large tanks of burning creosote.

The 'QL' sites were provided with apparatus to give the impression from the air of the restricted lighting in the target area they were supposed to represent. Widely spaced rows of white lamps shining on to large circles of sand gave the impression of the lighting typically found in railway marshalling yards, while the glow of a locomotive firebox was created by a hooded red lamp shining down on to a bed of sand. The electricity required for these illusions was provided by a pair of generators installed in a splinter-proof bunker built at least 400 yards away from the main site. The Norbin Barton bunker was built of concrete reinforced with steel arches similar to those used underground in the nearby ammunition depot. Although abandoned in 1944, it was not demolished until the late 1960s and its debris can still be seen beside the South Wraxall road.

An unavoidable hazard associated with all 'QL' sites protecting airfields was that friendly aircraft might mistake the dummy flarepath with the real thing, which would of course be blacked out, and attempt to land on it. This appears to be what happened on the night of 2 September, 1941, when Hurricane Z3576 of No.87 Squadron, based at Charmy Down airfield, crashed on the Norbin Barton decoy. The situation was made worse by the fact that the site, together with Kingsdown Common and the large fields nearby, had earlier been obstructed by rows of huge stone blocks to prevent enemy gliders landing in the event of the anticipated invasion.

INVASION IMMINENT

After Dunkirk the Chiefs of Staff realized that, with the whole of the Channel coast in German hands, some form of attack, either a full-scale invasion or perhaps a limited paratroop operation to destroy airfields and industrial capacity, was very likely.

On 27 May General Edmund Ironside became GOC Home Forces, charged with the task of preparing the country to thwart the expected invasion. Ironside and his staff quickly developed a plan for Home Defence which was put to the Chiefs of Staff on 25 June. The elements of the scheme which concern us are the fixed defence lines built to protect London and the industrial Midlands, consisting of continuous lines of pillboxes and anti-tank ditches that followed natural obstacles wherever possible. In Southern Command the main or GHQ line stretched from the Bristol Channel to beyond Reading, with subsidiary Command, Corps and Divisional lines running from the GHQ line to the coast, dividing the South of England into defensive boxes. Between Bradford-on-Avon and Reading the GHQ defences consisted of two parallel lines about twenty miles apart. The lower or 'Blue' line followed the Kennet and Avon Canal south of Corsham, while the 'Red' line followed a course which skirted north of Corsham and on through Great Somerford, Lechlade and Abingdon. A further, only partly completed line, the 'Green' or Bristol Outer Defence line, ran through Freshford, a few miles west of Corsham, and thence northwards into the Cotswolds. The Corsham Garrison was thus completely enclosed by the intersection of these various components of the GHQ line. Within this box a further system of defences, the 'Corsham Defence Scheme', was put in place as an integral part of the overall Ironside plan.

During the pre-war years security arrangements at the CAD were controlled by the War Department Constabulary, whose task was merely to dissuade the curious, suppress pilfering, and ensure compliance with the contraband regulations which prohibited items such as cigarettes and matches from being taken underground. Broad red lines painted on the ground ten feet in front of all entrances marked the points at which the contraband regulations took effect.

In the early months of the war a small military guard was provided by 'C' Company, 5th Battalion Somerset Light Infantry, who lived in freezing tented accommodation at Monkton Farleigh. The Somerset Light Infantry moved to Lydd in March, and during the late spring large numbers of Home Defence troops arrived at the Corsham Garrison. Guard patrols were arranged and work started on obstructing fields in the vicinity of the depots to prevent enemy aircraft landing. By 21 June the Garrison strength included 500 riflemen of the 8th Battalion Royal Welch Fusiliers and 750 men of the 5th Battalion Argyll & Sutherland Highlanders. The latter was a mechanized machine-gun Battalion and was camped in woodland near Hudswell. Additionally, 1,000 Pioneers stood guard over main road junctions and other key points in the locality. Their battalion headquarters was Ridge Quarry, with two companies at Monkton Farleigh and one at Thingley Junction. A further 350 members of the 99th Company, Royal Pioneer Corps, together with 700 men of the 63rd Ammunition Section RAOC, were detailed for ammunition movement inside the quarry, but could be called upon for defence duties if required.

Contracts to build pillboxes to protect the Hudswell area were issued on 9 September, and for all other sites ten days later. Construction was undertaken by the Devizes firm of W.E. Chivers, who were also responsible for building defences along the GHQ Blue line. Work at Corsham was completed, in a modified form resulting from the gradual abandonment of the Linear Defence scheme, on 20 March, 1941. Chivers also built a series of portable 'railway-blocks' which could be used to obstruct the mouths of Box tunnel and the entrances to the War Department sidings.

During the summer of 1940 the imminent attack was expected to take three possible forms:

1. Small, highly trained parachute units landing in the near vicinity.
2. Large numbers of enemy troops arriving in troop carriers or

gliders, specifically tasked to capture or destroy the quarries and nearby key points. It was expected that these forces would land at the recently opened airfield at Colerne, which would be overrun in the first assault. All other possible landing grounds in the immediate vicinity had already been obstructed by rows of stone or concrete blocks and old cars filled with earth.

3. Large bodies of troops moving overland from the south following a seaborne invasion.

During June the Royal Welch Fusiliers and the Argyll and Sutherland Highlanders were replaced by an Infantry Battalion of the 11th South Staffordshire Regiment, together with 14 group and 36 group Royal Pioneer Corps. The Staffordshires were camped under canvas in Kingsdown Plantation at Monkton Farleigh, where the remains of their zigzag slit-trench perimeter defences can still be made out in the undergrowth. By this time the local Home Guard units were integrated into the Corsham defence scheme under the general control of the Officer Commanding 11th South Staffordshire Regiment. Overall command of all the defences except that at Monkton Farleigh rested with Lieutenant-Colonel Sargeaunt, the Fortress Commanding Officer at Pockeredge House, where he had his operations control room and emergency telephone exchange hidden in the basement. Local forces at Monkton Farleigh were under command of the RAOC Garrison Commander, Lieutenant-Colonel Lister, but if communications became disrupted then the South Staffordshires would also come under his control. His battle headquarters were in a heavily protected semi-buried concrete telephone exchange at Monkton Farleigh.

Further changes were made in the spring of 1941, following the creation of the North Wiltshire sub-area of Southern Command, which became the administrative unit for the Corsham Defences from 1st February. Forces available to the sub-area commander, Brigadier J.C. Burnett, amounted to 26,000 regular troops plus a large Home Guard contingent. The 11th (Home Defence) South Staffordshire Regiment was joined by the 13th Battalion West Yorkshire Regiment and the 6th Battalion Suffolk Regiment in April, the latter taking over the static guard duties. The South Staffordshires maintained standing day patrols and, together with the Home Guard, made cycle patrols at night. They also manned permanent defence posts along the Bybrook Valley to guard

122

against enemy landings at Colerne airfield. Should a serious situation develop then the Wiltshire striking force, consisting of elements of the 7th Guards Brigade stationed at Redlynch House near Bruton, could be called upon.

Shortly after the creation of the North Wiltshire sub-district major changes to the home defence plans were introduced, which marked the abandonment of the 'linear' system introduced by General Ironside. All work on outstanding pillbox construction was cancelled and local commanders were urged to avoid using those which were finished as the primary line of defence. This change in policy materially affected the construction programme at Corsham. Whilst all the pillboxes facing the direction thought to be most vulnerable to enemy attack, notably those around Rudloe Manor and the Admiralty shafts at Gyers Lane, had been completed, those of lower priority around Neston and Ridge Quarry were never started. In compliance with the new policy work started on the preparation of fieldworks where pillbox construction was abandoned. By early August 'A' Coy, 63 Ammunition Section RAOC, under command of Captain Harris, was busy digging slit-trenches around Ridge Quarry and Monkton Farleigh, where the topography was well suited to this form of defence.

Summer saw the withdrawal of the South Staffordshire and West Yorkshire units from Corsham. The force now available to defend the depot consisted of:

1. 6th (Home Defence) Battalion Suffolk Regiment
2. 36 Group RMPC (12/21/33/99/167/177 and 283 Companies)
3. 284 Light Anti-Aircraft Battery, armed only with obsolescent Lewis guns.
4. 63rd Ammunition Section RAOC
5. War Department Police
6. A total of 22 Home Guard units from the 1st & 4th Battalions Wilts Home Guard and the 5th (City of Bath) Battalion Somerset Home Guard.
7. No.454 Searchlight Unit, manning positions around the sub-depots.

The Suffolks, together with certain Pioneer Corps units, manned road-blocks and checkpoints in and around the Garrison by day, being replaced by Home Guard units at night. Concertina wire blocks and anti-tank mines were held in readiness at each post but were not to be put in position until an alert was sounded. Stress was laid on the principle that security checks should not interfere with the efficient operation of the depot. There was to be no undue delay to bona-fide personnel at check-points; it was unnecessary to demand identity from known men or officers, but when four or more men, or two or more vehicles together approached a checkpoint, then these were to be challenged. Standing orders specified that:

> "Posts, **including Home Guard Posts,** will therefore only chal-lenge and examine passes when in doubt as to the identity of persons approaching their post."

The specific reference to the Home Guard in this order is an implicit recognition of its reputation, if not notoriety, for over-zealous officious-ness, already prominent so shortly after its foundation. It was not uncommon for serving Army Officers, policemen and ARP wardens about their night-time duties to be stopped and searched by Home Guard volunteers, or even for them to be stopped repeatedly on the same night by the same volunteer.

By July, 1941, the defence role of the RAOC 63rd Ammunition Section was well established and training of the mobile strike force was in hand. A cycle platoon was formed from the Headquarters Company for anti-parachute patrols and regular inter-troop parachute exercises were undertaken to test the defences. In the first of these, on 5 July, the defending forces were roundly defeated by the 'enemy' parachutists. A few weeks later a tactical exercise in which 'C' Company defended the depot against an attack from Suffolk Regiment 'parachutists' degener-ated into a pitched battle with inconclusive results.

During an attack communication between Garrison Commanders and the various defence posts was to be maintained by telephone, but should the land lines become disrupted then responsibility devolved upon a squad of motorcycle despatch riders. As a last-ditch resort, two lofts of carrier-pigeons were kept to maintain communication should even the despatch riders be unable to get through. After some negotia-tion, the two bird-keepers, Mr Bond and Mr Ashman of Pickwick Road in Corsham, although civilians, were authorized to indent for the birds' rations through the Royal Army Service Corps. All messages sent by pigeon were duplicated, using two birds in case one should lose its way en route, or, more sinisterly, be shot down by enemy action.

DENYING THE ENEMY

Contingency plans were prepared to deny the Germans ammunition which, it was feared, might be abandoned as the defending forces fell back in the event of a successful invasion. At first it was proposed to evacuate all ammunition stockpiles in advance of the invading army, but the logistic impossibility of this task soon became clear. The next plan was to evacuate only those types of ammunition and demolition explosives which were in short supply, and which coincidentally were most efficient for shooting German soldiers and stopping their tanks. Larger natures of shell were to be abandoned to the enemy, as it was argued that they would be of little use to them, but demolition explosives gave greater cause for concern. Initially the War Office was in favour of destroying the entire stock in a series of enormous explosions, but it was soon realized that the same panic that resulted in the demolition of numerous river bridges during the false 'Cromwell' warning of 7 September could similarly result in the British Army denying itself a vital weapon of war.

During the early months of 1941 the Home Defence Executive put forward a proposal for the destruction of the entire stock of filled ammunition and bulk explosives, should defeat seem inevitable, but this idea was firmly rejected by the War Office, which quite rightly saw it as a task of impossible magnitude, even more difficult than the total evacuation previously suggested, and infinitely more dangerous to implement. To illustrate their case they gave an indication of the country's current holdings in August. Stocks of bulk high explosive and propellants held at the filling factories amounted to 80–100,000 tons, while a further 10,000 tons of filled ammunition awaited despatch. The Home Commands had several hundred thousand tons stored in 140 Command and Corps ammunition dumps, and there were 300,000 tons of filled ammunition and bulk explosives stored in the Central Ammunition Depot.

Deterred only slightly by the War Office stance, the Home Defence Executive next focused its attention specifically on the underground depots at Corsham where it saw great scope for mass destruction. Sensing probable failure in pushing through their master plan, Officers of the Executive suggested a more moderate scheme involving only the mining and demolition of the entrance shafts to the quarries. This also was unacceptable to the War Office. On 13 October, 1941, they wrote to the Home Defence Executive that:

"We have considered this question fully and do not think that the Corsham CAD should be treated separately from other ammunition depots even though it does hold very large stocks of explosives. The proposals for blowing-in entrances to the shafts sound both dangerous and difficult to apply. We therefore suggest no additional action be taken."

10

PERSONNEL AND WELFARE

Although we have throughout this narrative referred to the Corsham Central Ammunition Depot as having been built by the Royal Engineers, it was in fact a project completed almost entirely by civilian labour, directed by a small staff of Royal Engineer officers and professional civilian managers. Labour for the first major task – clearing stone debris from the quarries – was drawn from the work force of the Bath & Portland Stone Co, supplemented by unemployed agricultural workers from the immediate locality and colliers from the Somerset coalfields. As early as the autumn of 1936 recruitment of civilian professional staff was begun, mainly from among colliery engineers and managers. During the mid-1930s the coal industry was in decline, with hundreds of marginal pits closing, and under these circumstances there were many highly skilled mining engineers either already out of work or seeking more secure employment. From this rich source the War Office, through the medium of the Ministry of Labour, was able to tap the cream.

As the pace of work gained momentum the local area was no longer able to supply sufficient labour, so men in their thousands were drafted in from the distressed areas of South Wales, Durham, Northumberland and Cumberland. Newly arrived batches of men were allocated work as far as possible in accordance with their trades, although many of them had no trade or had been unemployed through no fault of their own for many years, the most unfortunate having been unable to secure work of any kind since leaving school. Most had given up all hope of ever working and had to be gently broken in to the disciplines of employment. When each new batch arrived they were welcomed by the Shift Managers who addressed them in the following way:

"You have been drafted here for the purpose of work. You may not have been employed for some time, therefore we want you to break yourselves in gradually, and if you just 'tick-over' for the first few days we do not mind so long as we see you are interested in your job, and that collectively a fair measure of work is done. Regular attendance is most essential, and we do not want any man to work so hard one day that he is unable to present himself for duty the next day.

"You have come to live in beautiful surroundings, and we wish you to conduct yourselves properly. When you get your weekly pay, don't go 'painting the town red' but take care of any spare money so as to provide yourselves with new clothes, and send what you can spare to those at home who are probably in need of it. You will be living in new environments and if any of you have had bad habits, now is the time to discard them and set for yourselves new higher standards."

The men were warned that, whilst they would be treated with respect, they would be expected to carry out the instructions of their seniors without question.

The War Office was opposed in principle to establishing shanty towns of workmen's hostels, so the immigrant workers were found lodgings in the surrounding towns and villages, with special bus services laid on by the Bath Tramways Company to take them to work each shift. A fleet of thirty single-decker buses ran to the Monkton Farleigh site alone.

The welfare of the workmen was a particular concern of Major Minnis, whose wife was appointed as the first full-time welfare officer. Central to the welfare scheme were the numerous workmen's canteens established with money advanced personally by Major Minnis. The canteens, which provided wholesome, inexpensive food for the workers, were a huge financial success. All the profits were directed into the welfare fund, enabling the payment of a wide range of benefits at a level previously unknown in British industry.

Entertainment for the workers and their families was also laid on by the welfare committee with money from the canteen fund. Perhaps the most spectacular such event was the great children's Christmas party held at the Bath Pavilion on 15 January, 1938, which was attended by over 1,100 children and 500 mothers, and was described thus by a reporter from the *Bath Evening Chronicle*:

128

"Coming as most of them do from the distressed areas of Wales, Northumberland, Durham and Cumberland it was for many of the children the first party they had ever attended, and no effort was spared to see that they had a real good time. The sight of their happy faces and the sound of their excited voices was a fine reward for the two months strenuous work which the organisation of the party entailed."

Earlier that day five lorry-loads of food had been delivered to the Pavilion, including 5,000 fancy cakes, 5,000 buns and scones, 2,000 slices of cake and 2,000 mince pies.

Wages and conditions at Corsham alarmed colliery owners in the Somerset coalfield, who saw a steady drift of men out of their industry. The pit labour shortage was exacerbated by the fact that the move towards re-armament since 1937 had stimulated industry generally, greatly increasing the demand for coal. At a meeting of the Bath and District local employment committee in March, 1939, the secretary, Mr A.C. Baker, noted that "there is a demand for elderly men who had been formerly employed in the mining industry to return to work in the mines in North Somerset, but such men who have been out of work for some years are not anxious to resume work underground". In fact many of these 'elderly men' had been locked out and blacklisted after the strike of 1926, denied work in the only trade they knew for over a decade. These men now joined the stream of working miners from New Rock colliery and elsewhere who were lured by better pay and conditions at Corsham. Mr Fred Swift, the Somerset Miners' Agent, said that if the owners desired to keep the men then conditions in the mines, which were the most primitive in Britain, should be made more attractive. Corsham men, he said, got accident benefit, paid holidays on top of statutory holiday pay, sickness and injury benefit and maternity benefit, none of which were available in the collieries.

Councillor Steynor, chairman of the Bath Public Assistance Committee, spoke loud and long against the men from the distressed areas, and what he described as:

"the very debatable policy of the government for dealing with the 'industrial black-spot' problem, which is unashamedly the

129

depatriation of the unfortunate inhabitants of such areas to those more prosperous."

He was, he said, fearful that when the work was finished many of the 2,000 men who were lodged in the City, often with their families, would be loath to leave:

"preferring our equitable climate, natural attractions, unique voluntary social services and cultural entertainment facilities."

During the early months of operation there were problems in town on Saturday nights caused by a minority of the Corsham workers, though it was perhaps not surprising that young men with money in their pockets for the first time in a decade should be apt to celebrate to excess. Unfortunately these occasional cases of drunkenness were seized upon by the press in an attempt to damn the entire work force for the minor transgressions of one or two men. Lurid accounts of drunken brawls appeared weekly, and when the law intervened the penalties tended to be heavy. Sentencing two men for brawling in September, 1938, the chairman of the magistrates told the prisoners, in terms which today appear of almost ludicrous pomposity, that:

"The magistrates have the reputation of the City to look after. When they come to a place like Bath they should behave as Bath people behave. Bath people do not get drunk."

THE ROYAL ARMY ORDNANCE CORPS ESTABLISHMENT

Once construction was complete only a small Royal Engineer staff remained on site to oversee repairs and improvements. The ammunition depot was administered by No.2 Battalion of the RAOC, under the command of Lieutenant-Colonel A.H. Allen, CBE, who held the post until July, 1945, when he was replaced by Colonel G.C.H. Heron OBE. The battalion consisted of a Headquarters and three regimental companies, together with a technical company. Ridge and Eastlays were under the command of Major A.T. Green who had been at Ridge since 1936 and who had the difficult job of integrating the army and RAF requirements at that site. Tunnel sub-depot was commanded by

Lieutenant-Colonel H. Cripps, and Monkton Farleigh by Lieutenant-Colonel Knox-Wilson.

By the end of 1943, when operations at Corsham were approaching their peak, a staff of over 1,200 RAOC Officers and men, 400 Pioneers and 300 civilians were directly engaged upon ammunition examination and movement.

11

OPERATION, RUNDOWN AND CLOSURE

The pre-war function of the CAD was to maintain the reserve stock to levels agreed by the Army council, make topping-up issues to overseas garrisons, and process faulty and obsolete ammunition returned for repair, modification or disposal. Following the outbreak of war the CAD also became responsible for supplying the locally administered Home Command ammunition dumps.

Before the war the storage of ammunition was controlled by Army Council regulations which stipulated minimum separation for various classes of explosives, the maximum capacity of individual stacks or magazines, and the types of ammunition which could be stored together. The premature commissioning of the Corsham Depot made it impossible fully to adhere to the Magazine Regulations, and different groups of ammunition were mixed within single districts to an extent which would previously have been prohibited. Although certain types tended to be allocated to particular areas of the quarries (heavy shells, for example, were kept close to the rail lines and cordite in the air-conditioned districts), there was otherwise a marked degree of randomness about the allocation. As turnover increased, this apparently haphazard system was found to have advantages. Due to the operational flexibility of the conveyor systems it was possible to make simultaneous issues of similar items from disparate areas of the depot, which greatly accelerated the speed of despatch. For this system to work satisfactorily it was necessary for allocation records to be kept centrally, transmitted daily from each sub-depot by teleprinter. To this end a Selection Branch was brought into being at the Hudswell headquarters under the command of Chief Conductor Lieutenant-Colonel H. Cook. The Corsham system proved so successful that it was subsequently adopted for all large ammunition depots.

THE AMMUNITION SUPPLY DEPOTS (ASDs)

Capacity for War Office ammunition beyond that available at the CAD was provided by numerous 'Ammunition Supply Depots' or ASDs, which were established in increasing numbers as the war progressed. By 1944 the size of many ASDs had grown enormously, with storage capacities at some sites in excess of 100,000 tons. The factories and ports despatched new production to either the CAD to fulfil deficiencies in the strategic reserve, or to one of the ASDs. Overseas issues and issues to Home Commands were made from the ASDs whenever possible and from the CAD reserve in cases of extraordinary demand. Daily CAD stock returns sent by teleprinter to the War Office determined the routing of each consignment of ammunition.

All the ASDs maintained their stocks under field storage conditions, which meant that facilities were minimal, generally in small roadside or woodland stacks widely dispersed over areas as great as twenty square miles. An example of the dispiriting conditions prevailing at the ASDs during the winter of 1944 can be read in the War Diary of ASD Drymen, near Loch Lomond. In December the total holding was approaching 65,000 tons including nearly half a million rounds of obsolete 18 pdr shell. The Commanding Officer complained bitterly of being allowed insufficient dunnage and fencing; shell stacks were sinking into the boggy ground and cattle had broken down the flimsy fences and eaten the tarpaulins.

Security in these rural locations was a further problem and pilferage was rife. A routine inspection of No.31 ASD at Buckingham in December, 1944, revealed that boxes of 4.5" anti-aircraft ammunition in unguarded roadside stacks had been broken into, rounds split apart and the cordite charges removed. Four boys from a local public school with a penchant for pyrotechnics were subsequently arrested and charged with the theft.

Safety precautions under field conditions at the ASDs inevitably fell below the standards of the permanent storage depots, resulting in several major explosions involving loss of life and extensive destruction. The explosion of a laden ammunition truck at Catterick Bridge station, the main railhead for No.23 ASD Bedale, in April, 1944, is well documented, but other disasters were less widely publicized. On 20 September, 1944, an officer and eight soldiers were killed by an explosion at No.31 ASD while emptying foreign mines in the workshops at the Olney sub-site. The last major incident occurred at No.22 ASD Savernake Forest, an extensive woodland site twenty-five miles east of Corsham. At the time of the disaster in January, 1946, No.22 ASD was working in co-operation with CAD Corsham on the collection and disposal of surplus stores. An ammunition train standing in the interchange sidings exploded, killing eight soldiers and injuring many others. It was estimated that the initial detonation involved 200 tons of explosives and great credit was paid to the RAOC personnel whose bravery in fighting the subsequent fires and moving the remaining wagons prevented the explosion of a further 800 tons of shell and cartridges still on board the train.

As well as storing current and future production, the War Office was also faced with the problem of accommodating the vast quantities of ammunition returning from battlefield dumps. Disposal arrangements were put in hand at the CAD as early as 21 June, 1944, in anticipation of the first large-scale returns from the Mediterranean. Ammunition from this source, together with salvage from Normandy, had to be handled in such a way as not to interfere with the enormous flow of issues to the allied forces in Europe. Large outward movements had begun on 6 June, and during the week ending 19 June 1,100 railway wagon loads were despatched from Thingley Junction. So great was the flow that for the first time since the depot was opened both underground platforms at Tunnel Quarry were loading simultaneously. Nearly 200 men of the Wiltshire Home Guard were called in to help the RAOC stencil packages for Operation 'Overlord' in large white letters to make them clearly legible on the darkened beaches. The last week in June saw record issues of 10,500 tons of ammunition, and statistics collated after the war indicated that Tunnel and Monkton Farleigh had each issued 32,000 tons during April and May, while Eastlays handled 15,000 tons.

All returns to the CAD were routed by rail to Thingley Sidings, from where they were transferred by road the short distance to Mynte Wood in the grounds of Lord Methuen's Corsham Court for primary sorting. Ammunition in satisfactory condition was despatched directly to store and the balance transferred by road to Monkton Farleigh where a detailed pre-examination was undertaken at a temporary site in

Kingsdown plantation, the location of the Staffordshire Regiment camp in 1941. Suspect ammunition was destroyed in the demolition pits beyond Farleigh Clump, south of No.20 District loading platform. After the war a huge quantity of ammunition was disposed of here, the pits being active until 1964. Prior to the sale of the depot this area was supposedly cleared and returned to an agricultural standard, but despite this it is still littered with military debris. Fuses, brass cartridge cases ripped open like bananas, and complete pyrotechnic mortars are regularly turned up by the plough.

Disposal became the principal activity of the CAD during the two years following the end of hostilities. As well as sorting, re-packaging and demolishing ammunition returned from abroad, the problems of de-commissioning the temporary Ammunition Supply Depots and reducing the inventories of the Command dumps also had to be addressed. Enormous quantities of ammunition were prepared at Monkton Farleigh for deep-sea dumping off the south coast of Ireland in transports despatched from Barry or Sharpness Docks. A great deal of serviceable but obsolete ammunition was disposed of by sale to foreign countries, much of it going to Spain and South America. The War Office was, however, conservative in its disposal policy and much was retained that was of no further utility. Numerous marks of projectile for the 9.2" gun were still held at Monkton Farleigh at the end of 1959, although not a single round had been fired since 1943.

RE-ARMAMENT

The rationalization of warlike stores was nearing completion by the end of 1947. Much of the obsolete and excess stock had been dealt with and that which was to be retained under the current programme was checked, re-packed where necessary and set aside for indefinite storage. It was evident by this time that the political tensions in Europe and in the East were escalating at a rate so dangerous that the risk of another armed conflict was just beyond the horizon. The wisdom of the post-war Labour government in not allowing the armament industry to become moribund was vindicated when, in 1947, a re-armament programme was instigated. The only drawback was that the arms and ammunition that formed the core of the post-war programme were the same arms and ammunition with which the war had been fought. New weapons were under development, but these would be a decade or more in coming and meanwhile the depot filled with 25 pdrs, 7.2" howitzer, 40mm Bofors, 17 pdr anti-tank and many millions of .303 small-arms rounds.

Rearmament gave the impetus to start the improvements at the CAD first proposed three years earlier. Works authorized at this time included the upgrading of the temporary districts at Monkton Farleigh, pillar strengthening in Tunnel Quarry and enhancements of the air-conditioning and ventilation in all the quarries. A further £135,000 schedule of new works, principally the improvement of the various 'temporary' loading platforms, was not proceeded with due to financial restrictions.

The Korean War highlighted the importance of the North Atlantic Treaty Organization, which had been formed in April, 1949, after the breakdown of the Control Commission in Berlin. Within NATO Britain still saw her role as a conventional force, doing her bit for the defence of Western Europe and defending her remaining Colonial interests against Soviet-inspired communism, nascent nationalism and anti-imperialist internal dissent. To meet these substantial commitments an increased re-armament programme was announced in 1951 costing £4.7 billion.

The post-Korea programme remained in force until the end of 1954, by which time world events and the progress of scientific research made further adjustments necessary. High-speed aircraft and the development of guided missiles rendered conventional anti-aircraft artillery obsolete. In 1955 Anti-Aircraft Command was disbanded and its principal function of defending the bomber airfields transferred to the RAF. At the CAD the process of de-stocking heavy anti-aircraft ammunition was completed by 1959.

In 1956 NATO confirmed that the nuclear bomb would constitute the prime defence of Western Europe. The use of conventional forces would be limited and the extensive reserves which such forces would otherwise require were to be drastically reduced. Stockpiling of ammunition for the fifty-six NATO divisions previously envisaged was stopped and ammunition already to hand was added to the war reserve of the forty divisions then in being.

The following year the government issued a momentous Defence White Paper entitled "Defence: Outline of Future Policy" which detailed the most far-reaching changes to the British armed forces since the 1930s. Britain's policy was defined as:

(a) The exercise of her responsibility within NATO to defend Western Europe against Soviet aggression by the use of nuclear force.
(b) The defence of her Colonies against external or internal aggression by limited conventional operations in overseas territories.

The White Paper affirmed that:

"The aim must be to provide well-equipped forces sufficient to carry out their duties, while making no greater demands than are absolutely necessary upon manpower, money and national resources."

To contribute satisfactorily to NATO the government concluded that it must possess a powerful nuclear capability. This capability would not come cheap, and the government, sorely pressed financially, complained that it was already contributing more than its fair share to Western defence in terms of conventional forces. It was feared that increased expenditure on nuclear defence, together with continued improvements in conventional weaponry, would be beyond Britain's financial capability and would unbalance the economy. Conventional weapons, it was argued, could no longer protect Britain in a nuclear conflict and the country could no longer sustain defence expenditure at the previous level. If the need arose then the United States would be called upon to provide the conventional weapons under the terms of her treaty obligations.

A requirement for conventional ammunition still existed for fighting 'limited wars' to defend the remnants of the Empire. In November, 1959, the Chiefs of Defence Staff Committee produced a memorandum for the Minister of Defence headed "U.K. Forces' Requirement for Limited War and the Strategic Reserve" which stated that:

"Our opinions are based on the belief that the international situation and the climate of world opinion will tend to make the use of force unattractive to the major powers, except perhaps China, but that there will be a continuing need for the U.K. to show her determination to defend her interests by force in the last resort. The

137

decision to use nuclear weapons in a limited war of course must be governmental. Their use in limited wars in Africa or the Middle East (except against Russia) is not at present envisaged.

"In the Far East the only possible military means of halting all-out Chinese aggression would be by the use of nuclear weapons, although their use might carry the risk of global war."

Subsequently the Chiefs of Staff issued a schedule of ammunition requirements for the overseas garrisons, calculated to be sufficient to fight the theoretical 'limited war' for sixty days in the Middle East, ninety days in the Far East and ninety days south of Suez. A strategic home reserve was required sufficient to replenish the above for six months at a two division contact rate. It was proposed to maintain home reserves sufficient to replace each of the theatre reserves once within two years. As an economy measure duplicate stocks were to be held only for those natures of ammunition which could not be manufactured by the Royal Ordnance Factories or purchased on the open market within the two-year period.

Eventually, after analysis of the implications of the various proposals, a decision was made which marked the end of CAD Corsham. In August, 1960, the Cabinet Defence Committee announced that:

"In the last three years decisions have been reached on the size, deployment and equipment of the regular forces in the light of the new defence policy announced in 1957.

"It might be possible to close an ammunition depot and a small technical stores department. Capital saving on Works Services is estimated at £1.3 million. Savings on ammunition stocking costs would amount to £28 million. New purchases will be reduced from £20 million to £17 million per annum."

CLOSURE CONFIRMED

Once the case for closing an ammunition depot was proved, the War Office found no difficulty in determining where the blow should fall. The underground complex at Corsham, enormous in both its capacity for ammunition and its voracity for public funds, was immediately high-lighted. Large enough in which to lose the small residual stocks demanded by the new Army, cumbersome in operation, and fighting a lost battle against the subterranean elements, the Corsham Depot was a dinosaur in the new age of military technology.

Before the end of 1960 a timetable of closure was prepared and thought given to the eventual disposal of the depots. It was hoped that some other government departments might express an interest in using one or more of the sub-depots, and in pursuit of this end a descriptive schedule of each site was drawn up, like an estate agent's pamphlet offering for sale a suburban semi. The particulars prepared for the Monkton Farleigh site gave the depot a nominal value of £6,000,000, plus a further £1,000,000 for electrical and mechanical services. Annual running costs were estimated at £110,000.

Temporary tenants were found for Monkton Farleigh in the form of the General Post Office which took over No.19 District for a while in the early 1960s. Huge stockpiles of used postal orders, balls of string, dog licences, elastic bands, sealing wax and all the other anachronistic paraphernalia endemic to the old-fashioned British Post Office were shipped in. The venture was an absolute disaster. No.19 District, being the dampest and most marginal of all the storage in the CAD, was totally unsuited to the material the GPO wished to store and in next to no time all the organic material was reduced to a sloppy pulp.

Formal announcement of the impending closure was made in the press on 26 January, 1961. It was reported that the Depot would close by April, 1964, and that the run-down would result in the loss of 658 civilian jobs. The statement continued:

> "A reorganisation of the United Kingdom Base has been decided upon, as a result of which it will be necessary to close certain depots.
>
> "The need for a reorganization of this nature has been brought about by several factors. The most important are the reduced military manpower that will be available and the reduced holding of stores that will be necessary for the smaller Regular Army of the future.
>
> "The overall reorganization will be phased over several years and it is anticipated that it will not be completed until October 1964."

Clearance of the 300,000 tons of ammunition was scheduled to take four years to complete. Stocks of current ammunition were transferred to the smaller, more modern surface depots; markets were found abroad

139

for certain serviceable but obsolescent types, and huge quantities of clearly obsolete stock were prepared for dumping at sea or destroyed locally in the Monkton Farleigh demolition pits. The extensive and remote nature of the Monkton Farleigh site made it ideal for this purpose and material from the other sub-depots was regularly transferred there by road for disposal. The thunderous explosions emanating from Farleigh Down echoed around the hills of Bath and were a constant reminder of the Army presence in North Wiltshire at that time.

Another disposal site was developed in the woods behind Main West building, where an open quarry near Brown's Folly was adapted for the systematic destruction of obsolete cordite charges. The plant was commissioned in 1960 and remained in continuous use until the depot closed. Although propellants for all types of gun were destroyed there, the greatest quantities were of those for the 4.5" field gun and the 5.5" howitzer. These charges were stored in sealed, card-lined steel cylinders, each about two feet long and marked with the dates of manufacture and subsequent re-packing. The contents of hundreds of thousands of these packages were destroyed in the incineration pit between 1960 and 1964. Each one was broken open, the contents thrown down a chute into the incinerator and the containers tossed into a deep gully which in earlier years had been the entrance to the camp air-raid shelter. Often at this time one would see great white flashes among the trees around Brown's Folly as another particularly large batch was thrown in the pit by an over-enthusiastic disposal squad. To the residents of Bath, most of whom knew nothing of the War Office works at Monkton Farleigh, these unexplained phenomena were a source of wonder and consternation. All was finally explained in an article in the *Bath Evening Chronicle* on 25 July, 1962, under the headline "Monkton Farleigh Mushroom Clouds":

"Vivid flashes of light, mushroom clouds and shooting flames and smoke have been sighted from the heights of Bath. Now the CAD at Corsham has supplied the answer to the mystery. Bath is not being used as a centre for testing nuclear devices – it is just the CAD's way of getting rid of unwanted explosives. The sky phenomenon came from the direction of Monkton Farleigh, where, said a spokesman for the CAD, supplies of old cordite are being burned up. 'We have been burning unwanted supplies of old cordite every day for the last eighteen months, and we shall go on getting rid of it for at least another year,' he added."

The mounting pile of empty cordite canisters eventually filled the quarter-mile-long gully to a depth of thirty feet.

With the demolition and disposal process finished, Monkton Farleigh sub-depot finally closed at the end of September, 1963, after an active life of twenty-five years. Clearance of the relatively small holding at Eastlays continued smoothly and was completed by the end of 1962, at which time the sub-depot passed quietly into the care of the Ministry of Works and Buildings. The evacuation of Tunnel Quarry meanwhile continued apace and a small ceremony in the MSLP marked the passing of the last box of ammunition on Friday 4 December, 1962. It was announced on 6 September that with the ammunition disposal operation drawing to a close, the sidings at Thingley Junction were no longer required. In 1966 most of the track was lifted, leaving only the most northerly sidings and a single connection to the up running-line. This connection was severed in August, 1969, although the remaining sidings were left in situ.

While Tunnel Quarry was destined to remain indefinitely in the possession of the Ministry of Defence it was obvious that Monkton Farleigh and Eastlays would never again figure in the defence of the United Kingdom. Having retained the depots in mothballs for ten years, the government decided in 1972 that in the current climate of financial stringency the cost of continued maintenance was indefensible. In November the two properties were put in the hands of the estate agents Henry Butcher & Co. National newspapers advertised:

"VAST UNDERGROUND PREMISES: WILTSHIRE
TWO PROPERTIES OFFERING UNDERGROUND CLEAN,
DRY, LEVEL SPACE".

The depots were offered for sealed tender either individually or together, tenders to be received by the PSA Land Agent at Durrington by 2 May, 1975.

The press advertisements generated a certain amount of lay interest, mainly among the curious who were intrigued to learn more of what had been the secret beneath their feet, but very few commercial enquiries. The agents had already highlighted potential stumbling blocks, noting in their Particulars of Sale that, despite several months of negotiation:

> "The County Council, as the Planning Authority, have said that they are unable to agree any use of these underground workings unless certain pre-conditions can be complied with, such pre-conditions are not readily capable of translation into formal planning conditions."

Both sites were purchased by EMF Farming Associates, a speculative consortium headed by Mr H.W. Clothier, a successful Somerset farmer. News that the consortium were in negotiations with Darlington Mushrooms to convert Monkton Farleigh into the world's largest underground mushroom farm, with an annual harvest of 7,000 tons, was described in the local press under the headline: "Mushroom plan for the Caves of Death". The owners were also trying to establish a secure warehousing venture at Eastlays in association with a Doncaster-based haulage company.

Negotiations with an increasingly intransigent County Council Highways Authority regarding road access for commercial vehicles to both sites rumbled on for over four years to no avail. Late in 1980 both schemes were abandoned and, seeing no resolution to the traffic problem or any immediate prospect of putting the depots to profitable use, the consortium tried to recoup a little of their investment by scrapping most of the surface and underground plant.

The outlook for Eastlays seemed bleak until, early in 1981, a sales caravan and several security men armed with walkie-talkies suddenly arrived on site. Soon it was leaked to the press that Guernsey-based Rusepalm Developments were going to transform Eastlays into a 'nuclear condominium' where those who could afford it could buy protection against thermonuclear war and radioactive fallout. The quarry was to be subdivided into thousands of luxuriously equipped family units, like hotel suites, enough to house a population of 10,000 lucky people. This enclosed community would be served by shops and cinemas, hospitals, sports facilities and air-treatment systems to remove the least trace of radiation or noxious gas.

In the press the Caves of Death became instead 'Doom City'. Locally the scheme was viewed with growing outrage and, bowing to constituency pressure, the Conservative MP Richard Needham questioned Parliament about the ethics of allowing a wealthy minority to buy protection from the holocaust while government did nothing to protect the majority. In public houses around North Wiltshire there were many militant mutterings, much talk of the odds against the wealthy few ever taking up their places in "Doom City" in the face of a panicked population armed with pitchforks, rook-guns and a grim determination to survive.

The Rusepalm proposal went before the Wiltshire planners at the end of March and was passed without a hitch. Even the surface car-park for 3,000 cars caused no qualms in the Highways Department. Perhaps the prospect of universal annihilation and a county laid bare, smoking and aglow with radiation, made quibbling about traffic density seem a bit irrelevant. The matter was academic anyway, for on 10 April newspaper headlines read: "DOOM CITY PLAN FOR WILTS IS SUNK". Rusepalm was in financial difficulty and the company collapsed soon after, along with the dreams of those few who had already paid £8,000 each to buy their privileged positions in the post-holocaust world.

The only bright spot during this gloomy period occurred late in 1978 when the BBC selected Eastlays as the location for filming *The Fourth Arm* and an episode of the science-fiction series *Blake's Seven*. Most of the *Blake's Seven* action takes place in No. 24 District, where a troop carrier upon which the security forces of the 'Earth Federation' arrive to disrupt a dissident meeting was in fact a cut-down electric milk float, its bodywork suitably adapted with cardboard and fibreglass to convey an air of totalitarian menace.

During the 'mushroom' period at Monkton Farleigh pilot studies of growing techniques were undertaken which required the delivery of materials to the mine by lorry at peculiar times, an activity which in the insecure atmosphere of the period gave rise to vague but sinister speculation. Voice was eventually given to this speculation by the Chairman

143

of the local Residents' Association, who wrote to the County Council that:

"It is a growing rumour in this area that the old Depot will be used for either (a) atomic waste or (b) an atomic shelter for Royalty. I have been informed that a very large supply of food has been installed within the Depot for use by Royalty in the event of an atomic attack."

The rumours were of course quite groundless.

The presence of a permanent caretaker saved Eastlays from the rampant theft and vandalism that destroyed Monkton Farleigh quarry in the mid 1980s, and in 1985 new owners were found in the form of Cert plc, a South Wales based logistics company in search of a secure bonded warehouse. Cert adopted a firm stance with the local planning authority and has subsequently established a thriving business at Eastlays which appears to guarantee a secure future for the quarry.

Between 1980 and 1984 the sprawling, unmanageable complex at Monkton Farleigh was virtually destroyed by vandals, the most devastating damage occurring in the powerhouse where the transformers were smashed apart to recover their copper content. In the autumn of 1984 the stricken quarry was taken over by a company with the intention of operating the mine as a tourist attraction, and a programme of repair and restoration was initiated. Six years' work and much material help from the Property Services Agency saw the project progressing well despite tight financial restraints. Thousands of visitors flocked from all over the world to marvel at the mysteries of the subterranean citadel. But in 1990 disaster struck. At the height of the property boom the freehold of the quarry was purchased by a group of East Anglian property developers. Within months inauspicious property purchases elsewhere had reduced the new owners to bankruptcy. With the property in receivership the tourism venture collapsed too.

The next few years saw a period of ugly litigation with the ownership of Monkton Farleigh mine in dispute and the site once again abandoned and prey to vandals and thieves. Then, in June, 1996, the premises were acquired by Wansdyke Security, a company which since 1957 has specialized in the secure storage of archives and data in underground vaults, first at its headquarters site in the old Admiralty ammunition depot at Brockleaze, and also since the early 1980s in the abandoned British Museum repository at Westwood Quarry. Wansdyke Security came armed with many years experience and the indications are that this company will at last succeed where others have so signally failed.

12

BEAVERBROOK'S FOLLY –
THE UNDERGROUND FACTORIES

By the early autumn of 1940 the nation's ammunition reserves were already buried in huge bomb-proof arsenals below the hills of Wiltshire, Staffordshire and Caernarvonshire, deep concrete citadels were burrowed under London for the War Cabinet and Chiefs of Staff, and belated plans were laid to transfer much of the aircraft industry (upon which survival was to depend) into a series of great underground factories beyond the reach of the heaviest German bomb.

Planned in haste and panic and propelled to reality by Beaverbrook, a man as autocratic in war as in peace, the underground factories were in retrospect to be ranked amongst the greatest squanderings of precious wartime resources. Greatest of them all, the Spring Quarry factory at Corsham, designed as a dispersal factory for the Bristol Aircraft Company with an estimated budget of one million pounds, was, by the war's end, to have cost twenty million pounds and prompted an unprecedented inquiry by the House of Commons public accounts committee.

With so many parties involved in its development, the Corsham engine factory evolved, like the camel that was a horse designed by committee, into a monster bearing little resemblance to its original conception. Under the jealous and expansive influence of the Ministry of Works & Buildings a modest plan for a dispersed engine factory in a small Corsham quarry developed into a vast scheme which was to include not only acre upon acre of factory space for numerous armament manufacturers but also underground warehouses and magazines for the Navy and Ministry of Supply, underground vaults for the dispersed treasures of the British and V&A museums and the National Gallery, storage for state

146

archives from several East European governments in exile, temporary storage for tens of millions of French francs with which to replace German occupation currency, and ultimately, in the immediate post-war years, to provide atom-bomb proof emergency war headquarters for central and regional government.

BEAVERBROOK LAYS HIS PLANS

Plans to relocate much of the British aircraft industry into heavily protected underground factories evolved from the dispersal schemes contrived in the summer of 1940 to counter the German bombing offensive which was aimed at crippling the supply of new aircraft to the RAF. Unlike the War Office, which had argued since 1917 for secure underground storage facilities to protect its ammunition stockpile, the supply departments, particularly the Air Supply Board, gave scant attention to the aerial threat until it was too late. A policy of dispersing large production facilities into numerous isolated locations far from the established industrial centres was agreed during the summer of 1940, but little practical progress was made with this voluntary scheme ahead of the devastating German bombing campaign of the following winter.

Heavy raids in September on the Supermarine Spitfire plant at Southampton and the Vickers Weybridge factory, followed by attacks on the BAC works at Filton on the 25th and 27th, which seriously disrupted production and killed 160 people, highlighted the urgent need for factory dispersal. This need was reinforced in November with the destruction of Coventry and the sustained bombing of Birmingham during which the BSA Small Heath works, then the principal source of Browning machine guns required to arm the Spitfire and Hurricane, was severely damaged. In two raids on the Small Heath works on the nights of 19 and 22 November over 1,600 machine tools were destroyed – more than were lost in the whole city of Coventry ten days earlier. After this progress was more rapid; in Birmingham, for example, machines still serviceable were raked from the rubble of Small Heath before the ashes had cooled to be sent off to hastily requisitioned premises as far afield as Stoke-on-Trent, Leicester, Tamworth and Kidderminster.

The feasibility of providing underground factories was first discussed at a meeting of the Air Supply Board in September, 1940, where the concept was seized upon enthusiastically by the Minister of Aircraft Production, Lord Beaverbrook, a man of overbearingly powerful personality and a close confidant of Winston Churchill. Churchill's near obsession with underground citadels is legendary and may explain in part the relative ease with which many of the factory schemes were authorized, despite vehement opposition from the Treasury and elsewhere.

Following consultation with the Ministry a number of companies engaged in aircraft manufacture were invited to submit plans for going underground, and on 24 October, 1940, an official of the MAP was able to write enthusiastically to the Treasury that "My Minister has before him a number of schemes for underground factories." These initial proposals included:

1. A plan put forward by the Bristol Aircraft Company to move into Monk's Park Quarry, a disused stone mine about eighty feet below ground at Corsham at an estimated cost of £1,000,000.
2. An aircraft component factory for the Plessey organization, to be built in a three-mile length of completed but unopened Central Line tube tunnel between Wanstead and Gants Hill stations in East London.
3. An Austin Motor Company plan to construct 25,000 square feet of new tunnels behind their works in Birmingham at a cost of £67,650.
4. A scheme prepared by the Folland Engineering Company to move production into chalk cliffs twelve miles from their works at Hamble near Southampton. This plan was abandoned at an early stage.
5. A scheme put forward by the Birmingham Small Arms Company to convert 12,000 square feet of the abandoned limestone workings below Dudley Zoo into a safe refuge for its Browning gun barrel production line.

Within a few days, on 1 November, the Treasury replied that it was "definitely opposed to the plans for a variety of reasons". Not the least of these objections was the prospective cost, which would have to be met entirely from the public purse. Over the past four years the Treasury had been coerced into funding the ever-spiralling costs of the War Office underground works at Corsham and was wary of any similar development there. Officials insisted that the principal method of protecting industrial capacity should be by dispersal and echoed the Government's general policy regarding deep-shelter protection for civilians. What, it was argued, would be the reaction of workers who remained in the relatively vulnerable surface factories, to those who benefited from the protection afforded by the underground factories?

Under pressure from Beaverbrook and his Ministry the Treasury relented to a degree, suggesting that it would accept proposals concerning production facilities which were of vital national importance provided that they could be built cheaply and very near to the existing works. Concern had already been raised when considering smaller-scale dispersals regarding the logistic difficulties of transporting large numbers of industrial workers to locations remote from home.

Meanwhile further schemes were coming forward for consideration. The Parnell Company of Yate near Bristol, makers of Frazer-Nash turrets, proposed to build a semi-underground factory on derelict ground adjacent to its existing site. This plan was abandoned at an early stage when the company became involved in an alternative development in the Corsham quarries. Similarly the Mollins Machinery Company was dissuaded from following up a plan to build a 20,000 square foot concealed factory in a disused gravel pit near Dartford in Kent, when it was instead offered space in Monk's Park quarry at Corsham. The original plan of the Mollins Company, whose production line was adapted from the manufacture of cigarette machines to the building of feed mechanisms for Hispano cannon, was to build a £37,000 reinforced concrete factory in the bottom of a deep gravel pit and conceal it under twenty feet of shingle.

Three further proposals emerged the following year. In mid-April the Air Supply Board informed the Treasury that they intended to build an underground factory of 250,000 square feet at Drakelow near Kidderminster, into which it was intended to transfer some vital part of an aircraft component factory. No end user was specified, a MAP memorandum noting that:

"No specific works is in mind, but it would doubtless be one of the engine or gun factories in the Coventry or Birmingham area."

On 11 June a suggestion was put to the MAP by the engineering firm of Sir George Godfrey and Partners Ltd regarding some tunnels near Henley-on-Thames. Godfreys was the sole manufacturer of hydraulic components for the Phillips Master trainer at its works in Hanworth, which was a very vulnerable location in West London. They had located a disused chalk quarry adjacent to a whiting works near Henley-on-Thames, and had prepared a plan to provide 30,000 square feet of underground workshop space at a cost of only £23,025.

What proved to be the last proposal was passed to the Treasury on 23rd September 1941. Short Brothers had contacted the MAP regarding their seaplane works at Rochester seeking authority to build a new underground works in tunnels excavated under chalk cliffs behind their existing MAP extension factory. Space was urgently required for seventy-five new machine tools, and their works were full to capacity. The tunnels were intended to create 12,000 square feet of workshop space at a cost of £20,000 which, it was acknowledged, was somewhat higher than new surface building but stress was laid upon the vulnerability of the Medway estuary.

Of the ten schemes put forward for consideration three were stillborn; two, the Austin Tunnels at Longbridge and the Short Bros. Factory at Rochester, were small scale developments, and the Plessey scheme in East London involved the temporary occupation of an underground infrastructure already constructed for another purpose. The four remaining proposals, Corsham, Drakelow, Dudley and Henley-on-Thames, were much larger engineering tasks involving enormous excavations in virgin stone or the conversion of vast areas of abandoned mine workings into modern production areas with all the services and facilities of equivalent surface factories. Of these four projects, which are the core subject of this study, the Corsham scheme was by far the biggest, most costly and most controversial.

13

THE SPRING QUARRY PROJECT

In the mid 1930s the War Office had been able to acquire, by purchase, the necessary quarry space for its Central Ammunition Depot under very different circumstances than those that faced the MAP in 1940.

In October, 1939, the Admiralty negotiated leases on two other small Corsham quarries at Brocklease and Pickwick, together with Bethel quarry at Bradford-on-Avon. The workforce of the Bath and Portland Stone Company, which owned virtually all the quarries in North Wiltshire, was then concentrated on stone extraction from the firm's remaining quarries at Limpley Stoke and from the west side of Spring Quarry, a 3,000,000 square foot area of workings containing some sixty miles of underground roadways below land between Corsham and Box.

Early in November, 1940, both the Ministry of Supply and the Ministry of Aircraft Production were seeking advice from War Office representatives at Corsham regarding Monk's Park Quarry which, at the time, was the only unallocated underground working in the area which it was thought might be available for government use. The intention of the MAP was to develop it as a dispersed factory for the Bristol Aircraft Company, whilst the MOS planned to develop a factory in the quarry to be operated by BSA, making Oerlikon gun barrels for the Admiralty. The Admiralty had authority to build 300 Oerlikon guns per month; these were currently being manufactured at the BSA expansion factory at Ruislip, established in the London Transport carriage sheds which had been requisitioned for this purpose in June. Admiralty staff were not satisfied that the monthly gun quota was adequate and were also concerned about the vulnerability of the Ruislip site and the militant attitude of the men employed there. Monk's Park was seen as a safe refuge

151

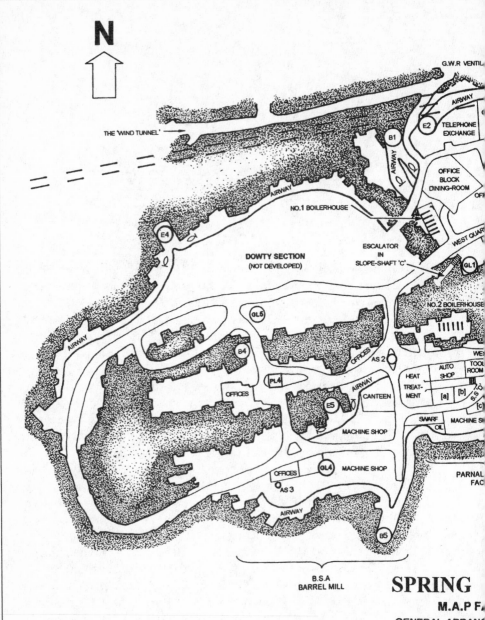

N

THE 'WIND TUNNEL'

G.W.R VENTIL

AIRWAY

E2   TELEPHONE
     EXCHANGE

B1

AIRWAY

OFFICE
BLOCK
DINING-ROOM

OFI

NO.1 BOILERHOUSE

WEST QUAR

E4

DOWTY SECTION
(NOT DEVELOPED)

ESCALATOR
IN
SLOPE-SHAFT 'C'

GL1

NO.2 BOILERHOUSE

GL6

AIRWAY

B4

OFFICES   AS 2

WE

PL4

AUTO
SHOP   TOOL
       ROOM

HEAT
TREAT-   [a]   [b]
MENT   [c]

OFFICES

AIRWAY
       CANTEEN

E5

SWARF
OIL   MACHINE S

MACHINE SHOP

OFFICES   GL4   MACHINE SHOP

PARNAL
FAC

AS 3

AIRWAY

B5

B.S.A
BARREL MILL

SPRING

M.A.P F.

GENERAL ARRANG

Februa

0   100   200   300   400   500   600   700   800   900   1000 feet

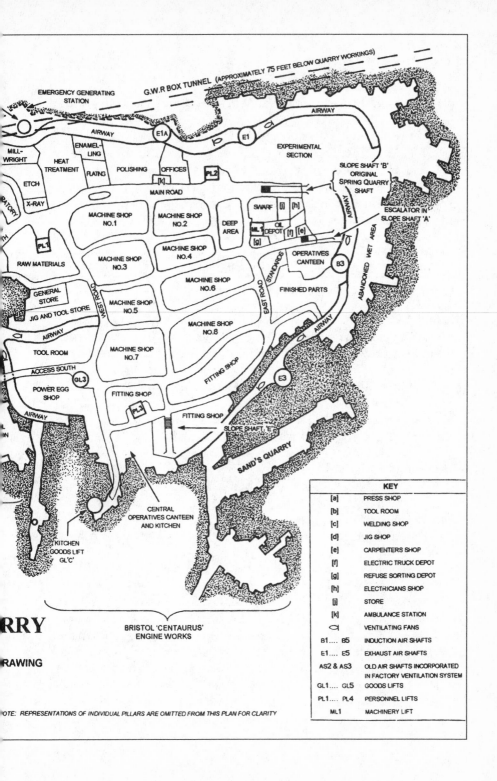

EMERGENCY GENERATING STATION

G.W.R BOX TUNNEL (APPROXIMATELY 75 FEET BELOW QUARRY WORKINGS)

AIRWAY

AIRWAY

E1A

E1

EXPERIMENTAL SECTION

MILL-WRIGHT

HEAT TREATMENT

ENAMEL-LING

PLATING

POLISHING

OFFICES

[k]

PL2

SLOPE SHAFT 'B'
ORIGINAL SPRING QUARRY SHAFT

ETCH

X-RAY

MAIN ROAD

ESCALATOR IN SLOPE SHAFT 'A'

MACHINE SHOP NO.1

MACHINE SHOP NO.2

DEEP AREA

SWARF

[j] [h]

ML1

OIL DEPOT

[f] [e]

AIRWAY

RAW MATERIALS

PL1

MACHINE SHOP NO.3

MACHINE SHOP NO.4

[g]

OPERATIVES CANTEEN

B3

ABANDONED WET AREA

GENERAL STORE

JIG AND TOOL STORE

MACHINE SHOP NO.5

MACHINE SHOP NO.6

FINISHED PARTS

EAST ROAD

STANDARDS

WEST ROAD

AIRWAY

MACHINE SHOP NO.8

AIRWAY

TOOL ROOM

ACCESS SOUTH

GL3

MACHINE SHOP NO.7

FITTING SHOP

E3

POWER EGG SHOP

FITTING SHOP

PL3

AIRWAY

FITTING SHOP

SLOPE SHAFT 'E'

SAND'S QUARRY

KITCHEN GOODS LIFT GL'C'

CENTRAL OPERATIVES CANTEEN AND KITCHEN

RRY

BRISTOL 'CENTAURUS' ENGINE WORKS

RAWING

OTE: REPRESENTATIONS OF INDIVIDUAL PILLARS ARE OMITTED FROM THIS PLAN FOR CLARITY

KEY	
[a]	PRESS SHOP
[b]	TOOL ROOM
[c]	WELDING SHOP
[d]	JIG SHOP
[e]	CARPENTERS SHOP
[f]	ELECTRIC TRUCK DEPOT
[g]	REFUSE SORTING DEPOT
[h]	ELECTRICIANS SHOP
[j]	STORE
[k]	AMBULANCE STATION
◁	VENTILATING FANS
B1.... B5	INDUCTION AIR SHAFTS
E1.... E5	EXHAUST AIR SHAFTS
AS2 & AS3	OLD AIR SHAFTS INCORPORATED IN FACTORY VENTILATION SYSTEM
GL1.... GL5	GOODS LIFTS
PL1.... PL4	PERSONNEL LIFTS
ML1	MACHINERY LIFT

and as an opportunity to obtain experience of manufacturing underground, although the MOS noted in an internal memorandum that the capacity was not currently vital and was "at the moment just an insurance". The Mollins Engineering Company, which had earlier been considered as a sub-tenant of Monk's Park, subsequently found more suitable premises elsewhere and declined to take up its option.

By early December there was intense interest in the Corsham Quarries from all quarters and to safeguard its interest the Admiralty peremptorily requisitioned Monk's Park on Monday, 2 December. Five days later the MOS requisitioned all the remaining quarries, much to the surprise of the Bath & Portland Board. The following Monday Mark Pictor wrote to inform the company land agent that:

"On Saturday the District Valuer arrived at our office and requisitioned the whole of our Bath Stone quarries with the exception of Monk's Park, which had been requisitioned a few days earlier by the Admiralty. This has come as rather a surprise to us as we did not anticipate the Ministry of Supply stepping in at all.

"No question of terms were discussed as he said that would be dealt with later. I tried to find out whether we should be allowed to do the clearing but could get no reply on that point. As you can imagine we are left rather high and dry, but I suppose we shall hear something this week.

"Meantime of course it is somewhat difficult to know what to do with the men as I do not want to disperse them knowing how difficult it will be to get them back again, but with all the quarries requisitioned it leaves very little work to which we can put them."

Work in the quarries stopped immediately and was for the most part never to resume. Lamps and tools were left where they lay by the quarrymen laid off at a moment's notice. Half-cut blocks of stone were abandoned in the working faces with the large steel saws or 'frig-bobs' still in the groove. In other places great blocks of stone were left hanging from the old wooden cranes or stacked on wagons waiting to be hauled to the surface. Nearly sixty years on, in the unconverted parts of Spring Quarry, Copenacre, and Hayes Wood mine at Limpley Stoke, the tools still remain untouched, awaiting the quarrymen's return.

To avoid possible conflicts a meeting of all the parties interested in the

154

various quarries was held on 3 January, 1941, at which it was agreed that the MOWB would take overall control, agree allocations and deal with compensation claims arising from the requisitioning.

Prior to this meeting consideration had been given to the idea of converting parts of Monk's Park which were surplus to the needs of the BSA company into dispersed accommodation for the Bristol Aircraft Company under the aegis of the MAP. On 27 December the MAP informed the Treasury that they had discussed the Monk's Park scheme with Lord Reith, the Minister of Works & Buildings, and had jointly concluded that the nearby Spring Quarry would be a better option. That site offered a nett usable floor space after clearance of 2,200,000 square feet, sufficient to contain the whole airframe and engine production facilities currently at Filton. Costs were estimated at £2,341,000, including the cost of 8,000 workers hostels. "You will observe," noted Lord Reith, "that the estimated cost, which is based on a competent technical opinion, works out at between 18/- and £1 per square foot." This, he continued, compared favourably with the cost of constructing a new, conventional surface factory. Recommending the scheme, the MAP stated that the estimates had been prepared by Lord Reith's technical adviser, Mr Brian Colquhoun, and had been favourably reported on by the Director General of Factories, Mr Alan Quartermaine. (Quartermaine was previously Chief Engineer of the Great Western Railway.)

Despite these optimistic assessments the Treasury was wary of initiating further large-scale underground expenditure. Eventually, however, the Treasury was forced to give way, a memorandum from the Minister concerned noting that:

> "I think there is no alternative but to sanction the scheme in principle, but to ask that a close watch be kept on the development . . .
> it should be, if necessary abandoned if difficulties begin to show themselves on a scale likely to vitiate the estimates substantially."

Back at Corsham the MOWB had completed a cursory survey of the recently acquired quarries and prepared a provisional allocation table. Those quarries already occupied by the War Office and Admiralty were included for completeness, although the former continued successfully to prevent the MOWB interfering in the management of their sites.

NAME	TOTAL AREA (SQUARE FEET)	AREA CAPABLE OF DEVELOPMENT	END-USER	AGENCY
SPRING	3,343,948	2,271,200	BAC	MAP
SANDS	138,234	59,320		MAP
HAYES WOOD	493,680	227,190	Air Ministry	MAP
WESTWOOD	719,270	148,969	Royal Enfield Ltd	MOS
COPENACRE	514,260	288,619	Admiralty	MOS
TRAVELLERS	20,042	20,042	Admiralty	MOWB
RIDGE PARK	183,000	183,000	W.D.	W.D.
ELM PARK	66,500	66,500	Air Ministry	MAP
BROWNS	43,000	43,000	R.A.F.	W.D.
GROUNDSTONE	46,290	31,600	W.D.	W.D.
PICKWICK	81,675	81,675	Admiralty	MOWB
BROCKLEASE	40,000	40,000	Admiralty	MOWB
TUNNEL	1,633,500	1,633,500	W.D.	W.D.
RIDGE	203,000	203,000	W.D.	W.D.
EASTLAYS	871,200	871,200	W.D.	W.D.
M. FARLEIGH	2,591,820	2,069,100	W.D.	W.D.
MONK'S PARK	519,600	109,500	BSA Ltd	MOS
PARK LANE	548,800	548,800		
BETHEL	120,000	100,000	Admiralty	MOWB
CLUB HOUSE	17,000	17,000	Not allocated	
CLIFT & NO.4	3,335,500	Unworkable	"	
KINGSDOWN	116,670	Unworkable	"	
HOLLYBUSH	6,000	Unworkable	"	
WESTWELLS	101,000	100,000	"	
BREWER'S YARD	34,000	Unworkable	"	

Following these provisional allocations, preparation for the start of the ground works proceeded rapidly. Sir Alexander Gibb and Partners were appointed consultant engineers to oversee completion of the entire project on behalf of the MOWB. Most of the major underground building contracts were let to Alfred McAlpine Ltd, with the exception of the Westwood Quarry contract which was completed by George Wimpey. Construction started at Spring Quarry in April, 1941, with a scheduled completion date of August, 1942. Due to numerous minor difficulties, starts at the other quarries were staggered over the next few months, but thereafter work continued simultaneously at Spring Quarry and all the smaller sites.

During the immediate pre-war years Spring Quarry was the largest and most important of the Corsham quarries, producing fine quality, soft stone in large blocks ideally suited to the mason's needs. Quarrying had continued for many decades and the underground workings extended over nearly ninety acres. Despite its size there was only one slope-shaft entrance to the quarry and that was at the eastern extremity of the workings, furthest from the active working faces. The northern boundary of the quarry is marked by the line of the Box Railway Tunnel. Workings beyond the railway tunnel, comprising the former Tunnel and Huddswell quarries, were, by 1940, in process of conversion by the Royal Engineers to form the No.1 sub-depot of Corsham Central Ammunition Depot. Disputes regarding safety, security and rights of access at this boundary continued to cause friction between the MOWB and the War Office for many years.

Spring Quarry is divided into three major sections separated by geological faults. The eastern section encompasses over half the available area, while the two smaller areas to the north-west and south-west are roughly the same size, with gross areas of 500,000 square feet each. Each of the western areas is connected to the east quarry by two wide haulageways which traverse the fault, while a single north-south haulageway connects the two smaller areas. Ventilation in stone mining days was by means of ten air shafts located at intervals around the southern and western perimeter of the workings.

The first major engineering challenge was the clearance from the underground galleries of an estimated 500,000 tons of waste stone dumped there by quarrymen in earlier days, a task sub-contracted by McAlpine to the Bath & Portland Stone Company. Following the practice adopted by the War Office, it was decided to transfer as much waste as possible into the unusable wet areas to the east of the quarry. With only limited space available underground, the majority of the waste stone debris had to be brought to the surface for dumping, but it was obvious that the single, steeply graded slope shaft could handle a maximum of only fifty-tons per hour. At that rate clearance would take at least three years to complete.

To overcome this bottleneck the firm employed several portable steam cranes brought up from its Portland quarries to raise waste stone via eight of the old ventilation shafts along the southern perimeter of the quarry. As work progressed it became apparent that the quantity of debris had been greatly underestimated. Revised estimates indicated that at least two million tons remained, the removal of which was beyond the capacity of the Bath & Portland workforce, so increasing numbers of directly employed labourers were drafted in by McAlpine's and four new slope-shafts were constructed with gradients more favourable than the original Spring Quarry shaft. Two of these shafts were designed only for the evacuation of stone waste and were supposed to be sealed once construction was complete, but, following changes in the way the factory was to be worked, both were kept open.

Stone debris brought to the surface via Spring shaft was loaded into standard-gauge railway trucks and hauled by a contractor's locomotive the short distance across the lane from Westwells to Corsham to be tipped on land at Westwells, but the bulk of the waste arising via conveyor in the new shafts was dumped over open ground surrounding the south-west corner of the factory site. Eventually the tip covered an area a quarter of a mile long and over fifty feet high. Little effort was made to disguise the conspicuousness of this vast heap of virgin white stone, which acted as an aerial beacon for many miles around and caused alarm at the nearby RAF and RAOC establishments.

MANPOWER

The magnitude of the contract, which was worth over £7,000,000 to McAlpine's, was such that the locally available labour force was totally inadequate, all the eligible men from the sparsely populated surrounding areas having already been mopped up by the nearby War Office works. By 1940, however, with the growing labour demands of the resurgent armament industry and the imminent call to arms, there was no longer a pool of unemployed men available and McAlpine's had to look to Ireland, its traditional source of labour, for its work force. A recruiting office was opened in Dublin and over 10,000 men enlisted, many of them the legendary, hard-working but hard-drinking 'Mayo Men' who, in the words of Alastair Kennedy, the site agent, "would draw a knife if you looked at them crossways".

Accommodating this great influx of Irish labour proved difficult in the insular towns and villages of Somerset and North Wiltshire. Considerable resentment had been generated by the arrival of the 'Men From The North' who came down a few years earlier to build the War Office ammunition depots; these poor men were looked upon disparagingly as rough and ill-bred, but billets were eventually found for over 7000 of them without the need for labour camps, the erection of which the War Office successfully opposed. Admiralty staff evacuated to Bath in September, 1939, took up the last remaining billets and fared no better, for Bath people, conspicuously conscious of their place in society, found these later interlopers rather too snobbish and cosmopolitan for their taste. Anyway, McAlpine's were aware that it would be dangerous, in the words of the Company historian Tony Gray, "to let such an army of workers, many of them Irish and heavy drinkers, loose on the surrounding towns and villages". Plans were made to build eight huge temporary camps provided with canteens, bars and cinemas in an attempt to keep the men voluntarily confined.

CHANGE OF POLICY

In December, 1940, it was proposed to move all of the BAC engine development and production departments to Corsham, together with most of the airframe construction department, as a government-financed dispersal scheme. Accommodation was also to be provided underground for hostels to house 2,000 factory employees. The engine building and development shops were to be concentrated in the East Quarry with airframe construction and hostels in the south-west and north-west areas respectively.

Excavation and construction work proceeded in accordance with this plan, but before the work had advanced appreciably it was suspended following the announcement of a radical change to the aircraft expansion programme. It was realized that to move the entire engine production line from Filton to Corsham would entail an unacceptable disruption to production at a time when the consequent shortfall would be very damaging to the accelerated big bomber programme. At one point, as the ferocity of the German air attacks on Bristol receded, it was rumoured that BAC would not require *any* of its underground allocation at all, but, following a series of Cabinet discussions, the Ministry of Aircraft Production was instructed to continue building, under the

159

presumption that some other manufacturer *would* undoubtedly require the space. Reporting on this decision to the Treasury some months later Mr Sam Brown, of the MAP, explained that:

> "While the discussions with the Cabinet were proceeding we felt it right to allow the work to proceed since, whichever aircraft programme was adopted, there were bound to be new factories of great importance which could be put underground. **The work of course proceeded on the basis of the Bristol layout since there was no other basis on which it could proceed.**"

The increase in the agreed bomber programme meant that there would, as predicted by Sam Brown, indeed be a requirement for additional engine, undercarriage and turret-building capacity which could possibly be allocated to Spring Quarry. Ultimately it was confirmed that BAC would transfer the whole of their development department as planned, but would install a completely new (but smaller) Pegasus and Centaurus engine production line underground, retaining the bulk of its capacity at Filton. The engine facility was reclassified as a *shadow* rather than a *dispersal* scheme. This change in classification, together with the fact that the whole BAC workforce was no longer expected to transfer from Filton, meant that the demand for living accommodation at Corsham was not so great and the scheme for underground hostels was abandoned.

Some of the redundant quarry space now available at Spring Quarry was to be taken up by BSA, a company which the MOWB had earlier expected to occupy Monk's Park Quarry. During the years 1940–42 the dilatory attitude of BSA was to cause much frustration to the various Ministries involved in the underground factory schemes. It appears in retrospect that the company was not in principle well disposed to any of the proposals, all of which would have been to their advantage, and showed little willingness to compromise. We shall see in a later chapter that BSA created so many difficulties in the West Midlands that a plan to utilize the Dudley Caverns had to be aborted after a great deal of money had been wasted. A similar scene was now being acted out in Corsham. After preliminary works began at Monk's Park to convert the quarry to specifications agreed with BSA the company then led the MOWB to understand that they wished to transfer a rather larger section of their capacity to Corsham than first proposed, suggesting a modest expansion into part of the now redundant area of Spring Quarry. Having apparently reached agreement on this point, BSA then announced that it would not after all take up its allocation at Monk's Park, as it did not wish to split its operations between two separate sites and would concentrate its activities in a smaller than anticipated area of Spring Quarry.

Meanwhile work continued in the East Quarry where BAC had confirmed their requirements. At the same time negotiations were under way with several other manufacturers in the aircraft sector in an attempt to fully utilize all the remaining space at Spring Quarry.

ESCALATING COSTS

Concern was mounting at the Treasury regarding the escalating costs accruing at Corsham, which were already far in excess of the agreed budget. By May, 1941, the estimate had risen from £2,341,000 to £3,553,165 with most of the excess attributed to increases in service installations and the decision to provide surface hostels for up to 12,000 workers. The hostels alone would cost an additional £1,220,000.

On 19 December, 1941, the MOWB presented the Treasury with new costings which took account of all the works currently in hand, including those being undertaken for the Ministry of Supply at Westwood and for the Admiralty at Corsham, as well as the main Spring Quarry project. The staggering total of £6,112,050 horrified the Treasury official responsible for compiling these figures, who noted to his Minister that:

> "I knew the Corsham expenditure was getting pretty big, but I didn't know it was getting this big! I suppose however that you did. There is I gather a good deal of other expenditure for the Admiralty, Museums and miscellaneous people, but it is small in relation to this."

In December, after studying the situation in more detail, worried Treasury officials questioned the MOWB regarding the enormous expense, noting that:

> "Quarry development at £2,227,000 looks **pretty sinister**. Is this a repetition of the War Office experience at Corsham? Why have we not been told of this enormous increase of cost at an earlier

stage? In view of the increase should the scheme be abandoned? I imagine the answer is most certainly 'NO'."

To compound the problem of expenditure apparently out of control at Corsham the Treasury suddenly realized that these huge sums of money were being spent on a property which had been requisitioned and about which matters of long-term tenure or ownership had not been properly addressed. An internal memorandum, expressing a notion which, prophetically, was to establish the post-war, cold-war future of Corsham for the next fifty years, noted that:

"As to the requisitioning position, one thing that was abundantly clear was that having spent such an enormous sum here we would want to buy out some of the quarries and keep some kind of permanent citadel for future emergencies."

Although this suggestion was eventually accepted, there was some concern at the time that making a post-war permanent establishment underground at Corsham would sterilize large stocks of building stone which would be in great demand for bomb-damage reconstruction.

Explaining the Costs
The Treasury made it clear that a Public Accounts Committee investigation was inevitable in view of the severity of the overspend, and recommended that the MOWB should start its own internal investigation in preparation for this.

As a footnote to the most recent accounts, submitted in December, 1941, Mr E.J.R. Edwards of the MOWB, explained that:

"The main reason for the underestimation of quarry development was that in neither December [1940] or January was time allowed for surveying the quarry adequately, ascertaining definite requirements or obtaining accurate information regarding the supply of services available in the District. Without such information detailed planning and accurate estimating was impossible."

In a subsequent, more detailed, defence, the MOWB stated that the original Bath & Portland quarry surveys upon which the working drawings

162

were based were very inaccurate, particularly with regard to levels. The roof slope was found to be nearer 1:7 than the expected 1:30, thus requiring much more cutting away to give sufficient head room, and extensive floor levelling was needed to provide horizontal machine foundations. Much more debris was encountered than had been expected, and removing this to the surface was very costly in time and material resources. Shafts which the engineers had hoped to use for the ingress of building materials were instead tied up for many months with the evacuation of stone debris, and a great deal of plant was similarly unavailable for more important duties.

Since the BAC section was to be run as two separate entities, a development factory and a production works, and a third independent factory for BSA was now also proposed, it became necessary to install three goods and machinery lifts instead of the one already planned, which greatly increased costs. An additional £32,500 was required to provide canteen equipment to replace that which was not, after all, to be transferred from Filton, following abandonment of the dispersal scheme. As production facilities were to remain at Filton, it was necessary to provide new plant and equipment (particularly transformers, switchgear and motor generator sets) rather than move them from the original site. Nearer the end of the project in 1943 a separate parliamentary vote of £3,000,000 was made for the purchase of new machine tools for the finished factory.

1942 – A YEAR OF FURTHER CHANGES

In the dawning days of 1942 a revised allocation of floor space at Spring Quarry was agreed, new tenants having been found for the areas no longer required by BAC or BSA. The new arrangements were to consist of:

1. A dispersed BAC development works established in the northern half of the East Quarry.
2. A new BAC engine factory with a designed output of 250 Centaurus engines per month in the larger, southern section of the east quarry.
3. A new factory operated by the Parnall Company, assembling Frazer-Nash turrets and vane oil motors in the south-west quarry.
4. A BSA dispersal factory, the erratic evolution of which is detailed

above, established in the south-west Quarry to build Oerlikon gun barrels for the Admiralty, using plant transferred from the company's Newcastle under Lyme works.

5. A new factory to manufacture undercarriages for Halifax and Lancaster bombers in the north-west Quarry, to be operated nominally by the Dowty Company but using sub-contracted BAC labour.

The group of factories were expected to employ 14,000 men, 8,000 of whom would live in hostels nearby and 1,300 in married quarters, with the balance transported daily from Bristol by bus. Initially the logistics of this arrangement were given scant attention, leading to a critical situation in the summer of 1942, at which time a number of emergency committees were convened to resolve the growing problems of accommodation and transport.

PROPOSED NUMBER OF EMPLOYEES	
BAC Development	800
BAC Shadow factory	9,000
BSA	700
Parnall	1,400–2,000
Dowty	2,000

MORE CHANGES TO THE DEVELOPMENT PLAN

By June, 1942, the month in which engine production was originally scheduled to start, clearance of the BAC experimental area was complete and building work was well advanced. Progress was such that the engine research department was able to start its move to Corsham the following month, although much fitting-out was still required.

There had been a temporary setback in April following complaints from Colonel Minnis, the RE officer in charge of construction at the War Office Tunnel Quarry ammunition depot. Slight roof movements had been spotted in the central section of Tunnel Quarry and some cracking of pillars near the boundary wall between Tunnel and Spring Quarries, and Brigadier Minnis was convinced that this was due to works currently under way in Spring Quarry. With the support of the Director General of Fortification and Works, Minnis initiated an inquiry by a committee of the Department of Scientific and Industrial Research, conducted by its secretary, Dr E.B. Baily.

Brigadier Minnis believed that, because of the downward slope of the rock strata from Tunnel Quarry to Spring Quarry, the incautious removal of backfill and support pillars in Spring Quarry was creating a tendency for a lateral movement of the quarry roof in the direction of dip. He further considered that the 20% ratio of roof support to gross area adhered to by the MAP was quite insufficient; in Tunnel Quarry a minimum ratio of 25–30% was insisted on. Minnis argued that given the lack of support a general or partial collapse of Spring Quarry was possible and that "It is likely that the collapse of any considerable area in Spring Quarry will start a roof movement down the dip which will be very difficult to arrest." Attention was also drawn to the widespread use of brickwork in support walls and pillars in Spring Quarry, which Brigadier Minnis thought very inferior to concrete.

Giving evidence on behalf of the War Office, the mining engineer Mr Foster Brown stated that there was evidence of a general 'adjustment' of the roof over a wide area, rather than failure of individual weak pillars. He recommended that two parallel, strong concrete support walls founded on solid rock should be built at the boundary between the two quarries to replace the lighter boundary wall (founded only on loose backfill) currently existing. Caution was advised in the way this was done, however, for the suspect area was directly above the GWR Box tunnel and it was thought that increasing the weight or loading there might distort the tunnel lining. In its circulated report, the inquiry concluded that:

"The main question that has been raised is whether failure of roof support in Spring Quarry is likely to cause trouble in Tunnel Quarry by initiating lateral down-dip roof slide. There seems no reason to anticipate such sliding, for failure in Spring Quarry would not open up any space to receive down-dip slide of roof. Careful examination has, moreover, not revealed any tendency to lateral slide: all movement or readjustment appears to have been vertical. It is agreed that the equilibrium of the roof of both Spring and Tunnel Quarries has been in the past liable to slight upset by any major operation, such as the removal of floor packing, removal or trimming of pillars, or sinking of a shaft. It is probable that use of explosives, train vibration, air conditioning have also all played a part. In the future vibration of machinery installed in Spring Quarry, and enemy bombing must be allowed for. Up to date no serious trouble has arisen. The yielding of supports has always been at a very gradual and manageable pace. The position seems satisfactory if constant vigilance is maintained. In general, corseting of pillars that show signs of weakness should meet requirements. If very heavy bombing does cause a roof fall, the effect is likely to be local and there is no reason to fear its propagation by lateral roof-creep."

Development of the production factory was also pressing ahead, although many months behind schedule. Machine shops 1–4 were completely cleared as were most of the ancillary areas to the north of the main haulage road, but the main shops south of this road, together with the south-east canteen area, were less well advanced.

Better progress was being made in the BSA area where clearance was virtually complete and two new twenty-foot-diameter ventilation shafts were being sunk. At the same time excavations began for the four shafts required in the east quarry. Development of the adjacent Parnall section was considerably less well advanced, with less than a quarter of the area cleared to the required headroom. Delays in this area were attributed to the fact that debris could only be evacuated via slope-shaft 'D', which was fully committed for some months to the removal of stone from the BSA area.

Hardly any progress had been made in the north-west quarry, which was allocated to the Dowty Company for the manufacture of aircraft undercarriages. Because of the size of these components a minimum headroom of 12'6" was required throughout the area, but by June little more than exploratory work had been undertaken, with only 5% of the 300,000 square feet having been cleared to even the minimum headroom sufficient for a detailed survey to be completed.

Completely new drawings had been prepared to take account of the most recent factory allocations. Access ways were realigned to take account of the four new goods lifts and pedestrian slope shafts, and new boundary walls built to separate the various factory units. Because of the limited headroom available it was not possible to install overall high-bay lighting as would have been normal in a conventional factory, so instead great care had been taken to prepare in advance the positions of all the machine tools required by BAC, and to design a system of individual lighting for each machine. These detailed plans were abandoned when the revised BAC requirements were announced in the summer of 1941, and were re-drawn at great expense when the new allocations were made early the following year.

Several other factors were to affect progress at Corsham from the early months of 1942. By this time the threat of invasion had evaporated and the German bombing offensive had dwindled to the extent that the risk to industrial capacity was minimal, making the whole concept of underground factories increasingly redundant. The manufacturing companies which had fallen over one another in the rush for protected accommodation at the height of the blitz were now noticeably lukewarm in their enthusiasm, and consequently made more stringent demands upon the MAP and needed considerable inducement before they would move underground.

All five tenants now required independent canteens for their workers – and these were not small establishments: the canteen specified for the Parnall area catered for 1,300 men, while the three in the BAC factory were even larger. Later a dedicated goods lift, designated GL'C', was installed in the main south kitchen to carry underground the huge amounts of food required each day and to dispose of the refuse.

The pace of progress at Corsham declined inexorably through the summer of 1942, to the extent that the Treasury once again questioned the viability of the project. Rumours were circulating in Bath regarding the waste, profiteering and endemic idleness at Corsham, a City Councillor telling representatives from the MAP that he had heard in his club that "Ten men did the work of one at Corsham". There were ugly rumours too about the recent visit of a Russian delegation to the underground works.

In reply to criticisms of the quality of labour at Spring Quarry, Brian Colquhoun stated that the problem lay with the Essential Works Order in force there, which made it virtually impossible to dismiss

167

unsatisfactory labourers, and under which machinery for discipline was non-existent or prohibitively cumbersome. He would have preferred the sanction of three days' unpaid suspension which was available in all other industries, but which was specifically excluded from building and civil engineering.

The more serious accusations of profiteering were investigated by the Treasury in the light of the most recent summary of costs, which had risen by April, 1942, to £8,578,702. It was explained that due to the previously untried nature of the work the MAP initially awarded contracts on a 'costs plus profit' basis, which in wartime was a notorious licence to print money. About half of the contracts were later renegotiated on a 'scheduled cost' basis, 80% of which involved a bonus incentive, (80% of which was achieved).

Referring to Mr Edwards' admission that inadequate account had been taken during the preliminary site survey of the sparsity of external services such as gas and electricity available at Corsham, the Treasury gave its opinion that the MOWB was subsequently too generous to the local authorities and utility companies regarding the provision of these services. The MOWB paid all the infrastructure costs and hoped to recover them at the end of the hostilities, the theory being that the enhanced supplies of gas, etc, to the area would greatly increase its post-war development potential. The prospect of large numbers of new customers would more than compensate the utility suppliers for the expense of acquiring the residual value of the pipes, cables and suchlike from the Ministry.

Early in July Mr Minns, the MOWB accountant at Corsham, forwarded yet another summary of costs to the Treasury which indicated a total of £9,917,387. This caused grave consternation, as an internal memorandum dated 25th July reveals:

"The really horrible thing is Mr Minns' letter of 17th July reporting that the cost of the scheme as a whole is now within sight of the £10,000,000 mark."

The truly horrible thing was that by 1945 this figure was to double.

Although criticism of the poor progress at Corsham was directed primarily at the MAP, whose project it was, it soon became obvious that the main culprit was the MOWB, who were in overall charge and who in retrospect were seen not to be up to the challenge. Due to what it saw as the most unsatisfactory financial control exercised by the MOWB, the Treasury questioned whether it should sanction any further work. Certain Treasury officers adopted a more sanguine view. Mr. Gatcliff accepted that many of the problems encountered at Corsham were unique, and that Spring Quarry posed particular difficulties. To some extent justifying the cost, Gatcliff wrote:

> "Perhaps I start with something of a prejudice in favour of this scheme, as I was long in favour of providing citadels in suitable mountains long before such schemes became fashionable, this by way of prelude. Unfortunately much of the best space seems to have already been used [by the War Office] and the quarries remaining are either physically less suitable or inconveniently wet."

In a critical but resigned conclusion he continues:

> "I should think right in saying that Mr Colquhoun gave a pretty bad preliminary estimate. One always assumes that a scheme of this kind will cost a good deal more than the preliminary estimate, perhaps 50% more, but 150% is another matter. I rather doubt that we should have taken a different line on this scheme if we had visualised the full cost at the outset. The scheme itself has not I think cost more than the cost of an ordinary factory building, and we get ninety feet of completely bomb proof protection thrown in for nothing."

Dismissing criticism regarding the utility contracts, he wrote:

> "As for the residual value of external services, it seems pretty clear that unless the war ends in an assured perpetual peace the Government ought to retain this citadel in some form by way of insurance, and I doubt whether it matters much that we have not succeeded in landing much of the cost on the local authorities."

Not only were costs mounting alarmingly but the scheduled completion date for the BAC section had slipped by almost twelve months. The company was initially expected to move into the partially completed factory in April, 1942, and attain full production within nine months. This was put back first to November, 1942, then February of the following year and then on into the autumn. The first engine eventually emerged from the factory in September, 1943, three months after production staff first took possession of the site, three years after the underground factory scheme was first proposed, and two years after its only justification for being built, the intensive, pre-invasion German bombing, had ceased to be a relevant factor.

Much of the delay was attributed to the shortage of suitable labour. By the middle of 1942 there were 8,500 labourers on site, but in order to keep to schedule the MAP needed at least 1000 more men. The MOWB was inexplicably reluctant to agree to this and was accused of working to its own agenda in not making sufficient labour available, effectively dictating completion dates rather than working towards them.

There was brighter news from the BSA section, which was scheduled for partial occupation in April and completion by June, 1942. Gun barrel production actually began only four months behind schedule in August, with full capacity attained by the end of the year. At its peak the factory achieved a monthly output of 1,500 Hispano barrels for the Admiralty and 500 Polsen barrels for the Ministry of Supply. The relatively rapid progress made in the BSA area generated its own problems for the BSA engineers. Because of the restricted dimension of access shafts into their section the engineers found it necessary to manoeuvre the larger items of machinery through the muddy, treacherous and undeveloped sections of the BAC factory, having lowered them down the large-diameter BAC shafts. This process was not without hazard, and on one occasion one of the largest pieces of equipment, a thirty-three-foot-long barrel rifling machine weighing nearly seven tons, slipped from its shackle and crashed to the shaft bottom where it smashed into three pieces, a three-ton section slicing through a workman's mess hut, luckily without fatality. BSA installed a total of 101 machine tools in Spring Quarry, including eighty-four transferred from their Newcastle under Lyme factory (required for Hispano cannon production), and seventeen new machines supplied by the Ministry of Supply as part of the Admiralty Oerlikon contract. In December, 1943, a new diesel-driven generator was delivered to the BSA factory to ensure continuity of electricity supply. This unit was brought underground in several pieces, the largest weighing eighteen tons, via the BAC machinery lift (ML 1).

170

Although virtually untouched to date except for the sinking of its ventilation shafts and an additional shaft for a goods lift (GL 5), the Dowty undercarriage section was still expected to be ready for occupation by March, 1943. Hardly before the workforce was put in place to implement the new arrangements there came more bad news for the MAP. In August the Director General of Airframe Production announced that Dowty would not after all be taking up their allocation, when it was found that undercarriage production could not begin at Spring Quarry for several months, whereas A.V. Roe had spare surface factory capacity available immediately. This was followed almost immediately by a further announcement that the 245,000 square feet earmarked for the Parnall turret factory would not be required either. When the allocation was first made there was an urgent requirement for 250 turrets per month, of which 100 were for home-built aircraft and 150 for airframes supplied from the United States. Subsequently, however, it was discovered that the American aircraft were shipped complete with turrets and it was found possible to arrange production of the remaining 100 units within Parnall's existing surface capacity at Yate.

Despite the loss of its prospective tenants it was decided that the Parnall area should be completed to the agreed standard and that it should be fitted out for the use of BAC who had hopes of taking on a contract from Napier's to build and repair Sabre engines. Nothing eventually came of this scheme but in anticipation of its successful outcome basic building work was completed. Clearance continued in the Dowty area for a couple of months after the undercarriage project foundered, because no authority felt competent to make a decision regarding its future. By the beginning of September 184,000 square feet had been cleared at a cost of £150,000 and it was estimated that a further expenditure of £300,000 was required to complete the task. The MAP, hopeful that some as yet unknown new user would come forward, authorized the continuance of debris evacuation, but only to the standard headroom of ten feet. Work went on for a while in a desultory fashion until halted by the integration of the only access shaft for this area into the BAC factory complex.

TROUBLE AT THE TEST PLANT

The mysterious designation 'Power Egg Shop' that appeared on a layout drawing of the factory submitted to the Treasury among other papers prompted the terse reply from a baffled official, obviously not familiar with current aeronautical terminology, 'What the hell *is* a power egg?'

The answer to this question lies in the Air Ministry's concern in the 'thirties about the inordinately long time required to replace a failed aircraft engine with another of the same type. Engine manufacturers were subsequently encouraged to build their engines as quickly interchangeable integrated power-plants (or *power-eggs*), complete with all the ancillary equipment specific to the aircraft for which they were intended. By adopting this scheme it was hoped to reduce the time during which an aircraft was immobilized by engine failure to only an hour or so. In December, 1937, this scheme was extended to allow interchangeability of engines of different types by different manufacturers, but of the same general performance, within forty-eight hours. The intention was to provide a second-line reserve in the event of failure of supply of any given type of engine.

Plans were prepared at an early stage to construct six huge concrete dynamometer buildings for full-load engine testing on the surface in a compound at the south-west corner of the site. Finished Centaurus engines were brought to the surface from the power-egg shop via the nearby goods lift GL3. From its inception in July, 1942, every aspect of the test house project was fraught with difficulty. Technical problems were encountered in designing a silencing system which could safely dissipate the 2,520 horsepower produced by the Centaurus at full power while maintaining acceptable noise levels.

There were gasps of disbelief from the MAP when the MOWB announced that a contract to build the test plant, initially worth £375,000, had been awarded to Wilson Lovatt, a firm with no previous experience at Corsham. The Director General of Airframe Production (DGAFP) was appalled at the choice of contractor and minuted that: "Our experience is that this firm are not speedy workers". He went on to deprecate the fact that a new contractor should be brought on site when existing firms were already established there with materials, plant, management structure and experience. In a postscript criticizing the ineptitude of the MOWB, the DGAFP noted that:

"It is interesting that one of the contractors on site at Corsham, **who was not invited to tender for the [test-plant] work,** was at the same time being asked by the MOWB to tender for another job at Kenilworth – where they have no plant or organisation existing – and which is near the headquarters of Wilson Lovatt."

Defending his Ministry's decision, Lord Portal stated that the test-plant contract was let quite properly. Of the five firms invited to tender Wilson Lovatt's was the lowest, and in Portal's opinion the firm was "one of the best in the country".

Progress with the test-houses, as with the rest of the project, was slow and expensive. By August, 1943, building was almost complete, but due to faulty design and implementation the plant was unusable. The main difficulty was with the silencers which had quickly become ineffective due to oil penetration. Meanwhile costs had escalated from £375,000 to £1,700,000 excluding the cost of dynamometer equipment. Impatient at the rate of progress, BAC pressed to have Wilson Lovatt removed from the site by the end of August, having decided to complete the work themselves. Later the firm of H.W. Cullum was brought in to design a more efficient silencing system, but there were doubts about the safety of the proposed new design as it would not permit workers an emergency escape route through the exhaust ducts in the event of a fire in the engine room.

Six Centaurus engines running in parallel dissipated in excess of a megawatt of power and Cullum's suggested that much of this wasted energy might be recovered by regeneration, i.e. using it to produce electricity that could be fed back into the grid. Gibbs insisted that Kennedy & Donkin should design a suitable regenerative system, but the MOWB replied rather testily that their own electricians were quite capable. Privately, the MOWB were sceptical of regeneration and believed that the problem of synchronizing the output of the test-house alternators with the grid frequency was an accident waiting to happen.

14

SPRING QUARRY 1943–46: FROM COMMISSION TO CLOSURE

The year 1943 began, like 1942, amid further accusations of financial mismanagement. The long-awaited inquiry by the Commons Public Accounts Committee got under way early in the year and announced its scathing findings at the end of July. Much of the evidence had been rehearsed long before and was supported by a recitation of the troubles caused by the continually changing priorities as prospective tenants dropped out and new ones were added. It was stated that at the planning stage partial progressive occupation by one user had been envisaged, and that piecemeal occupation over a broad front meant that a great deal of money was wasted on temporary works, especially in the provision of services. Examples of excessively costly items, exclusive of the cost of railway works and the £1,220,000 spent on hostel accommodation, were:

- Extra costs of factory occupation, including additional lifts, administration buildings etc., and the supply of new plant originally expected to be transferred from Filton   £991,500
- Increased price of materials, extra transport costs due to poor siding facilities, and costs arising from labour inefficiency   £265,000
- Cost of providing services, including new gas mains   £2,674,371
- Extra quarry excavation   £556,859
- Detail planning for multiple tenancies   £164,000
- Wage cost uniformity charges   £1,549,125

- Works for Postmaster General. (Underground
  telephone exchange, temporary surface exchange and
  sorting office)   £36,022

Special attention was drawn to the difficulties encountered in meeting the BSA demands for improved lighting levels in their section of the factory and the provision of dedicated bus parks for their employees. Soon after production began it was found that the sodium silicate paint used to render the walls and ceiling dustproof was virtually useless, and expensive remedial measures were taken to repaint the whole quarry with a specially developed, highly reflective and dust-free cement-based finish.

At an urgent meeting called on 4 May, 1943, the Treasury demanded that Alexander Gibb and the major contractors should be removed from site as soon as possible, as it was recognized that "as long as they remain new works continue to accrue". Most contracts were now coming to a close and there was a move to classify them as completed even if there were still minor works to be done. Six weeks later there was still little sign of the operation winding up and pressure was mounting on the MOWB, an official of the MAP urging that: "our Minister is anxious to liquidate the New Works Organisation at Corsham as quickly as possible." A schedule of outstanding contracts prepared in July indicated that, disregarding any new work in the as yet unused Dowty and Parnall areas, the project should be completed by late autumn. Finally, under increasing Treasury and MAP pressure, the MOWB decided on 8 November to withdraw all the contractors at the end of the month. Until that time numerous requests for alterations and additions were being made by the various tenants and the MAP despaired of ever finishing the project. Gibb and the remaining contractors eventually left on the 26th, after the MAP refused to sanction any further expenditure except by special parliamentary vote.

Since April, 1943, most of the remaining works were on the surface, principally the completion of the troublesome engine test-beds and fitting out the last of the hostels sites, the need for which was by now in serious doubt. Underground construction had come to an end, completion of the ventilation system was imminent, at least one of the two boilerhouses was on line, most of the BSA and BAC factory was occupied, and Waygood

Otis had completed installation of the personnel escalator in slope shaft 'C' in March. The escalator in shaft 'A' was commissioned two months later.

No longer required for day-to-day operations, the old Spring Quarry shaft was secured at the top and bottom, with the keys held at the police lodge for emergency use. Most of the original ventilation shafts which had until now been used for material movements were capped or blocked by the end of May, except for AS 2 which was integrated into the new ventilation system, and AS 8 which carried a 12" rising water main. It was proposed that slope shaft 'D', which was sunk solely for construction purposes, should be sealed once building was complete, but BSA pressed for it to be kept open, enlarged and fitted with a winch for the eventual removal of their machinery at the end of the hostilities. The new vertical shaft in the Dowty area destined for Goods Lift No.5 was slabbed over at the end of July, following the decision to suspend further development of that area.

FLOODING IN THE B.S.A. FACTORY
Spring Quarry suffered badly from the percolation of seepage water after heavy rain, and the noticeable dip of the strata meant that during particularly bad times flooding occurred in some parts of the workings to a depth of several feet. The MAP was ignorant of the severity of this problem when the BSA factory was planned and was unprepared for the serious flooding that occurred in January, 1943, when a thaw of lying snow was quickly followed by heavy rain. The situation was most acute in B5 ventilation duct and E4 and M5 plant rooms which housed the factory air-conditioning and ventilation equipment. The BSA heat treatment pits were also flooded and the equipment badly damaged. Two pumps (one diesel and one electric), each with a capacity of 70,000 gallons per hour, were quickly installed to pump the flood water into the disused wet workings at the eastern extremity of the quarry. Further floods on 2 February overwhelmed the original pump sets and larger ones of 100,000 g.p.h. capacity were installed in a more suitable position. Excess water flowed into the drainage adit ('the lake') below Box Tunnel originally constructed to drain the railway tunnel and approach cutting.

RENEWED INTEREST FROM OTHER QUARTERS
Several coincident events led the Navy to look to Corsham for secure storage accommodation and early in January, 1943, a representative

from the Admiralty approached the MOWB with a view to occupying part of the hitherto unused Parnall area. The Admiralty subsequently took 90,000 square feet on a short-term tenancy for the storage of optical and asdic equipment.

At this time building work in the Parnall area was complete, although only minimal lighting had been installed and most of the remaining electrical equipment had been sold to a local firm of electrical engineers. The finished but unused 1,300-seat Parnall canteen was maintained by Sir Alexander Gibb and Partners but was not made available to the Admiralty. Fixtures, fittings and furniture were stored by Gibb in another part of the quarry.

In September officers from the United States Air Force visited Corsham looking for temporary accommodation for tens of thousands of maps of Europe, needed for the forthcoming invasion. Horrified by the conditions they encountered, the Americans decided that the risk from fire and explosion in a conventional surface warehouse was preferable to the incipient dripping dampness underground.

A month later enquiries were received from the Air Ministry, which required storage space for magnesium alloy extrusions and other light metal stock. The MOWB suggested the remaining section of the Parnall area, but this was opposed by Mr Wright, the recently appointed BAC factory manager, ostensibly because of the fire risk, but actually because he had his own plans for the area and was probably already making unauthorized use of it for rough storage. Justifying his opposition, Wright explained that the initial factory contract was for 2,300 Centaurus engines plus spare parts, and that a second contract for a further 1,500 engines had just been agreed. The spares schedule of 55–60% was much higher than normal due to the need for large spare part dumps in the Far East. Wright stated that with the existing plant and labour force he could not complete the first spares contract until 1949, and implied that to reach the second contract quota he would need the Parnall area to accommodate additional machine tools and resources. Thus it would be impossible to agree to the Air Ministry scheme, and in all probability it would be necessary to throw the Admiralty out of the space they currently occupied as well. Later enquiries revealed that BAC had more than sufficient excess capacity at their Accrington plant to complete the contracts on time, but by that time there were more pressing demands on Spring Quarry.

177

OPERATION "CROSSBOW"

That the huge sums of money sunk into the Corsham quarries had not, after all, been as reckless a waste as the Public Accounts Committee had at first concluded became a fleeting possibility in the early winter of 1943. On 8 November the Minister of Aircraft Production read a top secret telegram from the War Cabinet 'Crossbow' Committee telling him that urgent information had been received 'on high authority that an intensified attack on London and the south-east counties was expected, probably from a new weapon against which no anti-aircraft device will be of any avail, and probably within the next few weeks." 'Crossbow' was established to co-ordinate passive and active counter-measures to the recently detected German secret weapons, the V1 and V2 missiles, and part of its remit was to organize the evacuation of vital industrial production capacity, totalling 1,500,000 square feet of factory space, from the vulnerable areas to locations in the north and west, beyond the estimated range of the German weapons. The MAP was instructed to hold the disused section of the Parnall area empty and at the immediate disposal of the 'Crossbow' committee.

Although a number of 'Crossbow' proposals were put forward for the Parnall area, none was implemented. Plans to utilize 200,000 square feet at Spring Quarry to store radio valves were abandoned due to the damp conditions; an earlier proposal to use the Austin tunnels at Longbridge for this purpose was withdrawn because there was insufficient capacity there. Among other abortive 'Crossbow' plans was one to transfer the precious metals processing plant of Johnson Matthey to Spring Quarry, the company later taking up more suitable premises in North Wales. The emergency lasted until May, 1944, when 'Crossbow' relinquished its absolute reservation on the Parnall area, although any tenancies negotiated in the immediate future were required to be held on seven days' notice.

Once the 'Crossbow' emergency receded in the late spring of 1944 the MOWB was inundated with enquiries from various departments regarding the vacant areas of Spring Quarry. First in the queue was BAC, seeking to legitimize its unauthorized occupation of some 60,000 square feet of the Parnall section, which it was currently using for raw material storage.

What was perhaps to be the most unusual enquiry came from the Foreign Office at the end of June. The American government had printed many millions of French francs needed to replace the German occupation currency after the liberation of France, and was seeking temporary storage for approximately half of this stockpile, amounting to 192 tons of banknotes. The other half would be distributed from the Mediterranean coast and was to be stored in Algeria. The MOWB did not, when first approached, consider Corsham, offering instead the use of 100 cells on the upper floor of Dartmoor prison. When this was turned down, the Treasury, always keen to see a return on the Corsham investment, suggested Spring Quarry. The MAP was at first inimical, but then grudgingly offered a redundant area of the BSA factory. The plan did not, however, reach fruition as, on 6 October, it was decided instead to arrange immediate distribution of the notes. Over a year earlier, in March, 1943, De La Rue Ltd, the security printing firm, took a lease arranged by the MOWB on Clubhouse Quarry in Corsham for the storage of replacement currency for a number of the occupied European countries.

Since February the Admiralty had sought to extend its rough storage capacity at Corsham and, aware that for the time being the Parnall area was sterilized by the 'Crossbow' embargo, negotiated instead for the use of 100,000 square feet of the unfinished Dowty section. No objections were raised by the MOWB, but the Admiralty was warned that the area was unfloored, unheated, unventilated and unlit, and that they would have to meet the full cost of any improvements required. Furthermore, access was not good as the lift shaft had been capped and the machinery for Goods Lift No.5, which was thought to be no longer required, had been sold off some months earlier. The nearest alternative lift, GL 4, was not available to the Admiralty as it was already working to capacity. In fact all the lifts were working to capacity and were suffering the effects of poor maintenance. An engineer's inspection in July revealed that the gears of GL 1 were worn dangerously thin, a problem attributed to the use of poor quality castor oil as a lubricant.

After reviewing the prospective cost of upgrading the Dowty area (estimated at £150,000 to bring it just to the minimum acceptable standard, plus a further £15,750 to purchase a replacement lift for GL 5) the Admiralty shelved the idea. The MOWB suggested that they should instead investigate the east side of Westwood Quarry which was still in the possession of the Agaric Company, but due to the remoteness of the location this suggestion was not followed up. Following an urgent request for temporary storage space for 100,000 tons of naval ammunition returning to Britain on merchant ships, the Admiralty was granted possession of a further 72,000 square feet of the Parnall area on 20 November. The remaining 39,000 square feet was finally absorbed the following December.

Production Draws to a Close

Having been gradually run down since the beginning of the year, production at the BAC engine factory finally ceased on 17 April, 1945. Work in the BSA factory continued for a few weeks to complete an outstanding gun barrel contract. During an inspection of the factory the previous month MAP officials were disconcerted to find BSA workmen, many of them skilled machine operators, engaged upon mundane building work, despite the fact that the factory was due for closure within just a few weeks. When questioned about this the factory manager replied that as he was obliged to employ the men on a rapidly diminishing task they may as well be given something to do.

BAC hoped to remain in occupation of the development factory for at least another two years to avoid disruption to the gas turbine development work which was initiated during the war and was now approaching fruition. During the summer of 1945, as men were being laid off at the production works, skilled men were being taken on at the development factory. The government, however, had different plans for Spring Quarry, and within a year, despite recent expenditure of several thousand pounds on the conversion of a Centaurus test bed for the Theseus turbojet engine, the entire development department was transferred to Filton and BAC's involvement with Corsham came to an end.

By the end of November, 1945, Spring Quarry, like all the other underground factories, was under the temporary control of the MOS, but the Treasury was making positive efforts to sell the site, preferably to another government department, either as storage or as a 'potential war factory'. The asking price was £70,000, less than 1% of its building cost, but heating and ventilating costs alone were estimated at £230,000 per year. Steps were taken to reduce the electricity consumption and plans made to convert the boilers to oil firing as this offered the opportunity for further economies in both fuel and labour. The Admiralty, which already occupied most of the south-west quarry, was the favoured department, the Treasury suggesting that the whole site could be

180

converted to permanent storage standards at little additional cost.

By the spring of the following year, however, there is evidence that the Government had decided to retain a part of the Spring Quarry complex as an emergency government war headquarters along the line suggested some five years earlier. A request from Sir Alexander Gibb & Partners to be allowed to show representatives from the Courtauld Company round the site in connection with a 'windowless factory' that Courtaulds intended to build was politely refused on the grounds that 'the future use of the site may be somewhat sensitive". In March Mr A.K. Davis, an officer of the MOS who dealt with the disposal of redundant government factory premises, when confronted with the files relating to the Spring Quarry factory, noted to his superior that:

> "I can find no aspect of factory disposal in them, in fact I gather that the policy is to hold on firmly to our best refuge from the atom bomb."

The greater part of Spring Quarry, however, was transferred to the Admiralty which consolidated its tenure during the early post-war years. Control of the site was exercised by the nearby Royal Navy Storage Depot Copenacre which was established in Hartham Park Quarry after the demise of the Fleet Air Arm interest there in 1945.

15

SPRING QUARRY – SERVICES

The problems likely to arise in a rural area with the supply of essential services were completely overlooked in the rush to go underground in 1940. We shall see later that the general shortage of water resources in the Melksham, Chippenham and Bradford-on-Avon areas seriously disrupted the hostel building programme in the outlying towns, and that this in turn had repercussions on the local railway system that were never fully resolved. Several additional reservoirs were required, new springs were tapped in the Widdenham valley and major extensions made to the Chippenham Corporation waterworks at Ivyfield and Westmead.

The demand for gas at the factory for heat treatment and other processes was beyond the existing capacity of the Bath gasworks. To meet this demand a bulk supply was obtained from Bristol gasworks, delivered via a new 12" compression main laid between Bristol and Bath and a duplicate 18" main laid from Bath to Corsham. In total some twenty miles of gas main were laid to supply the Spring Quarry complex.

Initially, when Spring Quarry was expected to provide the wartime home for several major engineering companies, the maximum electricity demand was calculated to be in the region of 25 megawatts, and negotiations with the Wessex Electricity Company began on that basis. By September, 1943, with the Dowty, Parnall and Monk's Park areas abandoned as productive units, this figure was reduced to 15 megawatts, but by this time most of the installation had already been completed based on the higher figure. Power was supplied to the quarry at 33 kV via two separate feeders. Thirty-one new sub-stations were required, together with over forty-six miles of high voltage cable. Although the cost of all the plant and cabling was met by the MOWB the high residual value of the equipment was taken into account, the supply company agreeing to reimburse this once the services were no longer required by the Government.

PROCESS AND HEATING STEAM

The planning, construction and operation of the two underground boilerhouses that provided steam to the factory epitomized the haphazard management of the Corsham project. The need for two separate installations was an unfortunate necessity of the quarry layout, requiring twice the number of stokers and attendants that would have been needed in a single plant, as well as duplicate flues, fuel lifts, and other peripheral plant. The boilerhouses were connected by a common 10" steam header, and no less than twenty-five miles of 8" pipework fed process plant, steam heaters and canteens.

Both boilerhouses came on line in the early spring of 1943, some months prior to the start of production, as it was anticipated that the heater batteries would be required to operate on full load for several weeks to dry out the fabric of the quarry satisfactorily and enable a consistently adequate level of relative humidity to be maintained. Shortly after No.2 boilerhouse was commissioned serious faults developed in the boiler footings which put it out of use until July, 1944. The normal practice with new installations is to allow six weeks for the footings to set with the boilers running on slow steam before applying full load. It appears that No.2 boilerhouse was fired up only three days after being set, resulting in rapid distortion and cracking of the brickwork, settlement of the boilers and damaged pipework.

As more sections of the factory came on line coal consumption reached the alarmingly high level of 487 tons per week. The general running of the boilerhouses did not meet the expectations of the MAP, and, sceptical of the technical competence of the MOWB, the MAP called in the world-renowned firm of F.A. Greene & Partners to produce an independent report.

Greene's investigation found that there were insufficient staff to run and maintain the plant properly; in particular care was not being taken to ensure that flue gas and boiler water analysis were carried out despite the presence of suitable monitoring instruments. Both boilerhouses were fitted with CO_2 recorders, 5-point temperature recorders, integrating steam-flow indicators and draft recorders, but most of this equipment was either disconnected or so badly calibrated as to be useless.

183

The surface coal-handling facilities were the subject of particular criticism. Coal was delivered to a large concrete yard which had two conveyor belts running its entire length, spilling on to two shorter cross-conveyors which fed two crushing plants. Crushed coal was transported underground to the boilers via inclined shafts. Dust extractors had been fitted at the bottom of these shafts but were not in working order, a situation that Greene considered dangerous to the health of the stokers. Fifteen men were employed loading coal on to the long conveyors, and it was suggested that with a suitable small crane and grab this work could be accomplished by just two men.

Each boilerhouse contained six secondhand Lancashire boilers, recently reconditioned by Hopkins of Huddersfield. Induced draught fans and economisers were fitted, although the latter soon fell into disuse because they were difficult to operate successfully by unskilled attendants. No.2 boilerhouse was fitted with Crossthwaite mechanical stokers, so badly set up that their operation verged upon farce. In a properly designed installation each boiler is fitted with a conical hopper at the bottom of which a variable-stroke ram pushes a pre-set quantity of coal into the grate. The hoppers are replenished by an overhead power conveyor, its rate set in accordance with the steam demand by automatic controls which vary the speed of the drive motor. At Spring Quarry, however, a fixed speed motor was used, which meant that at periods of low steam demand the hoppers over-filled, coal spilled off the end of the belt and had to be dug up and wheeled back to the start in hand barrows. Greene suggested that either a variable speed motor should be installed or the boilers should revert to hand firing. Following completion of repairs to the footings, the automatic stokers were removed in August, 1944, there being no economy with auto-stoking using the poor quality of coal then available.

The final matter raised by F.A. Greene & Partners concerned the disposal of hot boiler ash, which was brought to the surface in barrows using the wood-lined passenger lifts. This practice constituted an obvious fire risk and it was recommended that a proper ash disposal plant should be installed.

HEATING AND VENTILATION
The ventilation systems for the east and west quarries were designed to work independently of each other and their effects on one another were

negligible, communicating passages between the two sections being fitted with airtight doors. The south-west quarry had two inlet and two outlet fans plus a small (10,000 c.f.m) inlet unit to ventilate the BSA offices. Two further pairs of fans were planned for the north-west quarry, but, following the abandonment of the Dowty area, these were not installed. Five inlet and five exhaust fans were fitted in the east quarry, together with a large extract unit to remove dust and fumes from the heat treatment area. This plant, designated 'E1A', utilized a twenty-foot-diameter fan with a capacity of 500,000 cfm. Each fan was provided with a sixteen-speed controller, and it was arranged that the inlet volume should always be about 10% in excess of the extract volume to produce a slight positive pressure underground.

Incoming air was heated by large, four-bank steam radiators fixed across the airways on the discharge side of each inlet fan. Moderately accurate temperature control was maintained by means of motorized thermostatic valves in the supply lines to each radiator, although at the time of Greene's visit only one of the seven valves was working correctly. When the system was brought on line in March, 1943, the plant attendants were warned to take great care when adjusting the thermostatic valves as they were very delicate, of American manufacture (drawn from residual pre-war stock) and impossible to replace.

A further function of the ventilation system was to protect the workers against enemy gas attack. In the event of a warning being received all the inlet fans could be shut down remotely from the central ARP control room; the extract fans were then shut down manually by the plant attendants and the shafts sealed by closing massive, centrally pivoted 'butterfly' doors in the suction side airways. It was important that all process fans exhausting into the main (E1A) exhaust shaft were shut down before stopping the main fan. Failure to adhere to this instruction would result in the distribution of dust and noxious gases throughout the workshops via the ventilation system. All the inlet shafts were fitted with electro-mechanically-operated shutters on the surface which closed automatically when the fans stopped running.

SECURITY
At the time of the handover, security was the responsibility of a private police force recruited by Alexander Gibb and Partners, their main functions being to patrol the three miles of security fence which surrounded

the factory and man the four police posts guarding the main entrance roads. This force was supplemented in January, 1943, by the 12th Battalion Wiltshire Home Guard, formed solely from factory employees and under the command of BAC's business manager, Major C.H. Tucker.

A few months earlier an undercover investigation by Mr C. Liddell, an MI5 officer sent to Corsham following numerous complaints of laxity and poor security, revealed a miserable state of affairs. Liddell noted that none of the forty-two entrances (including air-shafts) were patrolled regularly, and that the site was protected by only lightweight fencing, in many places missing or torn down, apparently erected to prevent locals from accidentally straying into the works. He was much concerned, too, about the risks associated with the large numbers of Irish workmen who were free to return home at any time, commenting that as long as that situation persisted, "It was hopeless to imagine that general information as to the importance of Corsham could be kept secret." The War Office had voiced its concerns about McAlpine's workmen using parts of the underground galleries still worked by the Bath & Portland Co as a shortcut to the surface. Posing as strangers to the area, Liddell and his associate found that the shortcut through an entrance known as Clift Passage was indeed open to all and sundry. On entering with torches they soon met a group of workmen who, without questioning their identity, were only too pleased to tell them all about the Government works and direct them towards the War Office ammunition depot. Security arrangements were subsequently strengthened significantly.

After the war it was revealed that a German spy, Weighleim Wessman, alias William Edward Bowman, a native of California who had come to England to gather intelligence for Germany, had worked as an electrician at Spring Quarry for several months during the summer of 1942. Subsequently he moved on to similar work in Admiralty and RAF buildings in Bath. Apprehended for similar offences in the West Midlands, Wessman was sentenced to two years' imprisonment and recommended for deportation at Warwick Assizes in July, 1945.

TELEPHONES

In a secret minute of 6 June, 1942, the GPO sought sanction from the Treasury for funds to provide full postal and telegraph services to the Corsham factory. Because of the magnitude of the project and its association with other secret government works in the Corsham area it was felt that a dedicated exchange was required, and plans for its construction went ahead under the code-name "Hawthorn". Strangely, this name, chosen arbitrarily, has been adopted by the local authority for the west side of Rudloe village and now appears on the Ordnance Survey maps. The new works for the GPO included a very large manual switchboard established underground in a 24,000 square feet chamber in the north-west corner of Spring Quarry, and a mail sorting office built on War Office land at the junction of Westwells Road and Park Lane.

16

TRANSPORT

Plans to move the Filton production line to Corsham presumed that the workforce would also be transferred. A revision of the manpower requirements of the factory had been made since the early summer, and it fell to Mr Brian Colquhoun from the MAP to explain the current situation at a special meeting at the Ministry of War Transport on 7 August. BAC currently employed 32,000 workers at the Filton factory, 20,000 of whom travelled from the Bristol suburbs daily. It was proposed that 12,000 of these employees would transfer to Corsham and work a two-shift system. B.S.A. would employ 3,000 men on two shifts, and the MOS would employ a further 3,000 men also working two shifts. Hostel accommodation would be provided for 8,000 single men; there would be 2,000 married quarters and a further 2,000 employees would be billeted locally. The remaining 6–7,000 men would be transported to work daily from Bristol.

Buses previously employed carrying workers from the suburbs of Bristol out to Filton would be released to provide services for the twenty-five-mile journey from Bristol to Corsham. The Ministry of War Transport was keen to see responsibility for this daily traffic transferred to the railway, criticizing the bus scheme as expensive in fuel and tyre rubber. The existing rail facilities were quite incapable of handling the proposed weight of passenger traffic and during the summer of 1941 a number of schemes were put forward to overcome this problem. The War Office argued that any increase in traffic would inevitably cause congestion when added to the already intense activity generated from its own sidings at Thingley Junction, Beanacre and Farleigh Down.

The GWR was eager to see the movement done by rail, but admitted

188

that use of the existing local stations was not possible as the subsidiary lines through Bradford-on-Avon and Melksham were working to capacity and the main London to Bristol line had to be kept clear for priority ammunition trains. The railway company estimated that between six and eight trains in each direction per shift would be required.

Sir Alexander Gibb & Partners put forward three alternative schemes for discussion:

1. An extension to Corsham station, including lengthening of the existing platforms and provision of additional sidings. This was rejected by both the War Office and the GWR because it would increase the occupation of the main line by several hours each day while trains were waiting at the station, and could interfere with ammunition shipments.

2. A new terminal station off the Melksham line near Thingley Junction at a point four miles from the factory. One hundred specially designed articulated buses would be required to transfer workers from the station to the plant and provide internal transport within the factory site.

3. A new, three-and-a-half-mile-long double-track branch line starting from a triangular junction with the Melksham line near Lacock and finishing at a four-platform terminal station within the factory compound at Westwells. Construction would involve several cuttings of more than thirty feet in depth, long lengths of embankment up to fifteen feet in height, two over-bridges and six level crossings. It would take twelve months to complete at a cost of £250,000. Brian Colquhoun expressed concern about the cost in terms of steel production and labour, while the War Office doubted that the new work could be adequately camouflaged. It was also pointed out that as the factory was expected to be in full production within six months, and the railway would take twelve months to build, there was a period of six months during which the entire workforce would have to be bussed from Bristol anyway. This, however, was the scheme that the MOWT preferred.

It was obvious to the Treasury that all the plans were going to be controversial and expensive; an official noting to his Minister that "the railway scheme strikes me as quite fantastic. I strongly suspect that there are the makings of a large muddle behind this."

The MOWT continued to press its case for the Westwells branch scheme against opposition from the MAP and the Ministry of Works, and on 18 September the MAP minuted the Treasury regarding the MOWT stance, warning that "Apparently they are quite obdurate and will not provide road communication. The MOWT are running us into a railway scheme costing £250,000."

Despite the continued pressure from the MOWT it was apparent by 7 September that, given the dramatic cost increases arising elsewhere in the Corsham project, the Treasury was unlikely to sanction the Westwells Branch scheme. The MAP still insisted that road transport, using a fleet of 120 buses, was the most efficient solution, but agreed that if it must use rail then it would favour the alternative solution proposed by Alexander Gibb & Partners, involving a new station just east of Melksham.

Realizing that Treasury consent would not be forthcoming, the MOWT withdrew its backing for the Westwells Branch, noting in a terse message that "briefly the position is that the £250,000 scheme is dead".

No adequate railway-based solution was evolving, but it was not until 6 March, 1942, that the MOWT finally abandoned its insistence on rail transport and agreed that workers should be brought from Bristol by bus. Unfortunately, in the interim period large sums of money had already been committed to ancillary works which were considered essential to make rail transit viable. Over £18,000 had been spent on land between Clifton Bridge and Ashton Gate station in Bristol on which to build a new station to entrain the workmen and on which to lay sidings to stable the Corsham commuter trains.

In 1940, when plans for the factory were first considered, little attention was given to the workmen's clocking on and off procedure. The Corsham plant was thought of like any other factory; at five o'clock the men queue up, clock off at time recorders and file out to board buses; each bus would carry 30–40 men and when loaded would make its independent way to Bristol. This would occur at a number of entrance points and would be a relatively slow procedure. The exact time the buses left the works compound and their separation on the road were irrelevant factors.

When pressured to adopt rail transport the planners realized that different constraints would apply. Several trains each carrying nearly

1000 passengers had to be loaded and despatched with the utmost haste; this was vital in order to avoid congestion and slot into the already near-capacity timetable on what was one of the country's most strategically important lines. It was decided that the only way to get large numbers of workers to the surface quickly was by using high-capacity passenger lifts, supplemented by escalators in the slope shafts. Three pairs of lifts (designated PL1, PL2 & PL3) were proposed to serve the BAC development and production works, together with Waygood Otis escalators fitted in slope shafts 'A' and 'C', at a total cost of £61,400.

When an order for the escalators was placed with Waygood Otis the MOWB was told that suitable equipment could not be procured at short notice, but it later transpired that the London Passenger Transport Board had two such units on order from the company which were nearing completion. These escalators were destined for the upper flights at Holborn and St Paul's stations, where refurbishment had been authorized just prior to the outbreak of war. Following negotiations with Mr Hawkins of the LPTB it was arranged that the escalators would be delivered to Corsham, and the MOWB would place an order for replacement units for delivery to the railway when the necessary steel allocation permitted. A replacement escalator was eventually installed at Holborn in August, 1948, but the equipment for St Paul's was never provided, and the financial liability was not resolved until the 1950s, by which time the LPTB were asking for £41,000 compensation. A bronze plaque above the steps at St Paul's station now records the wartime adventure of the missing escalator.

FREIGHT TRAFFIC

Inward freight, excluding coal, was expected to reach a maximum of sixty wagons per day. The bulk of the despatches, mainly finished engines, would go by road, either to aircraft assembly plants or to small, temporary underground stores close to the main factory complex. Coal receipts would reach 600 tons per week when both boilerhouses were complete. No suitable freight facilities existed at the time, but the GWR representative suggested that land near Lacock Halt, being the only location with suitable road access, could be used for reception and mileage sidings, while the existing War Office sidings on the main line at Thingley could be extended to provide a sorting yard. War Office objections to this plan on the grounds that further extensive railway works in the vicinity could jeopardize the security of their own sidings were overruled. The meeting agreed to the construction of two groups of sidings at Lacock and Thingley and a new west-south chord line (the 'Air Ministry Loop') joining the main line to the branch at Thingley Junction, thus allowing through running for trains from Bristol to Westbury and beyond, via Melksham.

Lacock yard was completed by 15 February, 1943, but it was a further six months before the Air Ministry loop and the new sidings at Thingley Junction were brought into use. No sooner had construction work got under way when, early in May, the GWR announced that it might after all be unable to work the sidings at Lacock due to a shortage of locomotives and staff. The railway company had already been difficult over the operation of the Air Ministry sidings at Thingley, but offered to come to a working arrangement if the Air Ministry would accept a degree of 'common usage', by which the GWR could use the sidings for general commercial traffic. The Ministry retorted that the GWR was already making prolonged and unauthorized use of the sidings to stable empty trucks, and announced that McAlpine's had a couple of spare locomotives which they were prepared to lend for yard work until the railway could find more suitable motive power. Still prevaricating, the GWR cast doubt upon the condition of the trackwork in the sidings, threatening that if maintenance was not improved they would refuse to operate over it.

Aware of the already congested state of the railways in the area, the Admiralty, which had considerably increased its presence at Corsham since 1943, began negotiations with the MOWB in May with a view to agreeing joint usage of some of the existing facilities at Lacock. Such an arrangement would be most acceptable to the MAP, which had always argued that the scheme put together jointly by the GWR and MOWT was excessive, and which now hoped to off-load part of the cost on to the Admiralty. Eventually it was agreed that No.6 siding should be allocated to the Navy and the contract for a new loading platform was awarded to Ernest Ireland, who finished the job early in September.

Experience was soon to prove right the earlier warning about the extravagance of the transport committee plans. At a subsequent inquiry into costs of the project the MAP told the Treasury that the MOWT had knowingly overestimated requirements from the start and should foot the bill for the excessive siding accommodation. The MAP had calculated that the absolute maximum rail traffic to the factory would amount to a turnover of sixty wagons per day. The MOWT then added forty to this and doubled the total to 200 wagons daily, and it was on this basis that its plan, prepared in conjunction with the GWR, was approved.

In mid-August, 1944, the Bristol Aeroplane Company gave notice that it no longer wanted responsibility for Lacock sidings, which the company admitted it had never used. Since opening the previous year the sidings had been used mainly by the War Office, Admiralty, Air Ministry and the National Hostels Company, although construction and running costs fell almost wholly on the MAP. It was disclosed that from the inception of the scheme the existing sidings at Corsham station had proved sufficient for all the factory freight requirements. The MAP complained that rail access to Lacock Sidings was difficult because no access points had been provided at the south end of the yard, thus necessitating much shunting of long trains. With production running down and the factory over-stocked with raw material and rough castings, and with plenty of motor fuel available by the autumn of 1944, the MAP decided that henceforth all freight to and from the factory would go by road, thus avoiding the four-fold transhipment required with rail transport.

The Air Ministry loop and associated sidings at Thingley were taken out of use in February, 1955, although the sidings had fallen into disuse some time before. Tracks remained in situ until at least the summer of 1959. At Lacock the yard continued to see a certain amount of Admiralty activity until September, 1964, when they too were taken out of use, their function as the Admiralty railhead usurped by the recently decommissioned War Office sidings at Thingley Junction.

17

SPRING QUARRY – HOSTELS AND MARRIED QUARTERS

From the earliest days of voluntary dispersal the government was concerned about the logistic problems created by the daily travel of many thousands of industrial workers to factories in remote locations. The most satisfactory solution seemed to be the erection of temporary hostels and married quarters. Each site was provided with medical and catering facilities, a welfare centre, and in some cases also with shops, a cinema and a church. The hostels at Corsham, in common with those erected at Ordnance Factories and other sites throughout the country, were run by the National Service Hostels Corporation Ltd, an agency of the Ministry of Labour, under the directorship of Major Haughton.

Planning for the hostels was left in the hands of Sir Alexander Gibb & Partners, whose first drawings were issued in May, 1941, after provisional manpower requirements were confirmed and a schedule of accommodation prepared:

Site	Location	Buildings or Area	Type or Capacity			Additional Building	Remarks
			2 bed	3 bed	4 bed		
MQ1	Corsham	300 Bungalow	140	158	2	Community C.	Transferred to Local Authority
MQ1a	Corsham	106 "	52	54			April 1954.
MQ1b	Corsham	188 "	84	92	6	School	Redeveloped 1963/4
MQ2	Boxfield	116 "	48	56	6		Bungalows and shops cleared 1964, school demolished 1984
MQ2a	Boxfield	144 "	60	70	7	School, 4 shops & C.C.	

Site	Location	Buildings or Area	Type or Capacity			Additional Building	Remarks
			2 bed	3 bed	4 bed		
MQ3	Westwood	96 "	7	89			Transferred to Local Authority 1958 and subsequently redeveloped
MQ4	Quarry Hill	64 "		64			Abandoned before construction commenced
MQ5	Chippenham	11 "	70	40			Abandoned before construction commenced
MQ6	Chippenham	266 "	138	128			Transferred to local Authority April 1955
MQ7	Chippenham	174 "	90	84			
HS.1	Westwells	114,452 Sq Ft	1000 men				Transferred to National Hostel Corp. by 1947
HS.2	Gorse Farm	112,650	1000 men				Transferred to R.A.F. 1943
HS.3	Thorney Pits	130,690	1000 men				Transferred to National Hostel Corp. by 1947
HS.8	Potley	119,344	1000 men				Transferred to War Office 1943
HS.9	Westwood	107,424 Sq Ft				C.C. & Hall	Transferred to National Hostel Corp. by 1947 Community Centre let for light industry until 1972
HS.10	Kingsmoor	160,000	1000 men				Transferred to Admiralty 1943
HS.14	Rudloe	Retained by MOWB in 1943 for experimental work. Rebuilt as married quarters but not used. Transferred to Local Authority for redevelopment 1963/4					
HS.15	Lypiatt	122,837	1000 men				Transferred to War Office 1943
HS.16	Leafield	141,742	1000 men				Transferred to Admiralty by 1947.

A £150,000 contract to build hostel No.1 was let to McAlpine's in May and construction was nearly complete by the middle of July. Construction of Sites 2, 3 & 8 was entrusted to George Wimpey at an inclusive price of £450,000 a few weeks later, but by July the contract was £100,000 over budget with much work remaining. The next three sites, Nos. 10, 15 & 16, were not started until August, 1942, by which time there were grave doubts as to their necessity.

Meanwhile the designs for the married quarters were accepted and construction of site 1(a) commenced in October, 1942, on land between Pickwick Road and Priory Street in Corsham. The vast increase in housing capacity created by the Government Works changed Corsham from a rural village to a small town almost overnight, causing many unforeseen difficulties. A committee set up by Sir Alexander Gibb & Partners in November, 1941, identified sewerage and water supply as the major problems, particularly to the west of the area near Bradford-on-Avon and Melksham where the shortage of water was critical.

Some months later, when it was realized that the requirement for married quarters had been grossly overestimated, the building of sites 8, 9 & 10 in Melksham was postponed indefinitely. This was quickly followed by the abandonment of site No.5, one of the three developments at Hardenhuish Park in Chippenham, and of site No.4 at the bottom of Quarry Hill in Box, which was originally intended to be a small development of "superior married quarters for 'better class' workers owning their own cars". Work on the remaining sites began early in January, 1942. The War Office, which was becoming increasingly impatient of the MAP works, questioned the ability to camouflage the Box Fields development, but accepted that the buildings at Chippenham, which constituted extensions to existing local authority housing estates, posed no such risk.

Although devoid of statutory powers other than those held under the various Public Health Acts, Wiltshire County Council was deeply concerned about the development of the married quarters estates. Prior to the war there had been growing government concern about uncontrolled building development, and particularly about the so-called 'ribbon development' along arterial roads and the consequent urbanization of rural areas. A committee headed by Lord Justice Scott was set up to investigate this and related matters, and continued to sit throughout the war. In February, 1942, in reply to a query from Lord

196

Justice Scott's Committee, the Clerk to the Council stated:

> "I am not surprised at the anxiety shown by Lord Justice Scott's inquiry of what is happening to many of the beauty spots of this county. The position is an extremely difficult one because the town planning committee, whilst deprecating to the full the shocking development which has taken place not only in Corsham but also in many other parts of the County, they feel that nothing must be done to hinder the successful prosecution of the War."

When asked how much more development was planned for Corsham and the likely number of men to be drafted into the area, the Clerk replied:

> "It is almost impossible to give you an adequate picture of the present situation at Corsham. It must be seen to be believed . . . With regard to the number to be employed, owing to the lack of co-operation between the departments I have been unable to obtain reliable information. The numbers vary from day to day and week to week."

By the end of March some 3000 hostel places were complete, although of these 2000 were used as temporary accommodation for construction workers. 350 married quarters were also finished. At about this time concern was mounting at the Treasury regarding the cost of the project generally, and of the hostels in particular. An investigation concluded that ultimate responsibility lay with the poor planning and financial estimates prepared by Brian Colquhoun. Drawing attention to the high cost and over-engineering of external services, a Treasury report noted that:

> "The Ministry of Works & Buildings are still inclined to build if not for eternity, at any rate for twenty years when three would be more appropriate, and I suspect that Gibb are as bad if not worse."

Regarding the hostels, which constituted a disproportionate part of the cost, the Treasury wrote:

> "The superstructures could not have been done cheaper, but the criticism I have heard of some of these operations is that the

foundations and services are monumental and will last for ever. The trouble seems to be that the MOWB are inherently incapable of Jerry-building, even when the best Jerry-builders are appointed to their staff."

As morale and the workforce dwindled, the rate of progress in hostel construction diminished through the autumn and winter of 1942. Although a contract for Hostel No.16 was let early in August there was doubt that it would be required. An extension of the call-up at the end of November meant that the MOWB was compelled to release 400 men per week until 24 December and 550 each week thereafter; as a result the finishing date for sites 10 and 16 was extended from May to July, 1943.

As production started at the factory the unpopularity of the hostels and married quarters became apparent. Take-up was not as rapid as had been hoped and was a source of embarrassment to the MAP. Many of the workmen, particularly the older and more skilled operatives who owned their own houses, preferred to keep their homes in Bristol and commute daily. The expense of bussing so many men from Bristol to Corsham each day was raised and numerous proposals put forward to overcome the problem. Mr Jubb, the MAP finance officer, commented that:

"We cannot direct people where to live, but we can direct them to work. We are at liberty to withdraw the assisted travel scheme – we can thus virtually compel them to live in the hostels."

The works welfare committee suggested that hostel accommodation might be made more attractive by putting aside one site for 'white collar' workers. This was firmly squashed by Mr Jubb, who said it would be like differentiating workers as officers and other ranks, but the committee did elicit some concessions for the displaced men. Bristol workers unwilling to leave their houses empty and unattended were offered 'Housing Liability Grants' to subsidise transport and other expenses until their houses could be sold or suitable tenants found.

A rather different clash of values relating to workers' welfare had recently occurred underground, with regard to the paint scheme to be applied there. The MOWB proposed using white paint throughout on account of its reflective qualities, while the MAP inexplicably preferred

198

a rather dull shade of red. This gloomily oppressive suggestion incensed Sir Reginald Verdon Smith, the chairman of BAC, who insisted that white should be used in the workshops, but who employed a professional artist, Olga Lehmann, to decorate the canteens and certain other areas with vivid floor-to-ceiling murals. Most of the murals, which are of a distinctive style very much of the period, remain in fairly good condition to this day. Subjects include prehistoric cave paintings, horse-racing and cricket scenes, and an alarming picture in the development department canteen of a missionary clergyman being boiled alive by African natives with bones through their noses!

Of the eight hostels, confusingly numbered 1,2,3,8,10,14,15 & 16, only four (nos. 3,10, 15 & 16) were completed to the MAP specifications. Built to house 1000 men each, the maximum occupancy rates of the four completed hostels were only 60, 570, 600 and 200 respectively. For many years accommodation in Hostel No.15 at Lypiatt was used to house girls of the Women's Land Army, and site No.2 was lent to the RAF to house additional staff for the Rudloe Manor complex.

The influx of thousands of migrant workers families into the Corsham area, many with young children, placed an impossible burden on the existing schools, and by the spring of 1942 pressure was mounting for the MOWB to finance the construction of new primary and nursery schools on the estates in Box, Corsham and Chippenham. The buildings would be provided free by the MOWB to the Education Authority, which would then be expected to meet the maintenance and running costs.

Periodic surveillance flights over Corsham by Fighter Command confirmed fears about the conspicuousness of the MAP works, which the RAF considered to be "a danger to itself and other government departments nearby". While construction was in progress the great gashes in the white oolitic limestone and the huge spoil heaps (never adequately camouflaged) acted as beacons to the Luftwaffe, while at the completed factory the regimented rows of workers' housing and geometric bus parks looked equally incongruous in the otherwise rural landscape. The bus parks were later dispersed around the factory site, but, despite pressure from the RAF and Ministry of Home Security, no funds were released to improve the camouflage. Steps were finally taken in February, 1944, as a result of direct intervention by Churchill in connection with Operation 'Crossbow', the plan to disperse vital war production away from London in preparation for the expected onslaught from V1 and V2 missiles. We have seen that plans were laid to hold vacant certain areas of Spring Quarry in readiness to house some of this dispersed industrial capacity and to this end the War Cabinet was anxious to ensure that undue enemy attention was not drawn to the site. Men were set to work applying black paint to the concrete roads in the factory sites to make them look from the air more like old-established lanes, while over £50,000 was spent painting the flat-roofed married quarters in different tones to simulate the typical pitched-roof local authority houses of the area. Wire link fences were put up between the buildings in the vain hope of encouraging tenants to plant quick-growing creepers to further disguise the formal layout of the buildings. Grass was sown and shrubs planted on the spoil heaps but fifty years on this has still not proved very effective.

It was expected at the beginning of 1945 that all the living accommodation would be demolished within ten years. Many tenants, however, had no other homes to go to and, although the underground factories were closing, there was a general shortage of housing for workers in the new industries which had become permanently established in the area. Short-term arrangements were made by the Ministry of Labour to utilize the married quarters as temporary housing. Management was transferred to the local authorities in 1954/5 and a few years later the freehold sites were purchased by the Rural District Councils, with all tenancies transferred to the Housing Departments. Between 1962 and 1964 most of the estates were demolished and replaced by modern council housing.

At the end of the war the deeply unpopular workers' hostels were used to house Polish and other East European refugees, the last tenants not moving out until December, 1958. A tentative plan put forward the following year to use Thorny Pits hostel as a Borstal institution met with such vehement local opposition that it was withdrawn immediately. Foremost amongst the opponents was Lady (Kathleen) Fuller of Neston Court, one of the great landowners of the area whose way of life had been changed for ever by the wartime developments. In a letter to the local authority she wrote:

"I am very much against this and I hope everything will be done to refuse permission. My main reason is that for the past fifteen years this area had most unsatisfactory people in it who have given much trouble and caused the local people much annoyance and disquiet. It would not be fair to them to turn this area into a permanent site for undesirable families."

Of the remaining sites, Leafield was taken over by the Admiralty for a while but has recently been developed as a light industrial estate, Kingsmoor became the home of HMS *Royal Arthur*, a Royal Navy training establishment, and No. 10 site is now the Army's Lypiatt Family Hostel.

18

SPRING QUARRY IN RETROSPECT

Of the £20,000,000 spent at Corsham some £13,000,000 is directly attributable to the Bristol engine factory. For a brief period, which lasted only a few months, when intense German bombing posed a genuine threat to Britain's aircraft industry (and by extension to the successful outcome of the war), the underground factory scheme seemed a desperate necessity. But the planning and building delays which dogged the Corsham factory meant that, even before construction got properly under way, the emergency was over. Spring Quarry was then already redundant and should have been abandoned. Neither the Bristol Aeroplane Company nor the Treasury wanted it built, and the factory was only completed because of pressure from MAP and MOWB Ministers who would not admit the true situation to themselves or to Parliament.

Planning, construction and operation of the factory spanned a period of four and a half years, but by the time it closed in April, 1945, it had been in production for only eighteen months, and during that time output never exceeded forty-two engines per month, even though the factory was designed and equipped for a monthly output of 260 engines. Out of a total of 100,932 Bristol engines manufactured during the war only 523 were built at Spring Quarry.

This poor productivity was not typical of the shadow factories: Accrington, for example, achieved its target output of 400 engines per month within four weeks of starting production.

The conspicuously poor productivity at Spring Quarry was due to three distinct factors. Because of the physical layout of the factory, which was unavoidable due to the quarry formation, it was impossible to

FACTORY	SCHEDULED MONTHLY OUTPUT	ACTUAL AVERAGE MONTHLY OUTPUT	FACTORY MANPOWER	MAN MONTHS PER ENGINE
Accrington	400	347	10,000	29
Spring Quarry	260	25	6,000	240

arrange an efficiently flowing production line. The second factor was the inferior quality of labour available. Under the dispersal scheme it was intended to transfer *all* the necessary staff from the parent factory at Filton, but under the later 'shadow' scheme (which was not really a shadow scheme at all) only the development engineers and a small nucleus of skilled machine operators were transferred to Corsham. The great majority of the men working on Centaurus production were unskilled workers trained up locally, or men from other engineering disciplines not used to the requirements of aero engine manufacture.

The most important factor to drive down the productivity of the Corsham factory was the very nature of its staple product, the Bristol Centaurus engine. Since 1927, under the guidance of Sir Roy Fedden, the Bristol engine division had developed a superb range of powerful, lightweight radial engines which utilized the Burt-McCollum sleeve-valve arrangement rather than conventional poppet valves. Sleeve-valve engines incorporated fewer and lighter reciprocating parts than their poppet valve equivalents, and in a multi-cylinder engine this resulted in an appreciable saving in weight. The disadvantages were that they were much more complicated in design, and very accurate machining and heat treatment was required to prevent distortion of the thin-walled sleeves under service conditions.

The eighteen cylinder 2,500 horsepower Centaurus engine was the apotheosis of piston aero-engine design, but it was an immensely complex machine. Practical development of the Centaurus was under way by early 1938, but technical problems, compounded by the transfer to Corsham in 1942, bedevilled progress and the first production engines, in very small numbers, did not emerge from Spring Quarry until the end of 1943.

There was intense pressure from the MAP to get the engine into production as soon as possible. This pressure to undertake development and production *in parallel* meant that much of the development work was rushed, with components passed to the production stage without adequate testing. Often the production engineers accepted batches of machined components only to be told shortly afterwards that they were unsuitable in some respect and the engines incorporating them had to be dismantled, or else assembly went ahead before the defects were discovered and the completed engines failed under test. However, the problems were eventually overcome and in the closing stages of the war Centaurus performed admirably in the Hawker Typhoon, Tempest and Sea Fury, which it propelled to speeds in excess of 440 mph.

A lesser known aspect of the work undertaken at the Spring Quarry was the development of Bristol's first gas turbine engines. This work, although important, made no real contribution to the war effort and was to some extent an unnecessary distraction of resources.

Aware by the beginning of 1942 that there was little chance of Bristol breaking into the current pure jet development programme, the company pinpointed an opening in the field of high-powered propeller turbine engines of around 4,000 horsepower. By May basic design features of what was to become the Theseus turbo-prop were ready, but from this time forward progress was hampered by the dispersal of the Filton development facilities; the offices going to Tockington Manor, drawing offices to Somerdale, and the machine shops and laboratories to Spring Quarry.

The MAP authorized initial heat transfer research and released finance for the construction of a heat exchanger test plant in September, the Bristol board having earlier agreed to finance all the smaller test rigs and tooling. At about this time the Company decided to downsize the original proposal to 2,000 horsepower in order to make test plant construction more feasible. The following January the Ministry authorized construction of five Theseus engines and complete sets of parts for three more, as long as production of the Centaurus engine was not compromised.

Theseus was designed, detailed and manufactured in seventeen months despite terrible difficulties with the heat exchangers, which were never successfully overcome. During the spring of 1945 combustion chamber and over-speed test rigs were added to the heat exchanger test rig at Corsham, and in May the first engine (minus heat exchanger) was run on a converted Centaurus test bed, the terrific noise it produced causing consternation for miles around.

At this stage larger and more sophisticated test facilities were required, and in October a number of proposals were put to the MAP for new buildings at Corsham. Test facilities were also required for the Proteus high-compression engine, development of which had been running in parallel with Theseus at Spring Quarry since December, 1944. The end of the BAC's occupation of Spring Quarry was now in sight, however, and, although conversion work went ahead on one of the old Centaurus test beds, no new buildings were erected at Corsham. Further testing of Theseus was undertaken on a borrowed rig at Northampton and Proteus made its first run on a purpose built test bed at Filton in February, 1947.

DOWTY, PARNALL AND BSA.

Critics of the Spring Quarry factory scheme tend to concentrate only on the conspicuously poor record of the Bristol engine section, but it must be remembered that the quarry had other tenants whose performance bears investigation. The Dowty and Parnall fiasco can be quickly dismissed as fully justifying the Treasury suspicions of underground factories. The BSA barrel mill was a different matter, however, and must be regarded as the most successful aspect of the Spring Quarry venture, despite its dubious start.

It would appear that throughout the war BSA was shunted from pillar to post by the MAP. We have seen for example that, as early as November, 1940, plans to move Oerlikon barrel production into Monk's Park was not motivated by necessity, but more as an insurance against the risk of militant communist agitation at the Ruislip expansion factory. The Spring Quarry facility only came into prominence late in 1943, not on its own merits but as a result of decisions made by the MAP in connection with the development of the first Rolls-Royce jet engine.

After prolonged investigations into the availability of skilled labour, BSA decided early in the war to locate its new Hispano cannon factory at Newcastle under Lyme. The factory began production in April, 1941, but did not reach peak output until October the following year. Meanwhile development of the Rolls-Royce jet engine was approaching the point at which limited mass production could be considered, and in the early autumn of 1943 the MAP was searching for premises, machinery, and a pool of skilled labour with which to begin manufacture. The Newcastle under Lyme cannon factory was ideally suited to this requirement and negotiations began immediately to transfer the BSA work elsewhere. Premises on Tyneside were first offered but this location was turned down by the BSA board on two grounds: firstly it was too distant from the parent factory to be managed effectively, and secondly labour would have to be drawn from the predominant heavy engineering industry of the area, which was fundamentally different from the precision engineering disciplines required by BSA. Following a meeting between Sir James Leek, chairman of BSA, and the new Minister of Aircraft Production, Sir Stafford Cripps, it was decided that Hispano component manufacture and assembly would be moved to Redditch and the barrel mill to Spring Quarry.

Output from Corsham started well and showed progressive improvement. Between August, 1943, and June, 1945, the gun barrel works had, in sharp contrast to the aircraft engine factory, made a significant contribution to the war effort, producing half of Britain's entire output of Hispano and Polsen barrels.

19

ROYAL NAVY STORAGE DEPOT COPENACRE

To the casual observer today the most obvious feature of the mysterious and secret underground world of Corsham is the Copenacre Royal Naval Storage Depot, an incongruous group of sinister, squat, wartime bunkers and modern offices crouching beside the main A4 trunk road about a mile outside the town. In reality Copenacre, or Hartham Park as it is more properly called, is a relatively unimportant quarry with no physical links to the much larger Spring Quarry complex a short distance to the south.

We have already seen that Hartham Park Quarry was requisitioned along with all the other Bath & Portland property in Corsham early in December, 1940, even though there were no specific plans for its development at that time. The situation quickly changed, however, when, on 3 January, 1941, the MOWB received an urgent enquiry from the Admiralty regarding storage space at Corsham for Fleet Air Arm stores needed to replace surface capacity destroyed during the bombardment of Coventry and Woolston on the nights of 27 and 29 October the previous year.

The Admiralty was not keen on underground storage, particularly when access required the use of lifts or inclined shafts, and had already investigated alternative sites in Scotland and elsewhere before returning reluctantly to Corsham. Despite these reservations the Navy already had two small underground establishments in the Corsham area, Pickwick and Brocklease quarries, acquired early in October, 1939. These were needed as temporary stores for about 10,000 tons of naval ammunition in order to release some of the hundreds of railway trucks and hulks used for interim storage until the major underground reserve depots at Dean

Hill and Trecwn were completed. A third small working, Bethel Quarry in Bradford-on-Avon, was requisitioned from the Agaric Mushroom Company at the same time to supplement the unsatisfactory and widely dispersed surface warehouses in Bath used to store electronic and optical components.

Copenacre Quarry extended to a little over ten acres and originally had two access shafts, the small and steeply graded Copenacre shaft near the main road, which dropped into the middle of the workings, and Hartham Park shaft, which was situated some distance from the main quarry and communicated with it via a long narrow drift. The Admiralty initially sought to convert 160,000 square feet (just under one third of the total area) for storage at an estimated cost of £192,500, the task to be overseen by the MOWB. The works schedule included the regrading and enlargement of the existing Copenacre shaft and the sinking and lining of a completely new shaft, the old Hartham Park drift being considered unsuitable for conversion although it was later incorporated as an emergency exit. Additional access was to be by means of two electric elevators in vertical shafts. Electricity for lighting and for haulage, air-conditioning and ancillary plant was to be taken from the grid supply with a standby generator in a small underground powerhouse for emergency use. Surface offices were required for fifty men, and dining facilities for fifty officers and 200 other ranks. On 3 January the Treasury authorized the following expenditure, subject to assurances that the work would be completed within six months and within budget:

• Clearing rubble, surfacing floors, enlarging existing slope-shaft and sinking new one, providing haulageways, sanitation, and building work for air conditioning system.	£112,000
• Surface offices and garaging for twenty-four vehicles.	£13,000
• Electrical equipment, lifts and air-conditioning plant.	£50,000
• MOWB Agency fee.	£17,500

Within weeks of work starting costs had greatly exceeded the agreed budget, much of the difficulty arising from Admiralty insistence on excessively heavy surface works, particularly the tops of the lift and ventilation shafts for which they demanded massive concrete protection irrespective of the cost. Cognisant of its historic role as the 'Senior

208

Service', the Admiralty has always demanded the absolute best of everything in almost every sphere. In 1938, when the War Office was struggling to gain acceptance for a modest increase of £16,000 to provide standby generators for its underground depots at Corsham, the Admiralty was, with only muted opposition, granted six million pounds to build two hugely over-engineered reserve ammunition depots at Dean Hill on the Wiltshire/Hampshire border and Trecwn in West Wales.

Towards the end of March, 1942, it was apparent that costs were still out of control, despite a downward revision in the Admiralty storage requirement to only 120,000 square feet. Three months later, however, preparing the Treasury for more bad news, the Admiralty minuted that:

"I should tell you that a proposal is now going forward to extend our storage at Copenacre as an alternative to installing expensive plant and making other arrangements at our underground quarry at Bradford-on-Avon, to keep humidity and temperature there within acceptable limits, the present conditions being very inimicable to the storage of the valuable gear for which we have to find accommodation."

The move from Bethel Quarry in Bradford-on-Avon required an increase in floor space at Copenacre to 217,800 square feet, at an estimated additional cost of £100,000. After token opposition from the Treasury and the imposition of certain cost control conditions, work on the extension began on 21 July, 1942, and was finished by the year's end, when the quarry was officially opened as Royal Navy Storage Depot Copenacre.

Space was required not only to accommodate naval anti-aircraft stores, RDF equipment and Fire-Control gear previously kept at Bethel Quarry, but also Asdic equipment stored in requisitioned garage premises in Walcot Street and St John's Road in Bath, and at Batheaston slaughterhouse. The bombing of Bath on the nights of 25 and 26 April, 1942, underlined the vulnerability of these unprotected dispersed stores.

With Copenacre now in service, the far from satisfactory accommodation at Bethel was quickly run down. Like the other small quarries in Bradford-on-Avon, the two-and-a-quarter-acre Bethel Quarry in Frome Road was shallow and somewhat unstable. This potential instability, together with its relatively shallow overburden, meant that it was much more vulnerable to enemy bombing than quarries at Corsham. Towards the end of the war the quarry and a useful range of transit sheds erected by the Admiralty was returned to the Agaric Mushroom Company.

The Fleet Air Arm function of the Copenacre depot disappeared at the end of the war, but storage requirements for Asdic and other naval electronic equipment expanded enormously. So great was the expansion that in 1947 Spring Quarry was acquired from the MAP as a permanent store to supplement Royal Navy Storage Depot Copenacre. After a short period of retrenchment, rearmament and the onset of the Cold War created a demand for further expansion. The Corsham quarries, which, with almost 100-foot cover of solid stone, offered a substantially greater radiation protection factor than conventional surface warehousing, were considered ideal to fill this demand, and, despite the extra cost, consent was granted for a major extension of the Copenacre depot which would double its capacity. The work was undertaken by Farr's, a Westbury-based civil engineering firm, and was completed at the end of 1954.

Monk's Park Quarry had remained disused since development there was halted in 1941. After the war the Bath & Portland Company hoped to recommence quarrying, but the Admiralty's renewed interest in the Corsham area in the early 1950s rather upset this plan. The catalyst for this renewed interest was the decision to close the sprawling and hope-lessly inefficient naval storage depot at Risley, established on the site of the former ordnance factory at the end of the war.

Early in 1954 a contract was let to the Devizes firm of C.J. Chivers and Sons for the refurbishment of Monk's Park Quarry to provide ten acres of storage space, a task that took two years to complete and involved the removal of a further 250,000 tons of waste stone from the workings. A new slope-shaft and vertical lift shaft were sunk to serve the Admiralty depot, but before these were completed the original quarry shaft was made suitable for the transport of building materials and equipment. A large stone-crushing and concrete-mixing plant was built near the shaft bottom, crushed waste stone produced by this plant forming the aggregate in the concrete floors throughout the depot. When building was complete the old shaft was transferred to Bath & Portland to serve the area from which they were to restart quarrying.

Personnel access to Monk's Park was via a double-car electric lift, with emergency stairs adjacent to the slope-shaft and in a secondary vertical shaft. Goods were brought into the depot via the slope-shaft, which was fitted with a haulage winch and a specially designed rail-mounted truck with a horizontal platform. At quarry level the rails terminated in a pit, thus enabling the trolley to stop with its platform flush with the floor.

An important function of RNSD Copenacre was the testing and calibration of the electronic equipment held in store, and to perform this task comprehensive metrology laboratories were established underground at both the Hartham Park and Monk's Park depots. Specially prepared dust-proof test rooms were equipped with the necessary electromagnetic shielding and environmental control equipment. Special earth mats were required, buried in the asphalt floors, because, paradoxically, deep mine workings provide a notoriously poor electrical earth and special provision is needed to ensure adequate safety. Much of the equipment under test required stable, high-frequency power supplies at a variety of voltages. These were provided at each depot by elaborate power stations, erected centrally to minimize cable runs, in which there were row upon row of motor-generators, rotary converters and mercury arc rectifiers. Standby diesel generators were also installed although these could only meet a fraction of the full load.

Heyday and Decline of RNSD Copenacre

The closure of Risley and centralization of Admiralty electronic equipment storage at Corsham involved the transfer of some 10,000 tons of stores and 400 personnel from Risley and required the construction of a huge new administrative block on the surface at the Hartham Park site. This move was completed by 1960 and was followed six years later by the transfer of the Royal Navy Stores and Transport headquarters staff from London to Corsham in line with the then current Government policy of dispersal out of the capital. When the reorganization was completed in 1969 Copenacre was a self-contained unit dedicated solely to the storage, issue and testing of the entire range of naval electronic gear. With a staff of 1,700, it was the largest employer in North Wiltshire.

Within a year, however, doubts were raised about the future of the depot, following a series of underground fires elsewhere in the country which proved difficult to control. It was felt that, due to the nature of the equipment stored underground at Corsham, the potential for fire was unacceptably high and that, should such a fire occur, then the entire storeholding of Naval electronics could be destroyed. A two-year enquiry looked at several alternative approaches to the problem, as a result of which it was announced in January, 1972, that the underground depot at Copenacre was to close.

For different reasons two surface-storage sites at Eaglescliffe and Coventry were also earmarked for closure at this time. Stock from all three establishments would be transferred to the MOD depot at Hartlebury in Worcestershire which was currently being vacated by the RAF. The consequences of these proposals on local employment and trade caused immediate public outcry, and, whether in response to this outcry or for other reasons, the closure plans were rapidly restructured. Following a decision to move the Coventry facilities to Llangennech instead of Hartlebury, the Eaglescliffe decision was also rescinded, leaving only the Copenacre to Hartlebury plan intact, which made much less financial sense. Bowing to pressure from local MPs of all parties, union leaders and local government officers, the Government agreed in 1973 to hold a Public Enquiry into the proposals. Eventually a plan was prepared which was acceptable to all parties and on 25 October, 1974, it was announced that RNSD Copenacre would after all be retained in service indefinitely.

With the future apparently secure the depot settled into an efficient routine that was to remain unchanged for nearly twenty years. Receipts were centralized at Spring Quarry, whence slow-moving stock was trans-ferred to Hartham Park and the faster moving items to Monk's Park, where issues, testing and calibration was also undertaken. A mixed range was maintained at Spring Quarry. During the recession of the early 1990s drastic reductions were made in the budgets of all the spending Ministries. The MOD was particularly hard hit and in July, 1991, a major contraction of the surface and submarine fleets was announced. A number of land-based installations were earmarked for closure, including the Invergordon oil depot, RNAD Trecwn, and RNSD Copenacre, which was to close completely by the end of March, 1997.

Hartham Park was to be cleared by December, 1993, Spring Quarry by June, 1995, and Monk's Park by December the following year. Surface storage of large items at the former RAF airfield at Colerne, which had been used for overflow storage for several years, was to termi-nate in March, 1997, although this site was later reprieved and is now the only RNSD establishment in North Wiltshire. Closure of the Copenacre depot was expected to save £23 million over ten years. Following a revision of the closure plans in September, 1993, it was decided that the underground areas would remain in use for a further two years, but only for the storage of slow moving items. Radar, sonar and communications test facilities were transferred to RNSD Exeter late in 1994, and the calibration support services split between MREE Faslane and Royal Navy Armaments Depot Gosport.

Destocking was completed at all three depots by the official closure date of 30 September, 1995. It had been intended to sell off the disused underground areas into the private sector as soon as possible after closure, but this was soon found to be an impracticable proposal in the case of Hartham Park where the surface offices were destined to remain under MOD occupation. All the ventilation and access shafts have been securely bricked up, leaving small openings for the colony of bats which are now the only inhabitants of the quarry. No attempt was made to recover any plant or equipment from underground, all of which has been abandoned to decay.

Monk's Park had none of the problems which encumbered Hartham Park, and the quarry and associated surface land and buildings were successfully sold early in 1997 to Leafield Engineering, a defence company long established in the Corsham area. At the time of writing Spring Quarry, as much a white elephant now as it was when it was first conceived in 1940, is still in government hands, although there are plans for its commercial disposal. The major obstacle would appear to be the maintenance cost, estimated at over £1,000,000 a year. Since the air-conditioning plant was closed down in 1995 conditions underground have deteriorated alarmingly and the cost of reparations will probably prove prohibitive. Staff charged with disposing of the site hope that the thirty acres of surface land will support businesses sufficiently lucrative to cover the cost of maintaining the minimal security of the disused and abandoned quarries below.

20

WESTWOOD QUARRY AND ROYAL ENFIELD
MOTORCYCLES

The 720,000 square foot Westwood Quarry lies fifteen miles west of Corsham below a precipitous hillside overlooking the incongruous, industrial hamlet of Avoncliff in the Avon Valley. It is the remotest of all the quarries requisitioned under the Corsham scheme, and, once the initial panic to go underground subsided, was the first earmarked for abandonment.

In June, 1941, the quarry was allocated to the Royal Enfield Cycle Company for the manufacture of No.3 anti-aircraft predictors. The company started making predictors and hydraulic control apparatus for Bofors anti-aircraft guns at its Redditch factory just before the war, but, due to the vulnerability of the site, dispersal to the West Country was proposed in 1940. It was planned at first to convert just 30,000 square feet of Westwood Quarry to provide capacity to build twenty predictors per month. Development was expected to cost £60,000, with a further £50,000 for new machine tools and £10,000 for gauges and hand tools. Later it was decided to also transfer part of the oil-motor capacity, which necessitated an increase of floor space to 41,000 square feet. By the end of the year the cost of quarry development alone had increased to £123,500, exclusive of the cost of site acquisition or of the workmen's hostels which were now required.

Although men from Royal Enfield had been on site acting as advisers for several months, in January, 1942, the company's interest in the project had become noticeably lukewarm. At the end of the month the original predictor scheme was temporarily abandoned, although the MAP was convinced that it would be revived later and instructed

214

the MOWB to continue with the conversion work, as they felt that even if Royal Enfield withdrew permanently 'some future end user would be found'. Three months later, in response to a Treasury enquiry, the MAP reported that too little work had been completed to query the costs and there were still doubts about completing Westwood. Shortly afterwards, when provisional figures were finally released, their disclosure prompted the normally tolerant Sam Brown to comment that "Westwood, which stands at £227,000 as compared with an original estimate of £60,000 for the same area, is rather horrible".

By the end of June construction was well advanced and it was decided that Royal Enfield would after all operate the factory. Building work was the responsibility of George Wimpey & Co, for whom this was the first underground contract, although the firm had built several of the hostels and other surface structures at Corsham. Wimpey's provided solid, top-quality workmanship at Westwood, a fact which may in part explain the excessive costs. Labour costs were increased by some £12,000 due to demands by the 200 Irish labourers for a 'uniformity allowance' which included subsistence and travelling expenses to guarantee that they were not worse off than men working at the main Corsham site.

Westwood Quarry consists of three independent workings which, over the years, have run into one another. Between the wars a large area was cleared by the Agaric Company for mushroom cultivation and about half of this section was converted for government purposes. A large area to the east, which suffered a serious roof fall during occupation by the mushroom company, was avoided, although an emergency exit from the factory traversed this area to reach an alternative entrance. Three new ventilation shafts were sunk, together with numerous boreholes to carry power cables, water pipes, coal shoots and flues for the small underground boilerhouse.

A great advantage of Westwood Quarry is that the main entrance is a horizontal adit into the hillside, which allowed plant and machinery to be moved in with comparative ease. The only disadvantage is that the ceiling height is much lower than in most of the other quarries, which made it necessary to set the larger machine tools in shallow concrete-lined pits. During the quarrying days blocks of cut stone were transported from the mine on a steeply inclined self-acting tramway which carried wagons down the hillside to loading platforms at Avoncliff Siding on the GWR, and beside the Kennet & Avon Canal, which

215

spanned the river and railway at this point by way of an impressive stone aqueduct. The 2'5" gauge tramway, which crossed the aqueduct on the canal towpath, was lifted in 1936. When the quarry was adapted for mushroom cultivation in 1928 most of the waste stone left underground was removed and tipped over the upper section of the tramway, obliterating all trace of it. This process was completed by the MOWB over the winter of 1941/2, when a further 200,000 tons of stone waste was cleared from the workings and added to the existing tip to form a broad plateau on the hillside to provide a lorry park and space for surface offices, a works canteen and motor transport sheds.

In October, 1941, two plots of land above the quarry were compulsorily purchased under the Emergency Powers (Defence) Act, 'due to the emergency of the project', upon which to build a hostel and an estate of married quarters for the factory employees. Later, as the number of workers increased, a community centre and dance hall was also provided. Three-quarters of the employees were women, the great majority of whom had never worked before, and whose training in precision engineering was undertaken with remarkable skill by the few experienced men transferred from Redditch or borrowed from the Bristol Aircraft factory at Spring Quarry. Workers at Westwood enjoyed excellent welfare facilities, including regular free medical check-ups and compulsory, weekly ultra-violet sun ray treatment in a specially prepared room underground.

Output of No.3 predictors began in July, 1942, and was followed by a range of other gun-control equipment, including tank oil-units and hydraulic control gear for the 40mm Bofors anti-aircraft gun. Towards the end of the war the Westwood factory was involved in the development of radar control equipment for the Bofors gun under the code name 'Red Indian'. A whole battery of guns could be directed automatically by one radar control unit equipped with parabolic reflectors which tracked the target. A tall lattice pylon erected in the yard just outside the quarry entrance carried antennae which transmitted signals to reflective balloons launched over the Avon Valley to test the prototype radar units. This pylon remained in situ long after radar work ceased at Westwood and was not demolished until some time after the factory closed in 1970.

Other defence contracts followed and were to continue for a decade or more after the end of the war. Among the new projects was the development of automatic fuse-setting equipment for the 4.5" anti-

216

aircraft gun. To test the experimental units built at Westwood a static-mount gun (with its barrel truncated) was acquired and set up in the yard, practice rounds being brought from Monkton Farleigh ammunition depot when required. During the 1950s Royal Enfield undertook a good deal of sub-contract work for BAC in connection with the Bristol Bloodhound surface-to-air missile which entered service in 1958, and also developed instrumentation systems for the Atomic Energy Authority at Aldermaston.

The staple product of Royal Enfield had always been motorcycles, and, despite diversification into other engineering fields such as the design and manufacture of a highly successful range of air-cooled diesel engines and the instrumentation work discussed above, this remained the case throughout the war years. Tens of thousands of 250 & 350 cc side-valve-engined bikes, together with the more modern 350 cc over-head-valve type and 125 cc 'Flying Flea', were built at Redditch for the War Department. At the end of the war several thousand were returned to Royal Enfield for rebuilding, most finding their way to Westwood, where they were stored in the disused and very damp mushroom area of the quarry pending overhaul. The bikes suffered badly in this dank atmosphere and, to prevent further deterioration, alternative accommodation was found in a disused warehouse in the centre of Trowbridge and in two premises in Bradford-on-Avon – an old Brewery in Wine Street and Greenland Mill in the centre of town. The latter was a beautifully proportioned eighteenth century woollen mill once owned by the forebears of General Sir Henry Shrapnel, inventor of the eponymous artillery shell, whose family seat, Midway Manor (its gateposts appropriately mounted with piled Shrapnel shell), lies within grenade-throwing distance of Westwood Quarry. Ex-WD motorcycles were stripped down in the Wiltshire warehouses, repainted, fitted with new Redditch-built engines and sold as new.

During the 1950s much of the Royal Enfield motorcycle work migrated to Wiltshire, with components for the 250 cc 'Crusader' made at Greenland Mill, which also produced Meteor and Meteor Minor motorcycles. By the early 1960s, however, the writing was on the wall for Royal Enfield. With an outdated range of production motorcycles, a conservative, patrician management and an over-diversified and dispersed structure, the company was not in a competitive position and quickly went downhill after the death, in 1962, of its managing director,

Major R.W. Smith. Under new owners a process of asset stripping commenced, accelerated by the formation of the Redditch Development Corporation, which was eager to take over the main factory site.

In 1963 all the outlying warehouses and old mills in Wiltshire were closed down and production of the 700 twin cylinder 'Constellation' motorcycle was concentrated at Westwood. With defence-related contracts now coming to a close, and despite the motorcycle work, there was plenty of spare capacity at the underground factory, which was taken up with any jobbing engineering work that the company could obtain. It was obvious, however, that the future was bleak for Royal Enfield, and no one was surprised when the underground factory finally closed in 1970. A small part of the works, complete with plant and equipment, was taken over by an engineering firm run by ex-Enfield employees, which continued to operate the site successfully for nearly twenty years.

The married quarters estate was purchased by the local authority in 1958 and a few years later Wiltshire County Council ruled that the workers' hostel and the ninety-four married quarters must be demolished by the end of 1965. At that time 70% of the tenants were Enfield workers, a substantial proportion of the 200 people still employed underground. The wartime huts were subsequently replaced by a permanent estate of council houses, but the community centre and dance hall remained and were later taken over by Royal Enfield as a drawing office and stores. After 1970 the surface buildings were used for a short time by a local rubber company, but in the early 1980s the land was partially cleared to make way for a housing development, which was later cut back substantially when concern was raised about the stability of the mine workings under the site.

21

DRAKELOW

The possibility of developing a bomb-proof underground factory below the sandstone hills of the Blakeshall estate at Drakelow near Kidderminster was first raised on 18 April, 1941, and subsequently an engineer's appreciation of the scheme was sought from Mr Brian Colquhoun.

Considerable new excavation would have to be made at Drakelow, which was expected to take a year to complete and require the labour of 1,200 men. Costs were estimated at £285,000 to excavate the quarter of a million square feet of tunnels, plus a further £140,000 for external services. The Treasury considered the plan for several months but remained sceptical, maintaining that their own scheme of dispersal to prefabricated factories, cheaply built at government expense on surface sites far from the traditional industrial areas, was the better option. This proposal later collapsed, following acrimonious inter-departmental misunderstandings.

Work began in June, 1941, but progress was very slow and it soon became obvious that there was no hope of finishing the job by the provisional completion date of 6 July, 1942. The first machine tools were installed in November, with full production achieved by May, 1943. Asked by the Treasury to account for the delay, the Minister of Aircraft Production explained that construction was overseen by contractors directly appointed by the MAP, which was not the usual practice. Such contracts were usually let by the appointed factory operator, but in this case, because no end user had been selected, responsibility fell upon the Ministry. Sir Alexander Gibb and Partners were contracted to superintend the project on the basis of costs plus £2,500 per annum. Gibb's

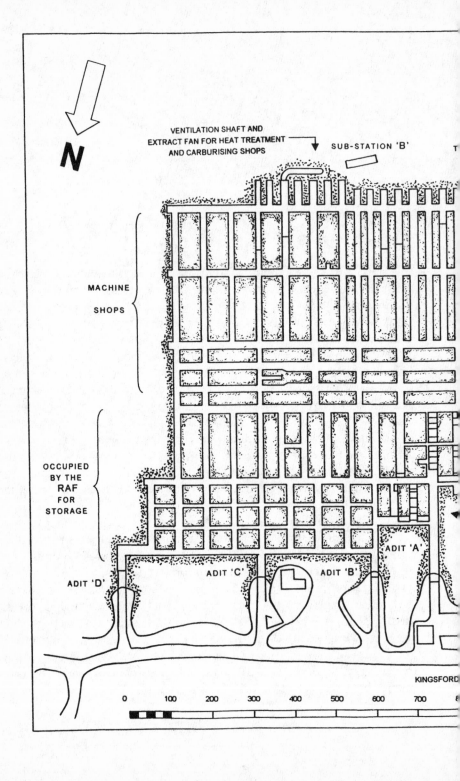

N

VENTILATION SHAFT AND
EXTRACT FAN FOR HEAT TREATMENT
AND CARBURISING SHOPS

SUB-STATION 'B'

MACHINE

SHOPS

OCCUPIED
BY THE
RAF
FOR
STORAGE

ADIT 'A'

ADIT 'D'

ADIT 'C'

ADIT 'B'

KINGSFORD

0   100   200   300   400   500   600   700

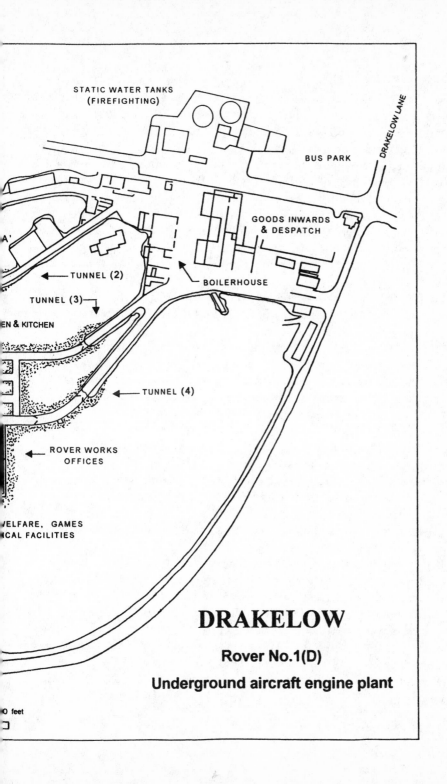

STATIC WATER TANKS
(FIREFIGHTING)

BUS PARK

DRAKELOW LANE

GOODS INWARDS
& DESPATCH

'A'

TUNNEL (2)

TUNNEL (3)

BOILERHOUSE

EN & KITCHEN

TUNNEL (4)

ROVER WORKS
OFFICES

WELFARE, GAMES
CAL FACILITIES

DRAKELOW

Rover No.1(D)

Underground aircraft engine plant

O feet

explained that the sub-contract for tunnelling work was first let to John Cochrane & Sons, but, due to delays attributed to a combination of inefficient management and poor quality Irish labour, this was subsequently withdrawn. The best original tender for the tunnelling contract was submitted by Robert McAlpine & Co. at £228,000, but because of commitments elsewhere they were unable to undertake the work and thus Cochrane's bid of £238,000 had to be accepted. Following the termination of the Cochrane contract the job was passed to The Cementation Company, which had performed conspicuously well on similar contracts for the War Office at Corsham and elsewhere. The labour inefficiency, together with a premium payable to The Cementation Company, was estimated to have cost the government an additional £33,000.

Despite the change of contractor progress was still painfully slow. Sam Brown, writing on behalf of the MAP, told the Treasury that:

"It is unfortunately apparent that with these major underground schemes the nature of the work and the lack of precise knowledge of what will be, always results in the original estimates of both cost and time being greatly exceeded. Prior to the War there was little or no experience of similar work in this country."

By 3 July, 1942, costs had risen to £983,000, which was more than twice the original estimate. Brian Colquhoun indicated that a further expenditure of £184,000 was necessary to prepare the tunnels for use by the Rover Car Company, which had recently been selected to operate the site. Among the special requirements insisted upon by Rover were acid-resisting floors in the production areas and specially painted walls to prevent stone dust getting into the machinery.

Rover involvement in aero-engine construction dates back to the inception of the shadow factory scheme in April, 1936, when the company, along with Austin, Rootes, Daimler and Singer, were invited to form a group which would produce engines for BAC when the demands of war outstripped the limited capacity of the parent firm. The Rover No.1 shadow plant at Acocks Green was in pilot production by October, 1936, and in October, 1940, the first complete engines emerged from the much larger, sixty-five-acre, No.2 shadow factory at Solihull.

The bombing of Coventry on the night of 14 November, 1940, which severely damaged Rover's Helen Street works, precipitated the company into the scramble for dispersed factory accommodation, along with all the other engineering firms in the Midlands. Rover took up at least eighteen dispersed sites in the north of England, including Banksfield Shed at Barnoldswick where the Whittle jet engine was later developed. Six months later, when the MAP suggested that component production should be concentrated in the proposed underground factory at Drakelow, Rover was unenthusiastic, fearing a further disruption of output while plant and machinery was transferred from the existing sites. Negotiations between the MAP, Rover and several other not-over-keen prospective tenants dragged on inconclusively for over twelve months. By the summer of 1942, when construction of the tunnels was scheduled for completion, Rover, like BAC at Spring Quarry, questioned the relevance and necessity of the underground factory scheme. Eventually Rover was persuaded to accept the MAP proposals for Drakelow with certain reservations. The relaxation of the German bombing offensive towards the end of 1942 led to the decision that Rover would retain its dispersed surface accommodation and would take up only half the underground area prepared at such great expense at Drakelow.

Documents relating to the construction of Drakelow are scarce, but it is recorded that a pilot excavation for the 300-yard-long No.2 Tunnel was started first, after which all four main access tunnels were dug simultaneously, the cross passages being formed as work progressed. The tunnel routes were cleared by blasting, with debris being evacuated by conveyor belt and dumped on low-lying land north of Kingsford Lane. Compressed-air tools were then used to trim the rough excavations to a uniform, slightly arched section approximately 18' high and 16' wide.

Development had not proceeded far, however, when two factors, the reduced requirement of the Rover Company and the presence of unexpected geological weaknesses which resulted in a number of roof-falls, called for radical changes in policy and design. A brief inspection of the factory layout shows that only a small section was finished to the original specification and elsewhere only half the intended number of workshop spaces were provided, the much larger remaining areas of virgin stone offering greater overall stability to the structure. Ventilation equipment, electricity sub-stations and the boilerhouse were housed on the surface, the diminishing threat of enemy bombardment having made it less

223

imperative that such vital plant should be given underground protection. Much heavy engineering and shaft-sinking was therefore avoided, the only major work completed before the change of plan being the extract fan and shaft for the carburizing plant.

Ventilation of the factory was achieved by a comprehensive system of extraction trunking which filled the upper section of the four access tunnels, with branches into the workshop areas. At each main entrance the trunking terminated at prominent brick towers which housed the ventilation equipment.

Adaptations were made to the layout of the factory to the north of the main central area to accommodate the vagaries of the ground encountered there. Part of this area was occupied by offices, canteen and welfare facilities and even a concert hall where ENSA shows were staged, but the greater part was not required by the Rover Company and eventually some 82,500 square feet came under the control of RAF No.40 group for the storage of a wide range of aircraft components. Of the four subsidiary entrances accessing the north of the factory, adit 'A' served the Rover administrative area, 'B' & 'C' were vehicular entrances to the RAF stores depot, and adit 'D' was an emergency pedestrian escape route.

The factory, designated 'Rover No.1D' (for dispersal), employed 600 workers and achieved full production in May, 1943. Half the work force lived in a hostel built nearby off Sladd Lane, while the rest were either bussed in from the surrounding area or found digs locally. Drakelow was intended to manufacture components for the range of Bristol rotary engines being assembled at the No.2 Shadow factory at Solihull, including the sleeve valves which proved so difficult to machine successfully. By the time the underground factory reached full production in 1943 the Mercury and Pegasus engines were going out of production and the capacity of the Rover shadow group was concentrated on Hercules manufacture. Development of the Centaurus engine, which was to have been the salvation of the Bristol Aeroplane Company, was still dogged by technical problems which held up quantity production for another year, and consequently the production of parts for this engine made little demand on the Drakelow factory. With the conventional surface factories apparently able to meet the demand for components with greater efficiency and lower unit cost, Spencer Wilkes, Managing Director of Rover, informed his board and the MAP in May, 1944, that in his opinion Drakelow could no longer be operated economically.

Probably rattled by the 'Crossbow' emergency of the previous year, and in line with the current government policy of retaining all 'potential war factories', the MAP insisted that Drakelow should remain in production, if only on a limited scale. Some relief was afforded by the dispute that arose between the Rover board and Power-Jets Ltd over the former company's involvement in the development of the Whittle jet engine, caused in part by a personality clash between Frank Whittle and the Rover engineering team. The outcome was that Rover agreed to transfer all its interests in turbine engine development to Rolls-Royce in exchange for the development contract and all future rights in the Meteor tank engine, which was essentially a modification of the famous Rolls-Royce Merlin V12 aircraft engine. Later a shorter version, the V8 Meteorite, was developed by Rover and went into serial production. Apart from resolving an immediate problem, there was much logic in this arrangement. Rolls-Royce regained its mainstream position in aero-engine development, while Rover, which had no such history and had already intimated to the MAP that it did not wish to maintain its aero-engine capacity after the war, consolidated its position as a prime defence automotive manufacturer. Various marks of the Meteor engine powered the Centurion and later the Conqueror tank, while the Meteorite found numerous applications, including Thornycroft's 'Mighty Antar' tank transporter.

In September, 1946, the MAP agreement with respect to the No.2 shadow factory at Solihull was terminated and the plant was quickly put over to motor car production. Acocks Green continued to serve as Rover's fighting vehicle engine research establishment, and production of the Meteor continued at Drakelow which was still retained at Government insistence under the control of the Ministry of Supply. Early in 1951 the MOS suggested that the underground factory should be put over to large scale Meteor production, although the Ministry was at the same time using the site, which was now much too large for its intended post-war purpose as a repository for surplus machine tools and other redundant plant. Over the next couple of years Rover's defence contracts gradually dried up and at the end of 1952 it was announced that Meteor production would cease in two years. Although new contracts were sought, little was forthcoming. At the end of 1955 the Acocks Green factory was transferred to car production and Drakelow reverted to the MOS, which for the next three years utilized it solely as a transit store for redundant plant. By the end of the decade Drakelow, like all the other ex-MAP underground factories, was granted a new lease of life as one of the highly secretive chain of Regional Seats of Government to which the powers of Whitehall would devolve in the event of nuclear war.

22

DUDLEY CAVERNS

Following the severe bomb damage sustained by BSA at its Small Heath works in November, 1940, urgent discussions were held with the MAP at which a plan was formulated for the removal of 20% of the company's Browning gun barrel capacity into the long-disused limestone caverns at Dudley. 400 men would work underground, and the company required 30,000 square feet for machine rooms, with a further 2,600 square-feet for ancillary services. An optimistic forecast suggested that the conversion work, estimated to cost £28,750, could be completed within ten–twelve weeks.

The major construction tasks consisted of preparing the existing underground area by levelling the floors and strengthening the roof, driving two new entrance tunnels, and erecting a few surface buildings.

On the 24 December the Treasury agreed in principle to the outline scheme and asked BSA to produce detailed, fully costed plans, a request with which the company eventually complied towards the end of April. It transpired, however, that BSA had already contracted for work valued in excess of £30,000 without Treasury approval and that much more expenditure would be required to complete the job. A Supply Board investigation undertaken in August revealed that, because of further unauthorized contractual obligations made by BSA, the Treasury was committed to approve a revised estimate of £50,000. The company was sharply rebuked for what was regarded as a serious irregularity.

Reasons put forward to explain the increased costs were to become familiar as underground developments progressed elsewhere in the country. Conditions had been miscalculated during the initial survey. There was much less loose rubble in the floor than expected, necessitating

PRELIMINARY ESTIMATE FOR CONVERSION OF DUDLEY CAVERN	
Clearance	£2,000
Concreting floors	£3,000
Picking roof	£2,500
Boring new entrances	£2,500
External roads	£750
Building and fencing	£1,500
Heating & ventilation	£5,000
Sewerage	£3,250
Electricity	£4,000
Canteen facilities	£1,500
Water	£150
Gas	£100
Contingencies	£2,500
TOTAL	£28,750

tating expensive rock cutting, while the steeper than expected slope of the roof precluded raising the floor level where the layout plans demanded. The roof was found to be much more unstable than expected and roof falls were frequent. An extra expenditure of £7,000 was requested in September to erect scaffolding and boarding to protect workers and machines from the hazard of falling rock. This was accepted, but when, in June, 1942, as work was nearing completion, a similar request for a further £6,000 was made the Treasury refused, questioning the safety and viability of the whole project.

It was by now apparent that the Browning gun position was not as precarious as was at first feared, and justification for the Dudley scheme was not so immediate. Under pressure from BSA, who were never very keen on the project, the Air Supply Board therefore decided not to move their capacity to the tunnels and the site was instead offered to the Air Ministry for use as an ammunition store. Towards the end of July the Air Ministry also decided against Dudley as the tunnels were too small. The MAP then approached the MOS which also rejected the site, which was subsequently abandoned.

The Treasury reported that the final cost of the abortive scheme looked likely to be £65,000, and commented that:

"All this undoubtedly makes rather a sorry tale, involving as it does —

(A) A final cost of more than double the estimate on the basis of which the scheme was originally approved.

(B) A considerable constructive loss.

However, if the conditions which prevailed in 1940/41 continued, we would have completed the tunnels. The real issue therefore appears to be whether a more thorough and expert technical examination of the scheme at its inception would have been more practicable; and if so whether it would have led to a more realistic estimate of the difficulties and costs."

Much of the blame for the debacle was, rightly or wrongly, put upon BSA and it was felt at the MAP that the Treasury should 'impress upon BSA their displeasure', although it was thought unlikely that it would be possible to impose any financial penalty. The official history of BSA makes no mention of the dispute over finance, stating simply that:

"A considerable amount of work was carried out by the Ministry of Aircraft Production before it became apparent that, in the event of a bomb falling on the ground overhead, there would be a considerable risk of the roof collapsing. The project was accordingly abandoned."

23

HENLEY-ON-THAMES

One of the last independent proposals put to the MAP by an aircraft firm came on 11 June, 1941, from the Hanworth-based firm of Sir George Godfrey and Partners. Godfrey's was a small engineering firm manufacturing gearbox assemblies and hydraulic control components for the Phillips Master trainer, and was currently in very vulnerable premises in West London. Potentially suitable accommodation had been found in a disused chalk quarry at Park Place near Henley-on-Thames, offering 30,000 square feet of workshop space with an overhead cover of between forty and sixty feet. A survey prepared by the firm indicated that the larger tunnels required only minor adaptation and the provision of lighting and ventilation to convert them into very adequate factory space at an estimate cost of £23,025.

This scheme was approved by the Treasury on 20 June and a local firm of building contractors, Gordon Carrington & Co. Ltd, was employed to survey the site and produce accurate costings. Carrington's was initially contracted on a 'costs plus profit' basis, but for reasons not satisfactorily explained this was later changed to a 'measured schedule' contract. A few months later the financial arrangements were changed again and the company was pinned to a firm price quote of £18,723. At the completion of work this was found to represent a loss to Carrington of £5,707. In September, 1944, Sam Brown, always the voice of reason, tried to persuade the Treasury to compensate the firm for their loss, commenting that:

"There is no question but that Gordon Carrington's have given us a good job, and a very cheap job, at Henley."

230

He went on to suggest that the Treasury should make an ex-gratia payment of £5,000 to alleviate Carrington's loss, backing up their case with the argument that throughout the war they had undertaken a number of government contracts at very low margins. The Treasury, however, refused the ex-gratia payment, stating that the company had entered into the contract freely and should bear the commercial consequence.

A second quarry was subsequently developed for aircraft component manufacture at Warren Row near Henley-on-Thames. Throughout most of these workings the lower walls of the arched-section tunnels were lined with brickwork which supported a false ceiling. The upper, more markedly arch-shaped part of the tunnel above the false ceiling was used as an air-conditioning and service duct. In two or three locations the tunnels were high enough to allow the insertion of a first-floor level to provide extra office space. Originally the only access was by means of a gently sloping adit, but a steeper graded emergency exit shaft was later provided at the far end of the quarry.

Unlike the Corsham quarries, where the cavities left by the miners consisted of wide expanses of randomly shaped open areas supported by an occasional pillar, the workings at Warren Row consisted of more or less straight tunnels only fifteen to twenty feet in width, with a total length of about 600 yards. In the workshop areas machine tools and benches were lined up against the left-hand walls with narrow walkways to the right. Surface buildings were absolutely minimal, the main structure being a brick boilerhouse adjacent to the main entrance with an independent access tunnel into the workings.

After the war the Park Place factory remained in use as a privately owned engineering works, held on lease from the MOD until the early 1980's when the freehold was sold. Warren Row was maintained by the Ministry of Supply until 1958, when it was developed (and very soon became notorious) as RSG-6, another of the once secret and later highly controversial Regional Seats of Government.

24

WESTWOOD AND MANOD – THE ART
TREASURE REPOSITORIES

Two or three years before the war, when those in power knew conflict was inevitable, discreet and secret steps were taken to safeguard the priceless treasures kept in the galleries and museums of the Capital. Such discretion was required as much resentment was anticipated should it become widely known that the government, which had already voiced its antipathy to universal deep-level bomb shelters for the civil population, was more concerned about inanimate (and many would say elitist) trifles than about the masses it was elected to represent.

By the time of the Munich crisis over 2000 pictures from the National Gallery had already been sent to country houses and provincial centres beyond the range of enemy bombing, many of them finding their way to the Welsh National Library at Aberystwyth and the University of Wales at Bangor. Other pictures were sent to Crosswood House, which was later used by Birmingham Museum and Art Gallery to store paintings, and also to store treasures from the Royal Collection. Paintings from the Tate Gallery were spirited away to Muncaster Castle in Cumberland and Sudelely Castle near Gloucester, while others were housed in disused sections of the Piccadilly tube where they shared space with treasures from Westminster Abbey, the London Museum and the Royal Academy. Priceless artefacts from the Victoria & Albert Museum, the British Museum and Buckingham Palace were stored in the disused Aldwych tube tunnels, Skipton Castle in Yorkshire and Montacute House in Somerset, until more suitable permanent accommodation could be found. The contents of the Public Record Office were widely dispersed to safe houses nation-wide, but the most important documents,

232

including the Domesday Book, were secured in the basement of Shepton Mallet prison in Somerset. It is interesting to note that in 1942 the prison was seconded by the US Army 6833 Guardhouse Overhead Detachment, and in a room above the cellars where the nation's heritage was kept safe, twenty-one American servicemen were hanged, and two of Red Indian extraction executed by firing squad.

The ferocity of the London Blitz, the threat of invasion and the possible occupation of Ireland by the enemy (which meant that Aberystwyth could no longer be considered safe) demanded more secure and secret accommodation for the artefacts now rendered increasingly vulnerable. To the War Cabinet 'secure and secret' meant *underground*, and a search was immediately instituted for suitably remote sites.

In the early months of 1941 a meeting was arranged between Sir Eric Maclagan of the V&A and Sir John Fosdyke of the British Museum to discuss the storage of the contents of their respective museums in deep quarry repositories. At first it was thought that all the suitable underground sites had already been allotted to other government departments, but, following a lead from staff at Bristol University, it was discovered that space might be available at Westwood Quarry, part of which was currently being developed as a factory for Royal Enfield. Further accommodation was found in the Manod slate quarries deep below the desolate, mist-enshrouded mountains north of Ffestiniog. Hidden at the end of a tortuous five-mile mountain track, Manod was one of the most dramatic government sites in Britain.

WESTWOOD

On 6 March, 1941, Maclagan and Fosdyke met representatives of Sir Alexander Gibb and Partners, and Mr Bennitt from the MOWB, to discuss the difficulties of preparing an area of Westwood Quarry as a museum repository. It was agreed that an isolated heading with a floor area of 25,000 square feet would be sufficient to meet the needs of both museums, and the MOWB was satisfied that they could satisfactorily air-condition the area. At that time the best tapestries and carpets from the V&A were stored in the long gallery of Montacute House, but conditions there were far from ideal, the roof let in water and the carpets in particular were becoming badly affected with mildew. Sir Eric Maclagan initially requested an area of 15,000 square feet, which would be sufficient for all the material currently at Montacute, together with all the

233

items remaining at Kensington, and still leave an unobstructed area 45' × 25' for the periodic unrolling and inspection of the largest carpets.

The section of quarry available to the museums sloped markedly and it was decided that the eastern half, which was allocated to the British Museum, should be terraced to give a series of horizontal stacking areas upon which shelving could be erected. Other than a number of large sculptures, and the Elgin Marbles (which were transferred to Westwood from their temporary home in the Piccadilly tube), most of the British Museum artefacts were securely boxed and could be easily stacked. Ethnographic textiles were stored in a separate chamber where they were hung in open racks to facilitate regular insecticide treatment without contaminating the air in the main storeroom. Despite this precaution, however, an infestation of moths was discovered just before a visit by Queen Mary in March, 1943. There was only one entrance to the repository, and this was sealed by a lobby secured by two strong-room doors transferred from Bloomsbury. Within the storage area an early application of the 'Radiovisor' light-ray smoke detection system was installed.

Conversion work started in June, 1941, and was completed within six months. When cleared the area was found to have a very regular pillar formation which required little reinforcement; the main building task being the treatment of the whole exposed stone surface with a special waterproof sealing compound. It was realized from the outset that very careful control over temperature and humidity was required, and a contract to supply plant capable of maintaining a temperature of 65° and humidity of exactly 60% was awarded to the Norris Warming Company. The installed equipment was very sophisticated and very extensive, requiring a plant-room almost as large as the repository. Much of the plant was duplicated, for it was calculated that, should it fail for more than a half-hour or so, conditions would deteriorate so rapidly that the more delicate items would suffer irreparable damage. Experimental Cambridge humidity recorders continually monitored atmospheric conditions in the repository, but adjustment of the plant was performed manually and required great vigilance from the attendants. Men were employed whose sole job was constantly to inspect the walls and floor of the storage chambers checking for damp areas, which were treated with 'Stett', a proprietary damp-proofing compound.

There was some delay in delivery of the air-conditioning machinery, which was not installed until 30 October, three days before the great strong-room doors were finally put in place. By 10 November the plant was up and running, but humidity was far from under control, for if the plant was stopped for just a few minutes the humidity in the repository rose immediately to over 90%. It took several months for the quarry fabric to dry out adequately and it was not until 24 February, 1942, that the inward movement of artefacts could begin. A rota was organized under which the V&A and British Museum deliveries arrived on alternate days. A narrow-gauge railway was laid in the tunnel leading to the repository doors, and out in the yard a gantry was built by means of which the heavier packing cases could be transferred from the delivery lorries onto the railway trucks.

In mid-April conditions underground deteriorated rapidly, the British Museum side of the quarry being worst affected. It was obvious that there had been some major malfunction of the air-conditioning system, but the electrical recording instruments indicated that the plant was operating normally and conditions were good. Then it was realized that the plant and the recorders both worked off the same power supply, so when the power to the dehumidifiers failed the recorders also stopped. A standby generating set, which would have overcome this difficulty, was planned from the start of the scheme, but in 1941 such equipment was virtually impossible to obtain new and competition for secondhand plant was intense. A portable 18 Kw semi-diesel set was obtained at short notice for emergency use, but the firm of J.Gerber & Co were instructed by the MOWB to locate a more powerful alternator for permanent installation. On 15 September this firm arranged the purchase of a very old 74 Kw Vickers-Petter set from the Exe Valley Electricity Company of Dulverton for the enormous price of £860.

When delivered to Westwood the equipment was found to be very old and decrepit; the two-cylinder, two-stroke diesel engine dated from 1927 and the Holland alternator was made in 1931; there was no switchboard, starting, cooling, or voltage regulating gear, and the engine did not run. A thorough inspection revealed that all the main bearings and the pistons needed replacing, but when the engineers contacted Petters of Loughborough regarding spares for the plant which, the MOWB informed them was "being re-erected in connection with works of great national importance", they were told that "the engine as you are aware was originally manufactured by Messrs. Vickers-Petters Ltd of Ipswich, and as the engine type has been out of production for a good many years we have run out of spare parts and instruction books." The company undertook to manufacture the necessary components, but in June, 1942, the MOWB was still desperately telegraphing Petters: "Corsham Pistons Urgently Required."

By the autumn the engine was sufficiently complete to be coaxed into motion, but, despite all endeavours by the engineers, it refused to run for more than a few minutes. The cause of the problem was pinned down to a brickwork expansion chamber near the bottom of the exhaust shaft which had been almost filled with broken bricks and other debris by Wimpey's men in their hurry to complete the building work. Once this was cleared it was possible to keep the engine running, although the voltage produced by the alternator fluctuated wildly. After much trouble an automatic regulator was found and fitted and, on 12 December, preparations were made for the first test run of the completed plant. The engine was still difficult to start and, after five minutes' running on-load, unusual noises were heard coming from the cylinder-head, followed by an enormous explosion which blew out the side wall of the exhaust silencer, wrecking electrical gear in the plant-room under a shower of bricks and concrete and causing irreparable internal damage to the engine. After struggling for fifteen months the MOWB decided to abandon all further attempts to get the old Petter engine running and fell back on the services of the 18Kw mobile generator until the end of the war, when it was able to acquire a brand new Crossley-engined alternator set.

For some time after the quarry was handed over to the Museums there were complaints that the air-conditioning plant was not working satisfactorily and that traces of mildew had appeared on some of the tapestries. Independent tests conducted by the National Physical Laboratory concluded that the plant was adequate for its purpose and that the fault lay in its inefficient operation. To ensure future reliability and proper plant-room discipline, comprehensive operating instructions were drawn up which required the plant attendants to adhere to a set routine and maintain a minute-by-minute log of all their actions in response to changes in ambient conditions.

The British Museum occupied Westwood Quarry from February, 1942, until December, 1946, during which time the museum staff evacuated with the artefacts continued as far as possible with the routine tasks of cataloguing and conservation. Junior members were housed in the

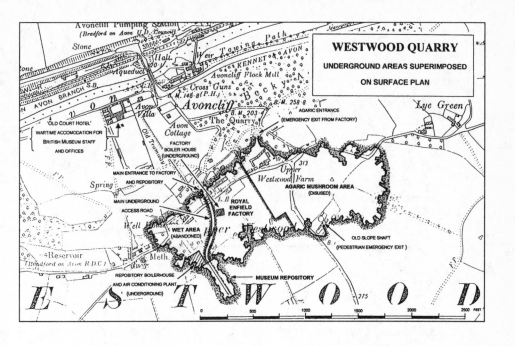

WESTWOOD QUARRY
UNDERGROUND AREAS SUPERIMPOSED
ON SURFACE PLAN

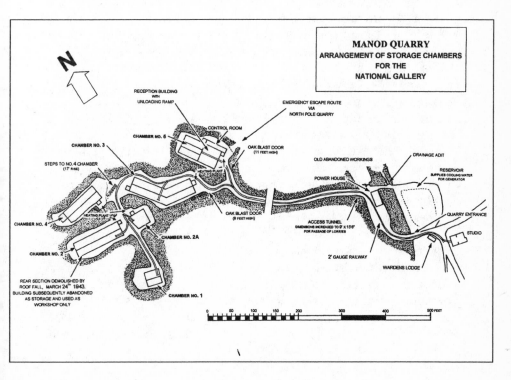

MANOD QUARRY
ARRANGEMENT OF STORAGE CHAMBERS
FOR THE
NATIONAL GALLERY

nearby workers' hostel built primarily for the Royal Enfield employees, but senior officers found better lodgings at Avoncliff in the recently requisitioned Old Court Hotel, a rambling eighteenth-century building that only a couple of decades earlier had been the Bradford Union Workhouse.

The museum trustees received requests for the safe-keeping of items of outstanding importance from numerous institutions and private individuals, and the quarry soon became a fabulous national treasure-house. Apart from artefacts from Bloomsbury and Kensington, Westwood also held collections from the Bodleian Library, the Imperial War Museum, and the Free French Museum of National Antiquities. Among the individual items to spend the war years in Wiltshire were the Rubens Ceiling from the Whitehall banqueting hall, the Crown Jewels, the Charles I statue from Whitehall and the bronze screen from the Henry VII Chapel in Westminster Abbey.

The V&A remained at Westwood for several years after the departure of the British Museum and, by 1954, concern was expressed that over £2,000,000 worth of artefacts were still stored in the quarry. The repository was finally vacated in 1957, although maintenance was continued well into the 1960s. Considering the incalculable value of the material interred in the quarry, security staff was modest, consisting of a Keeper or Deputy Assistant, with one warder by day, and one warder accompanied by one Wiltshire Police Constable at night.

Despite the demolition of all the accommodation and welfare buildings the surface area of Westwood Quarry has changed little. Many of the larger buildings have been adapted for light industrial use, while land immediately above the quarry has been partially landscaped following the contraction of an intended housing development. The area is littered with a fascinating profusion of red-brick buildings which mark the air-shaft tops, their peculiar shape being due to the incorporation of washing facilities for the complex filter panels. Elsewhere, tall iron flues rise from the two underground boilerhouses, while another shaft houses a chain hoist and skip to raise boiler-ash.

The Bath & Portland Stone Co re-acquired the property when it was de-requisitioned and, soon after, set up a branch of Wansdyke Security, its archival storage business, in the museum section. When Willet & Wilkins, the engineering firm which took over the Enfield workshops, moved to new premises in 1987, Wansdyke Security absorbed the vacant

238

area and is gradually extending its operation there. Meanwhile the extraction of stone has recommenced west of the main access passage.

MANOD

We have seen that at the start of the war most of the National Gallery collection had already been evacuated to the relative safety of North Wales, where temporary surface refuge was found at Bangor and Aberystwyth, pending the location of more secure underground premises. These arrangements were upset in May, 1940, not by the immediate fear of invasion or bombing, but by the threat of damage by fifth columnists and militant Welsh Nationalists, encouraged by German forces that might occupy neutral Ireland. Consequently a hundred of the most important pictures were secretly transferred to three secure and isolated country houses about ten miles distant from Bangor.

One of the great houses selected was Penrhyn Castle, which was offered on a one-year rent-free lease until 16 July, 1941. Shortly after the first pictures were despatched to Penrhyn it was announced that the War Office, oblivious of the National Gallery presence, had made plans temporarily to station at the castle 1000 troops of the BEF recently evacuated from Dunkirk. This put the government in something of a dilemma; National Gallery officials were not happy to have potentially unruly troops ensconced with their pictures, while the Government was unhappy about the political implication of public opinion regarding paintings being more important than soldiers.

Meanwhile Brigadier Temple-Richards, the Senior Civil Engineer of HM Office of Works Defence Architects' Department, had inspected a slate quarry at Manod and was convinced that it could be made ready to accept the pictures from Penrhyn when the lease there expired. The underground storage at Manod was scheduled for completion by Christmas, 1940, but work was impeded by the terrible winter weather and in November Temple-Richards reported that work there would not be finished before February, 1941. Labour difficulties involving the bricklayers and carpenters further retarded progress, but it was hoped that the first of the six storage chambers would be ready early in April and the last by the end of May. Further delays were experienced during construction of the five-mile approach road, due mainly to the low height of a railway bridge near the village of Ffestiniog. The railway company agreed to lower the road below the bridge, a task which was expected to involve simply cutting away a certain amount of solid rock. They discovered, however, that the bridge was founded on compressed shale and deep concrete footings were required to support the abutments. Near the quarry entrance a new access road which clung perilously to the mountainside collapsed twice during construction. As a result of all the delays it was impossible to move the pictures out of Penrhyn Castle by 16 July, when the tenancy there expired. Construction of the quarry repository was complete, but drying-out of the storage rooms took longer than expected and the standby generator was not yet operational. The additional delay caused friction with the MOS as it had already arranged a new lease of Penrhyn Castle with the Daimler Motor Company which was creating a shadow factory at Bangor, having already taken over the Crossville bus garage as a workshop. The castle was required for office and storage space. All the pictures from Penrhyn, Aberystwyth and Crosswood House were finally transferred to Manod on 18 August, 1941.

The slate quarry at Ffestiniog bore no comparison to the limestone workings in Wiltshire with which the MOWB was more familiar. At Manod the enormous chambers (over 400 feet long, sixty feet wide and up to 100 feet in height) were overlain by at least 200 feet of hard igneous rock. The store consisted of six interconnected chambers approached by a three-hundred-yard heading which was originally a small drainage adit but was widened and levelled to allow access by the five-ton pantechnicon lorries used to transport the paintings. The natural chambers were far too large and damp to be used for storage, so a series of six brick buildings were erected within the quarry, linked to one another by a narrow-gauge railway. The railway was extended through the access tunnel to serve a studio, built on a narrow plateau outside the quarry entrance, where large repairs were undertaken and the pictures photographed or viewed when necessary.

Only limited funds were available to complete the project, so the underground buildings were erected with the utmost economy. The proposed buildings were not heavy structures but they had to be absolutely dry and free from settlement, criteria which posed something of an engineering challenge. The cavern floors consisted of loose slate debris to a depth of twenty feet, but extensive spread-footings for the buildings could not be afforded and, in any case, there was no time for their preparation. The slate was scraped and levelled with a two-inch layer of concrete over which a continuous bituminous sheet was laid. Brick walls with an inner compo-board cavity were erected on shallow foundations and a concrete floor pad laid over the bituminous sheet, after which the slate chippings around the outside of each building were drenched with weak cement slurry applied by watering-can to grout the ground. Roofs were of light compo-board tarred and covered with bituminous felting. To prevent the risk of small rock falls penetrating the rooflight steel mesh was laid over the felt and bonded into the brick walls.

Five of the six buildings had a headroom of ten feet, while the largest was fifteen feet clear, to accommodate the largest canvases. The interior of each building had an inspection area, where small repairs such as the laying of blisters could be undertaken, and was fitted with timber frames built integral to the structure to support the pictures without the need for stacking. The largest chamber served as an air-conditioned reception hall where the pictures in their sealed cases were unloaded from the lorries on to a raised loading dock. Those assigned to other buildings were transferred in special air-tight railway wagons, the light railway system entering through curtain air locks.

Each storage building had its own air-conditioning plant room containing electric heaters and circulating fans which enabled humidity and temperature to be closely controlled to a RH of 57% and a temperature of 64°, with a variation not exceeding 3°. Warning indicators in a central control office activated if the temperature in any building fluctuated by more than 2°. To guard against any stoppage of the air-conditioning plant a 140-horsepower standby generator was installed in a chamber near the quarry entrance.

Although the cavern roof was carefully examined before construction began and any loose rock brought down, the risk of roof falls was an ever-present problem. To allow continuous inspection a spidery network of scaffolding and ladders was erected, and in certain places it was found necessary to secure sections of roof with great chains attached to eight-foot bolts which pierced the suspect strata and adhered to the sounder rock above. After conversion work was well advanced the MOWB learned that the Cwt-y-Bugail quarrying company intended to continue slate extraction from an open-cast quarry nearby, and that the government had no statutory powers to prevent this, despite the fact that the blasting might endanger the stability of the Manod store. After negotiation, the company agreed in future to blast with reduced charges, but the question of compensation payments was raised. As an additional precaution two sets of heavy oak doors were positioned in the storage-chamber approach-passages to lessen the effects of nearby blasting.

The pictures at Manod were returned to their respective galleries within six months of the war ending, but the government continued to maintain the empty site for a further forty years. Why such a desolate and patently unsuitable facility, dripping with water, shrouded in mist for most of the year and often cut off for weeks by impassable winter snowstorms, should be retained when other more amenable underground sites were falling vacant is difficult to understand. Even Brigadier Temple-Richards admitted that the conversion of Manod went ahead only "having regard to the difficulty of finding any other suitable site". The inhospitable nature of its surroundings may have been the very attraction of the site, but whatever the reasoning a new lease was negotiated in 1959, at much the same time as the government programme of nuclear bunker construction was gaining momentum nationwide. Manod was to function in the next war as it had done in the last, but despite the ingenuous parliamentary proclamations of Frank Allaun MP, in 1981, no major changes were ever made in the quarry; the great concrete bunkers with 'steel doors barring access' described by his correspondent never existed, and to the very end the only buildings within the quarry were the six flimsy brick structures erected in 1941. An improved electricity supply was laid on to the quarry in the 1960s, and a new standby generator and switchgear installed, but electrical services within the storage areas were unchanged since the war.

By 1990 Manod was abandoned and decaying, occupied sporadically by the nearby slate quarrying company as a store for derelict machinery. The railways have been lifted, cabling ripped out and all the buildings stripped of their window frames, timber roofs, doors and everything else of salvageable value, even the wooden racking for the pictures. Among the red-brick shells can still be found some reminders of wartime occupation, like the wrecked humidity recorders which monitored the atmosphere in each chamber to such fine limits, and the rusting remains of the fans and heaters, inexplicably ignored by the scrap merchants who were otherwise so thorough. Debris from a more recent adventure also litters the site. In 1989 Manod was the location for a spectacular television advertisement for BMW, in which a motor car bursts from the tunnel mouth at high speed, pursued 'Prisoner'-style by a monstrous and menacing bouncing white ball. When filming was finished much of the lighting and other electrical equipment was abandoned in the quarry.

25

COLD-WAR WARRIORS

In April, 1963, a small group of anti-nuclear protestors, calling themselves 'Spies For Peace', revealed to the world that the British Government had constructed for its own protection a chain of secret underground bunkers in which the favoured few would sit out the looming nuclear war while the civil population vaporized in the ensuing holocaust. In many ways this was a seminal moment for British society, the moment from which the nation, particularly the newly enfranchised intellectual younger generation, lost faith in the Establishment. Since then attitudes have hardened; commentators have ceaselessly promulgated the opinion that since the start of the Cold War, fifty years ago, government has been increasingly prepared with callous disregard to abandon the population to the consequences of its war-mongering brinkmanship. A more reasoned analysis, however, will show that this interpretation is a fallacy and that the post-war development of Civil Defence and the corresponding bunker construction programme is merely a logical progression of the system that had been in place since 1936.

Preparations to move certain Government departments from London to safer areas of the country were made early in the Second World War. The Admiralty, for example, moved to Bath and the Air Ministry to Harrogate in September, 1939, as part of the pre-war 'Yellow Move' evacuation plan. No sinister motive was read in to this precaution and it would have been no more sinister had the government gone a step further and transferred the departments in to *underground* accommodation at that time. Such a move would simply be another step on the same ladder. Within eighteen months several RAF Group and Sector Command

244

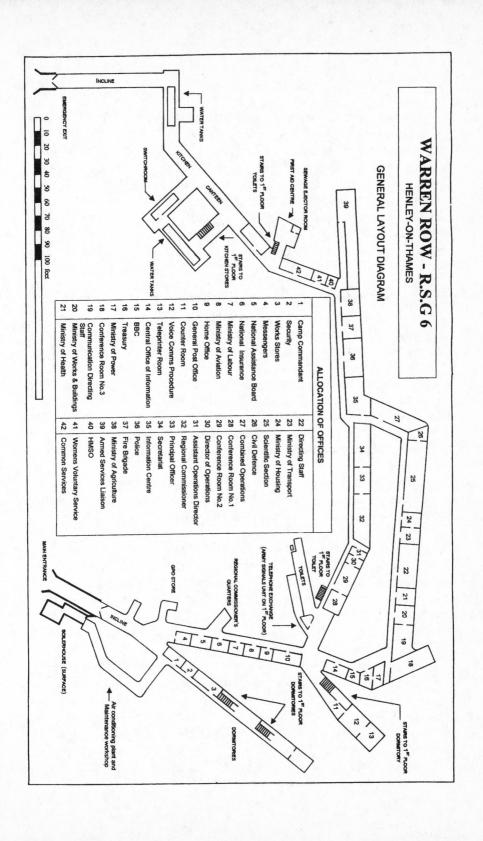

WARREN ROW - R.S.G 6
HENLEY-ON-THAMES

GENERAL LAYOUT DIAGRAM

ALLOCATION OF OFFICES

1	Camp Commandant	22	Directing Staff
2	Security	23	Ministry of Transport
3	Works Stores	24	Ministry of Housing
4	Messengers	25	Scientific Section
5	National Assistance Board	26	Civil Defence
6	National Insurance	27	Combined Operations
7	Ministry of Labour	28	Conference Room No.1
8	Ministry of Aviation	29	Conference Room No.2
9	Home Office	30	Director of Operations
10	General Post Office	31	Assistant Operations Director
11	Counter Room	32	Regional Commissioner
12	Voice Comms Procedure	33	Principal Officer
13	Teleprinter Room	34	Secretariat
14	Central Office of Information	35	Information Centre
15	BBC	36	Police
16	Treasury	37	Fire Brigade
17	Ministry of Power	38	Ministry of Agriculture
18	Conference Room No.3	39	Armed Services Liaison
19	Communication Directing Staff	40	HMSO
20	Ministry of Works & Buildings	41	Womens Voluntary Service
21	Ministry of Health	42	Common Services

INCLINE

EMERGENCY EXIT

0 10 20 30 40 50 60 70 80 90 100 feet

WATER TANKS

SEWAGE EJECTOR ROOM

FIRST AID CENTRE

STAIRS TO 1ST FLOOR TOILETS

SWITCHROOM

KITCHEN

CANTEEN

STAIRS TO 1ST FLOOR KITCHEN STORES

WATER TANKS

TELEPHONE EXCHANGE (ARMY SIGNALS UNIT ON 1ST FLOOR)

REGIONAL COMMISSIONER'S QUARTERS

STAIRS TO 1ST FLOOR TOILET

TOILETS

GPO STORE

STAIRS TO 1ST FLOOR DORMITORIES

STAIRS TO 1ST FLOOR DORMITORY

MAIN ENTRANCE

INCLINE

BOILERHOUSE (SURFACE)

Air conditioning plant and Maintenance workshop

DORMITORIES

centres *were* found underground accommodation, and, far from appearing sinister, this was seen at the time, and in retrospect still appears, to be an elementary precaution. And if the men and women who control the fighters should have underground protection, why should the men who control the controllers not be similarly safe?

At the same time that the plan for the 'Yellow Move' was under preparation further arrangements were being developed for a more extreme measure, the 'Black Move', or the evacuation of the central government nucleus to a secure location out of London. There is little doubt that this contingency was considered in connection with Spring Quarry as early as December, 1941, when the Treasury, faced with the inordinate cost of quarry development, commented that *"we would want to buy out some of the quarries and keep some kind of permanent citadel for future emergencies"*. We have seen already that in November, 1943, large parts of Spring Quarry were reserved by the War Cabinet 'Crossbow' committee, and, although documents so far released do not specifically mention using the quarry as a central government facility, the committee was at the same time making arrangements for the "maintenance of the machinery of government under rocket bombardment". Although it is irrefutable that Spring Quarry was never used as a central government dispersal during the war (the entire site being under control of BAC and BSA until 1945) the seed of an idea had been sown.

By the end of the war a number of coincident factors confirmed the government's interest in Spring Quarry as a nuclear citadel. At Corsham nature and Victorian enterprise had provided a vast, virtually unique, ready-made underground complex, the provision of which, in virgin ground, would have been financially prohibitive in the straitened post-war years. With the closure of the factories there was an abundance of vacant space and a plentiful provision of essential services. Spring Quarry was well provided with communications facilities, for in addition to those available in the adjoining RAF South West Control switching centre it also contained a 25,000 square foot GPO telephone exchange complete with its own emergency power station.

In 1945 large areas of Spring Quarry were absorbed by the Admiralty for naval storage, but the development factory and a range of machine shops in the north-east quarry were retained by BAC for a further twelve months. When moves were finally made to dispose of the development factory in September, 1946, the MOS officer charged with this responsibility soon learned, as we have already seen, that "the policy is to hold on firmly to our best refuge from the atom bomb". It is probable that the first moves towards establishing an emergency seat of central government at Spring Quarry were made in 1947, when East-West tension was reaching a peak, the Royal Observer Corps was reconstituted, and terms were being negotiated for American bombers to be stationed, it was then thought only temporarily, on British airfields. At the same time access to Spring Quarry was severely restricted, as "the future use of the site may be somewhat sensitive".

The perceived threat was Russian possession of the atomic bomb and the response seems to have been to prepare a revitalized 'Black Move'. The atomic bomb was at first seen as little more than a more powerful conventional weapon, but a weapon which could render whole cities untenable; hence the urgent need for an alternative seat of government outside London. Atomic war was, however, considered survivable and was expected to be a prolonged affair similar to the Second World War, requiring similar systems of civil defence and civil administration.

Over the next few years an increased air-defence programme was initiated in response to the Russian threat, an important feature of which was the 'Rotor' radar system, consisting of over seventy sites with hardened underground control bunkers. Most of the bunkers were purpose-built to a standard design, the exception being the Southern Sector Operations Centre, which was constructed in Brown's Quarry at Corsham in the old No.10 Group headquarters. The introduction of supersonic high-altitude bombers and the corresponding advances in radar technology meant that by 1958 the 'Rotor' system was already obsolete. Many of the now redundant bunkers passed to the Home Office which was then developing a network of nuclear-bomb-proof Regional Seats of Government (RSGs) for use in time of war, to replace the earlier and much smaller civil defence Regional War Rooms.

The advent of the nuclear bomb marked a quantum leap in destructive power, threatening cataclysmic material ruin and human misery on a scale that would destroy the entire fabric and structure of civilization. Civil defence in nuclear war, as in the Second World War, was to be a Home Office rather than a military responsibility. Great Britain would be divided into twelve regions, each administered from the safety of a blast- and radiation-proof underground headquarters by a Regional Commissioner, (at first a senior civil servant, but in more developed

247

versions of the plan a Cabinet Minister) who would assume full powers of government in his region if communication with central government was lost.

During the three decades since 1962 the number, administration and designation of these underground regional government bunkers have undergone several alterations, but their prime function and physical characteristics have remained constant. A full analysis of post-war civil defence policy is beyond the scope of this narrative, as is a detailed description of all the RSG bunkers newly built since 1958 or adapted from existing military installations. What concerns us is the integration into the system of central and regional government of the three underground aircraft engine factories which, by lucky coincidence, became available just as the various stages of the scheme were being developed.

Pursuing the long-practised policy of adapting existing, redundant, underground facilities to meet current needs, the Home Office pressed into use the disused factories at Warren Row to serve as RSG 6, controlling central-southern England, and Drakelow, as RSG 9, to control the West Midlands. Drakelow entered service in 1961, replacing the earlier War Room in Shirley, and Warren Row was ready for occupation by April, 1962, when it participated in Exercise 'Parapluie'.

Surrounded by high wire fences, RSG 6 looked, on the surface, remarkably unchanged from its wartime incarnation, inconspicuous on the edge of its woodland site except for a telltale aerial mast and an obvious MOWB brick boilerhouse which sat somewhat incongruously in an otherwise rural setting. Warren Row was infiltrated in April, 1963, by 'Spies for Peace', and the less-than-impartial interpretation of their discoveries there have clouded public perception of government civil defence planning ever since. 'Danger-Official Secret', the pamphlet widely circulated by 'Spies for Peace', (who were children of the first generation for decades to have been untainted by first-hand experience of the realities of war), while laudable in its idealism, is just that – devoid of pragmatism and unconscious of the genuine fears for the safety of the country as a whole, felt by those in power at that time. 'Spies for Peace' claimed that RSG 6 was *"not a centre for civil defence. It is a centre for military government"*, deftly ignoring the fact that of the sixty offices underground, which included accommodation for, among others, the Ministry of Health, Ministry of Labour, Ministry of Housing and the National Assistance board, only one was directly allocated to the armed

248

services. Avoided also was acceptance of the fact, however unpalatable, that in war or as a result of war the loss of cohesive government, even an unpopular government, leads instantly to anarchy and social dissolution, which are far greater evils.

Three months after the 'Spies For Peace' episode, in July, 1963, administrative changes were made to the system of emergency regional government that called for a greater number of hardened control bunkers each responsible for a smaller, more manageable geographical area. These new 'sub-regional controls' (S-RCs) would coordinate the recovery stage after a nuclear attack and would later, when conditions were sufficiently stable, hand over responsibility to a regional government headquarters established in suitable surface offices. Under this new system Warren Row became S-RC 61.

Following the disbanding of the Civil Defence Corps in 1968, the structure of emergency government was again re-examined. Most of the S-RCs were reduced to 'care-and-maintenance' status, except for Warren Row which, as the most unsatisfactory site from the engineering viewpoint and with an uncomfortably high public profile since 1963, was abandoned, its function having already been transferred to a new bunker below the recently constructed Civil Service Commission Headquarters in Basingstoke. In 1973 the S-RC organization was abolished and replaced by a system of 'Sub-Regional Headquarters' (SRHQs). Unlike the S-RCs, the SRHQs had no civil defence rescue function, but would, until full regional and national government was restored, become *"the highest level of internal government"*, responsible for the maintenance of essential services and civil order. The replacement S-RC61 at Basingstoke became SRHQ 6.2, responsible for the western counties of the old region, while a new bunker designated SRHQ 6.1, constructed in the Second World War tunnels below Dover Castle, took control of Kent and the eastern counties.

During the early 1970s maintenance of the disused Warren Row complex was progressively reduced and by 1978 it was apparently derelict, becoming prey, like so many other similar sites, to widespread vandalism and theft. In 1982, however, the bunker was quietly refitted at great expense as part of the final phase of civil defence planning and the emergence of the most sophisticated of the embunkered emergency administrations, the Regional Government Headquarters. Ten years later Warren Row, along with all the other RGHQs, was sold into the private sector following the end of government civil defence planning for nuclear war, and is now a secure commercial warehouse.

The evolution of Drakelow as an RSG for the West Midlands was broadly similar to that of Warren Row, except that unlike Warren Row, which, at 30,000 square feet, afforded barely adequate office space, the quarter-of-a-million square feet at Drakelow greatly exceeded requirements. None of the manufacturing section of the factory was utilized by the Home Office as sufficient space for RSG 9 was available in the old Rover offices and the adjacent RAF storage area. The original works canteen and kitchen were refitted by the MOWB in 1961 and incorporated in the RSG, but the rest of the underground area was sealed off except for emergency exit routes maintained via tunnels T4, T3 and T2. The main access points for civilian personnel were adits 'A' and 'B', while adit 'C' was used solely by military personnel staffing the armed forces liaison unit. Fitting out was finished at Drakelow by May, 1961, when it took part in Exercise 'Mercian Trump II'. The previous year 'Mercian Trump I' had been conducted from the WWII war room at Shirley.

Drakelow required a staff of 325 (including about 75 women), led by a Regional Commissioner of Cabinet rank, assisted by a Principal Officer from the Civil Service and two Deputy Commissioners. Virtually all the government departments were represented (except the Treasury and Foreign Office), together with the Regional Hospital Board and the 'Uniformed Services', a title referring not to the armed forces but the Police, Fire Brigade and other civilian services. A small GPO and PSA staff was retained to maintain the fabric and equipment of the bunker.

In the reorganization of July, 1963, Drakelow became S-RC 91 and assumed responsibility for the counties of Shropshire, Hereford and Worcestershire. It was intended that the eastern counties of the region would be administered from a new S-RC established at the redundant Royal Ordnance Factory at Swynerton. With the development of the Sub-Regional Headquarters in the 1970s Drakelow became SRHQ 9.2.

Major structural changes were made following the introduction of the RGHQ system in 1982, when a £2,000,000 refurbishment scheme was put in hand. With a reduced staff of only 134, the new RGHQ was only half the size of its predecessor. All the offices at the east end beyond adit 'C' were abandoned, as was most of the dormitory area, the old kitchen and canteen and the emergency connections to tunnels 'T4' and beyond. Blast and radiation protection was improved at the remaining entrances and two new 147 Kva generators installed, together with enhanced air-conditioning systems and improved water supply. A new, smaller and much more hygienic kitchen and dining room suite was provided in the area previously occupied by the female dormitories. Communications equipment in the headquarters was progressively updated throughout the 1980s, the last significant improvements being made late in 1989, only a few months before proposals were made to close down the site and transfer its function to the recently vacated UKWMO control bunker at Lawford Heath. The transfer went ahead in 1992 and the following year Drakelow was offered for sale by public tender. In 1994 Lawford Heath was itself closed down and that site also sold.

Over the years the area of the Drakelow complex required for its various roles has gradually diminished, and the fact that the unused sections have been simply sealed off and abandoned makes the site quite fascinating to explore. Apart from the removal of the machine tools the factory tunnels appear much as they did forty years ago when the last 'Meteor' engine was built underground. Electrical and ventilating equipment, offices, toilets and tea-bars, clocks, notices and tannoy speakers all remain (though gradually rusting away), and the distinctive smell of oil and cutting fluid still pervades the air. When the 1960s RSG was rebuilt on a more modest scale as an RGHQ in 1982, the redundant facilities from the earlier installation were isolated and abandoned with most of their fixtures and fittings intact. Among the disused sections are the RSG canteen and kitchens, already relics of the Rover period, complete with huge ovens, grills and boiler-pans. The original BBC radio studio at the east end of the depot was replaced at that time with an almost identical but slightly smaller suite next to the new communications room near adit 'C'. The communications apparatus was removed prior to the disposal of the complex in 1993, but all the other plant and equipment, including the fully fitted kitchen and even some food stock, was included in the sale.

Having traced the history of the two smaller factory sites throughout the Cold War era, we can now examine the role of the Corsham Quarries in those unstable times. Most of the underground RSGs were completed by 1962, and at their heart was RAF Rudloe Manor (situated in the now redundant 'Rotor' operations centre in Brown's Quarry) which functioned as a central reporting and communication hub. Later this establishment expanded into an adjacent area of Spring Quarry and became known as the Quarry Operations Centre, which had once served as the BAC operatives canteen and millwrights' shop. The 40,000 square foot QOC was manned by a staff of 600 RAF personnel and, like the RSGs it served, contained its own catering facilities and dormitories. The much smaller Brown's Quarry site subsequently housed the headquarters of the Defence Communications Network, further enhancing the national importance of this secret, subterranean area of North Wiltshire.

It would appear that some form of national government emergency headquarters existed in putative form in the north-east Spring Quarry from 1947. Controlled by the Cabinet Office, the autonomous facility at Corsham seems to have been a precursor to, but initially independent of, the later Home Office RSG scheme. Policy changes which were to establish the Corsham Government War Headquarters in its most complete, Cold War form occurred in April, 1954, when the government negotiated the freehold purchase of Spring Quarry from the Bath & Portland Stone Co. Until that date the whole complex was still held under the original wartime requisition. Significantly, the existence of a 'Central Government War Room' is first mentioned in a Civil Defence circular of 1954. Detailed plans for the new headquarters were prepared early in 1956, with construction scheduled to proceed over the next three years. The role of South-West Control, the underground RAF communications centre established during the war at the west end of Tunnel Quarry, also expanded enormously at this time, just as the 'Backbone' microwave communications network was being put in place. The functional importance of this site came to public notice in July, 1957, when the *Bath Evening Chronicle* reported that

"It is confidently expected that the Air Ministry will confirm that a regular airman at the RAF's Southern Sector radar headquarters at Rudloe Manor is under close arrest, accused of handing over to a contact in Bath, acting as a spy for a foreign country, information regarding a new atom-powered submarine."

The area of quarry space available to the Cabinet Office amounted to some 550,000 square feet gross, or about 300,000 square feet net, after making allowances for support pillars. This is much less than 2,000,000 square feet suggested by some commentators and postulates a staff of only 7,500. This figure could be reduced further when account is taken of the substantial areas dedicated to telecommunications apparatus and essential electrical, ventilation and sanitation equipment, as well as the dormitories, dining rooms, kitchens and licensed bar (which was a feature also present in all the RSGs).

During the forty-year period from 1954 to 1994 the function of the emergency National Seat of Government seems to have undergone an inversion. Until 1973 it appears that the country would be run via a hierarchical structure from the top down, a structure made clear in the notes published in 1963 for the Government Scientific Intelligence Officers, which stated that *"a Regional Commissioner appointed in the emergency period will, in wartime, **be responsible to central government** for the administration of a civil defence region"*. It seems therefore that the government at that time felt competent to oversee the regional civil administration of the country as well as deal with foreign relations and prosecute nuclear war; a strategy that implies that the National Seat of Government would be a large civil/military establishment. The pivotal role of the Corsham complex (referred to in contemporary documents as the 'Central Government War Headquarters') is evident from the briefing notes prepared for Exercise 'Mercian Trump I' in 1960, which state that:

> "Central Government is being run from the Central Government War Headquarters through the RSGs, Regional Commissioners are exercising all the essential executive functions of government and are answerable to the Central Nucleus".

The same document notes that:

> "Regional Commissioners were appointed with specific powers **when the government moved to its wartime headquarters** and were given all the powers of government except those specifically reserved such as the control of the Armed Forces and foreign relations".

The co-location at Corsham of the communications hub for the RSGs, an important military signals centre, and the central government nucleus, all within a physically discreet underground complex certainly fulfilled all the requirements for such a strategy.

By 1984, however, central government had almost completely divested itself of responsibility for regional government during and immediately after a nuclear war. Responsibility for the re-establishment of social order and the provision of essential services devolved upon the Regional Commissioners, who would report to, rather than receive instructions from, central government. This policy allowed central government to concentrate on the key tasks of managing international relations and, within NATO, coordinating the military effort. This transformation in policy robbed the Corsham emergency headquarters of its civil government function, and the dismantling of all civil defence planning in 1992 reaffirmed the redundancy of the site, although it appears that it was already mothballed by 1989. The quarry operation centre (the old RSG communications hub) fell into disuse some five years earlier and is now stripped and abandoned.

Since 1973 the government has gradually disposed of the majority of its underground estate. All the small, temporary storage depots in quarries in Wiltshire and North Wales were returned to their owners by 1955, but after that, although some of the most significant sites, like the CAD sub-depots, all the RAF depots (except Chilmark) and the mustard gas tunnels at Rhydymwyn, fell into disuse in the mid 1960s, they were retained under 'care & maintenance', the government being, for nearly a decade, reluctant to make further disposals. Perhaps these sites figured in some vague, and probably undefined, future civil defence plan which is not as yet open to scrutiny. That they were eventually sold (and the rail connection to Tunnel Quarry severed) in the early 1970s, at a time coincidental with the shift in emphasis of civil defence thinking, may be of more than marginal significance. A series of stringent Defence Reviews since 1990 have highlighted the costly irrelevance and anachronism of the remaining underground sites, nearly all of which date from the Second World War and reflect thinking from an even earlier generation. Most, like RNSD Copenacre, RAF Chilmark, RNAD Trecwn and all the Regional Government Headquarters, are now gone too, leaving only RNAD Dean Hill, a sprinkling of post-war military command centres, and the communications centre at Corsham (now RAF No.1SU and associated units). The Spring Quarry emergency headquarters still remains in government hands, although an increasing irrelevance in this

254

time of instant, nodal communications. But one day, perhaps in twenty or fifty years time, it *might* be needed again to counter an as yet undefined threat, so its possible disposal, after a half a century of development, lays a tremendous responsibility upon the official who may have to determine its future.

INDEX

257

Ammunition:
    25 Pdr, 90
    Admiralty storage of, 180
    American, 112
    Anti-Aircraft (disposal of), 136
    D-Day issues, 134
    Howitzer, 7.2", 90
    Naval (storage in hulks), 207
    Recovery & disposal, 69, 134,
        140
    Sale of surplus, 135
    Storage policy, 103
    Storage requirements, 20–21
Ammunition Depots, Home
    Commands, 132
Ammunition examination, 69
Ammunition Selection Branch
    (Corsham), 132
Ammunition storage depots, 7, 8
    Dispersal of, (WW1), 12
    Investigation of underground
        sites for, 8, 11, 13
Ammunition Supply Depots
    (ASDs):
    Accidents at, 133, 134
    De-stocking, 135
    Drymen, 133
    Security at, 133
    Unsatisfactory conditions at,
        133
Anti-aircraft Command,
    disbandment, 136
Anti-aircraft predictors, 214, 216
Area Commands, 15
Argyll & Sutherland Highlanders,
    121, 122
Army School of Preliminary
    Training, 68
Arthur Scull Ltd, 98
Ashton Gate station (Bristol), 190
Assisted travel scheme, 198

Atomic war, Civil Defence during,
    246
Austin Motor Company, 148, 150,
    222
    Longbridge tunnel,178
A.V. Roe, 171
Avoncliffe, 214–215

'Backbone' microwave system, 252
Bailey, Dr E.B., 165
Bainbridge, Colonel, 12
Baldwin, Stanley, 16
Bangor, 238, 240
Banksfield Shed, Barnoldswick,
    223
Barry Docks, (deep-sea dumping),
    46, 135
Basil Hill barracks, 68
    Fires at, 69
Basingstoke, Civil Service
    Commission Headquarters, 249
Bath, 208
    Admiralty evacuation to, 244
Bath & Portland Stone Company,
    11, 16, 17, 48, 127, 151, 154,
    186, 207
    Royalty plans, 28
Bath Evening Chronicle, 128, 140,
    252
Bath gas works, 182
Bath stone, 25
    Quarrying techniques, 26
Bath stone industry:
    Organization of, 26
    Decline of, 17
Bath Tramways Company, 128
Beanacre sidings, 70, 112, 114,
    117, 189
    Closure of, 115
    Proposed RAF bomb store at,
        114
Beaverbrook, Lord, 146, 147

Colwall tunnel (Herefordshire), 2
Committees:
  Cabinet Defence Committee,
    138
  Chief of Defence Staff
    committee, 1959, 137
  House of Commons Public
    Accounts Committee, 146,
    162, 174
  Lord Justice Scott's Committee,
    196–197
  Treasury Inter-Service Joint
    Committee, 19, 60, 108, 110
  War Cabinet 'Crossbow'
    Committee, 245
  Geneva Disarmament
    Conference Standing
    Committee, 16
  Committee on Army Supply
    Depots, 1920, 12
  First Committee of the Army
    Council to Consider . . .
    Magazine Regulations, etc,
    11
  War Office Tunnel Quarry
    Committee, 28, 55
'*Conqueror*' tank, 225
'*Constellation*' motorcycle, 218
Construction labour:
  CAD Corsham, 127
  Spring Quarry project, 158
  Conditions of employment, 128
Conveyors:
  Monkton Farleigh, 82, 83, 89,
    92–3
  Tunnel Quarry, 66–67
Cook, Lieutenant Colonel H, 132
Copenacre Quarry, 154, 210
  Conversion costs, 208
  Description, pre-war, 208
Cordite storage at Tunnel Quarry,
  59

Corsham, 2, 3, 15–18, 20, 35, 38,
  41–42, 148, 150–151, 246
  Clerk to Town Council, 197
  Role in nuclear war, 251
  Station, 48–49
Corsham Court, 68, 134
Corsham defence scheme, 120
Corsham Garrison, 116, 121
Corsham Quarries, 149
  Air conditioning, 22
  Requisitioning, 154
  Table of allocations, 156
  Telephone services to, 186
'Corsham System' of ammunition
  storage, 132
Cotterell, Sturge, 11, 17
Counterfeit coinage, 53
Courtauld's 'windowless factory',
  181
Coventry, 207
  Admiralty storage depot, 212
  Bombing of, 147, 223
Creighton, Squadron Leader, 114
Cripps, Lieutenant Colonel, 131
Cripps, Sir Stafford, 206
'Cromwell' warning, 125
Crossthwaite mechanical stokers,
  184
Crossville Bus Company, 240
Crosswood House, 232, 240
Crown Jewels, 237
'*Crusader*' motorcycle, 217
Cwt-y-Bugail Quarrying Company,
  241

'*Daily Express*', 5
'*Daily Mail*', 5
Daimler Motor Company, 222
'*Danger – Official Secret*', 247
Darlington Mushrooms, 142
Dartmoor prison, 179
Dartford, Kent, 149

Risk of German occupation, 233
Irish labourers, 215
    Threat to security at Corsham, 186
Ironside, General Edmund, 120, 123
Ivyfield waterworks, 182

J. Gerber & Co Ltd, 235
Jennings, Captain, 17
Jerry-building at Corsham, 198
John Cochrane & Sons, tunnelling contract at Drakelow, 222
Johnson Matthey Ltd, 178
Jubb, Mr (MAP finance officer), 198

Kennedy & Donkin Ltd, 61, 110, 173
Kennedy, Alistair, 158
Kennedy, Sergeant-Major, 28
Kenilworth, 173
Kensington, 234, 237
Kidderminster, 149
Kingsdown common, 120
Kingsdown plantation, 122, 135
Kingsford Lane, 223
Kingsmoor hostel, 201
Knox-Wilson, Lieutenant Colonel, 131
Korean war, 136

Laboratories, surface, 69, 70, 74
Laboratories, underground, 69
Lacock goods yard, 192
    Closure, 193
Lacock halt, 191
Ladbrook valley, 108
'Lancaster' bomber, 164
Lawford Heath (UKWMO bunker), 251
Leafield Engineering Ltd, 213

Leafield hostel, 201
Leek, Sir James, 206
Lehmann, Olga, 199
Lend-lease Act, 42, 112
Lewes, Lieutenant Colonel P. K., 11
Liddell Hart, Captain B. H., 14
Liddell, C (Guy), 186
Liege, 7
'Limited War', 138
Limpley Stoke, 113, 151
Linear defence scheme, abandonment, 121, 123
Lines, Squadron Leader F. R., 41, 103
Linley RAF reserve depot, 39, 43
    Collapse of, 39
Lister, Lieutenant Colonel, 122
Llanberis RAF reserve depot, 39, 43, 47
    Collapse of, 40
    Court of Enquiry, 40
    Recovery of bombs from, 43–44
Lloyd George, David, 10, 13
Loch Lomond, 133
London Blitz, 233
London galleries and museums, 232
London Museum, 232
London Underground, Central Line, 148
Long Newnton airfield, 46
Longparish, RAF ammunition dump, 115
Lyddite, 12
Lypiatt family hostel, 201
Lypiatt workers hostel, 199

Maclagan, Sir Eric, 233
Magazine Regulations, 132

265